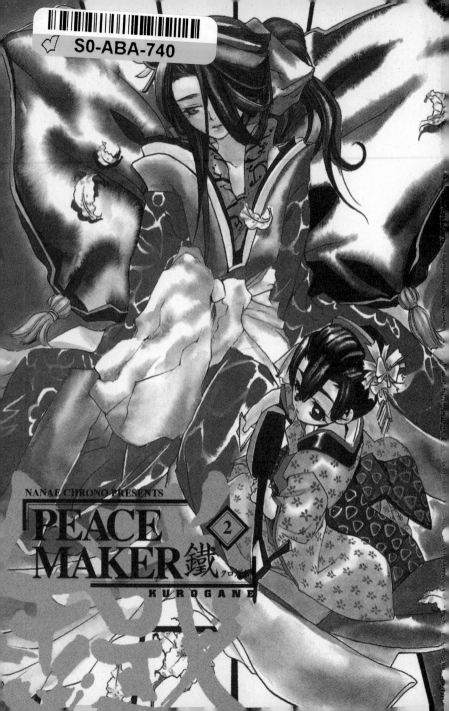

NANAE CHRONO PRESENTS

PEACE MAKER 鐵 ② KUROGANE

CONTENTS

縄声雪雨難

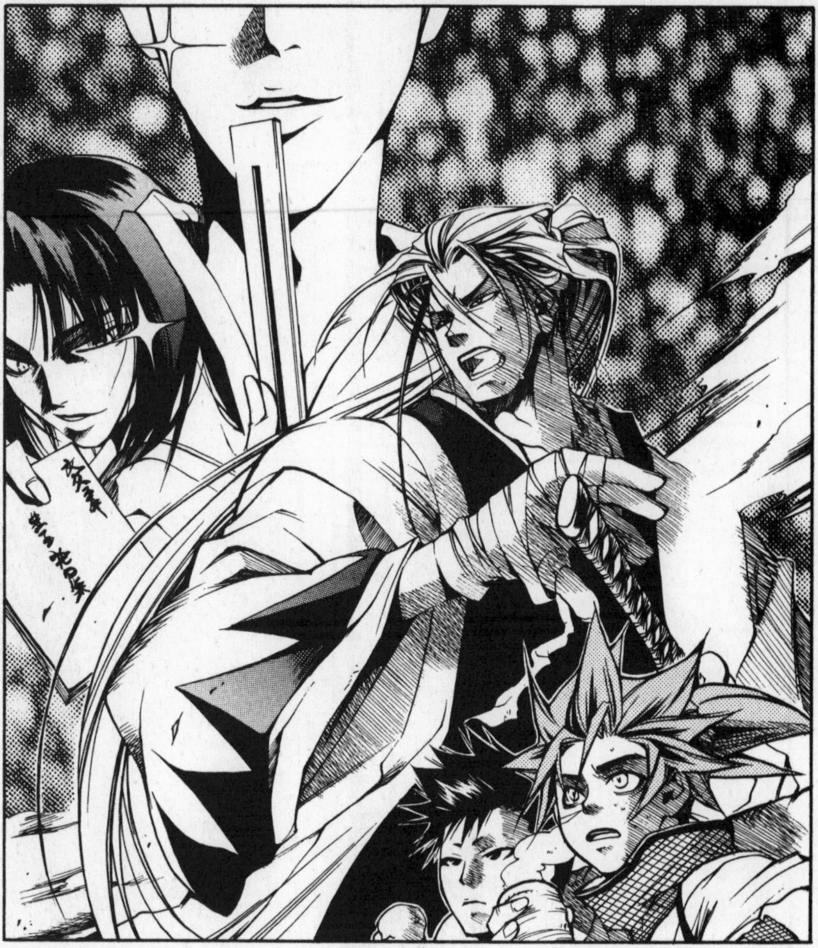

CHAPTER 6

HARDSHIP 鐵

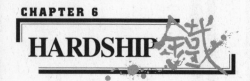

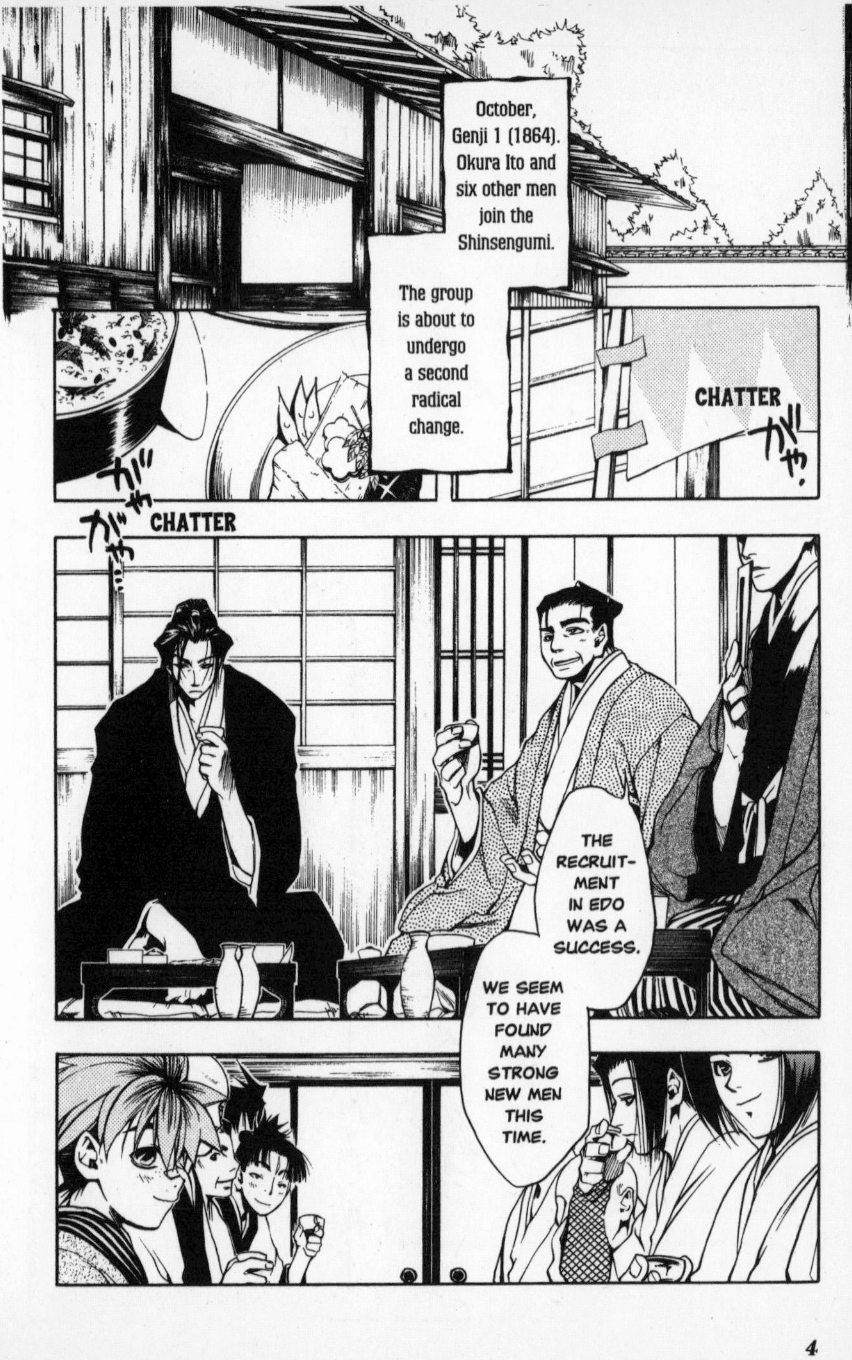
October, Genji 1 (1864). Okura Ito and six other men join the Shinsengumi.
The group is about to undergo a second radical change.
CHATTER
CHATTER
THE RECRUIT-MENT IN EDO WAS A SUCCESS.
WE SEEM TO HAVE FOUND MANY STRONG NEW MEN THIS TIME.

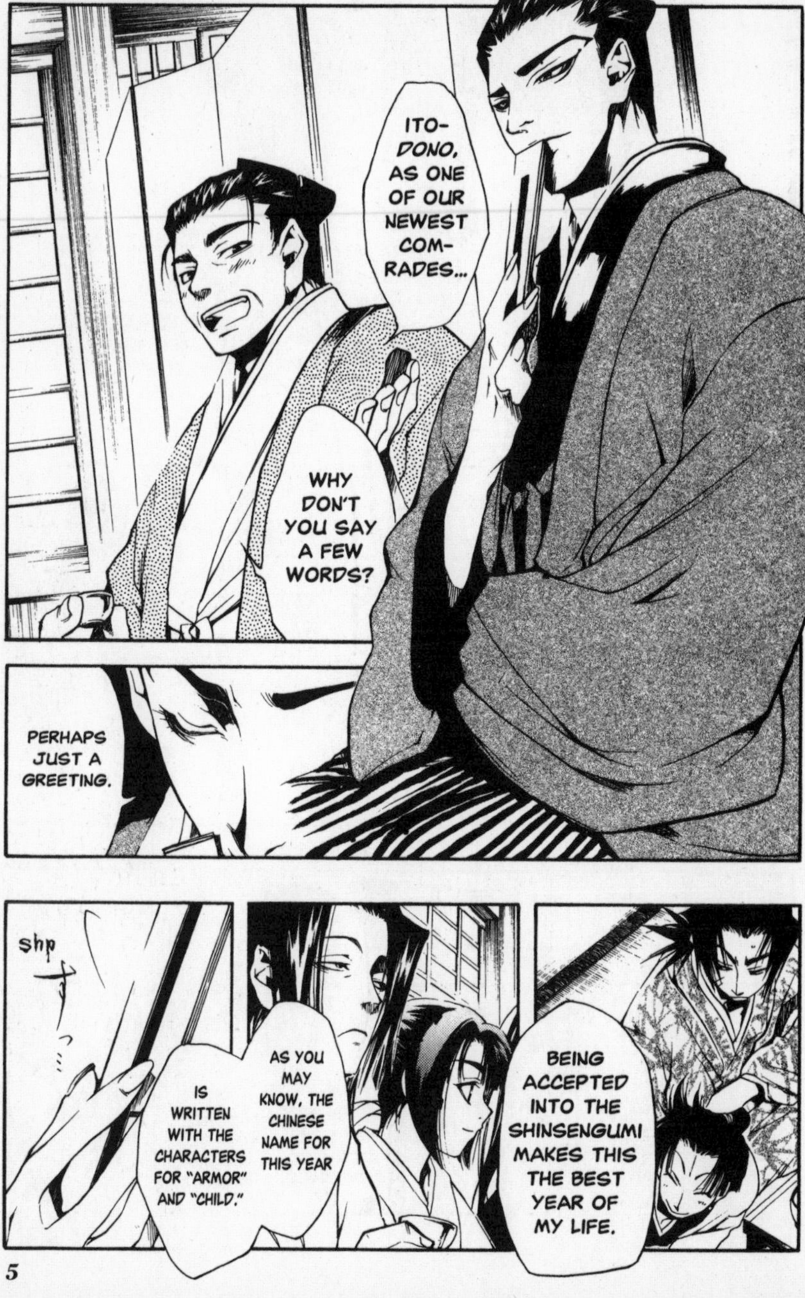
ITO-DONO, AS ONE OF OUR NEWEST COMRADES...
WHY DON'T YOU SAY A FEW WORDS?
PERHAPS JUST A GREETING.
BEING ACCEPTED INTO THE SHINSENGUMI MAKES THIS THE BEST YEAR OF MY LIFE.
AS YOU MAY KNOW, THE CHINESE NAME FOR THIS YEAR
IS WRITTEN WITH THE CHARACTERS FOR "ARMOR" AND "CHILD."
shp

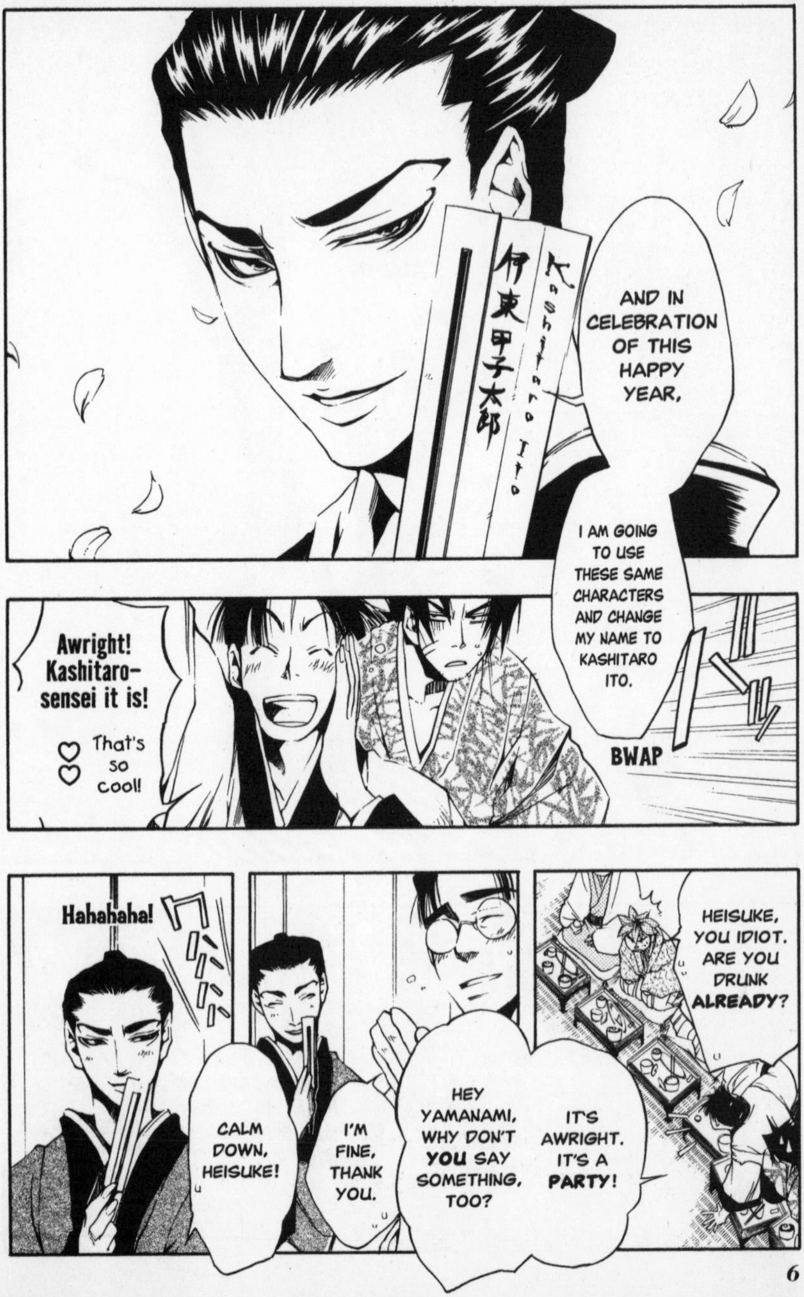
伊東甲子太郎
Kashitaro Ito
AND IN CELEBRATION OF THIS HAPPY YEAR,
I AM GOING TO USE THESE SAME CHARACTERS AND CHANGE MY NAME TO KASHITARO ITO.
BWAP
Awright! Kashitaro-sensei it is!
♡♡ That's so cool!
HEISUKE, YOU IDIOT. ARE YOU DRUNK **ALREADY**?
IT'S AWRIGHT. IT'S A **PARTY**!
HEY YAMANAMI, WHY DON'T **YOU** SAY SOMETHING, TOO?
I'M FINE, THANK YOU.
CALM DOWN, HEISUKE!
Hahahaha!

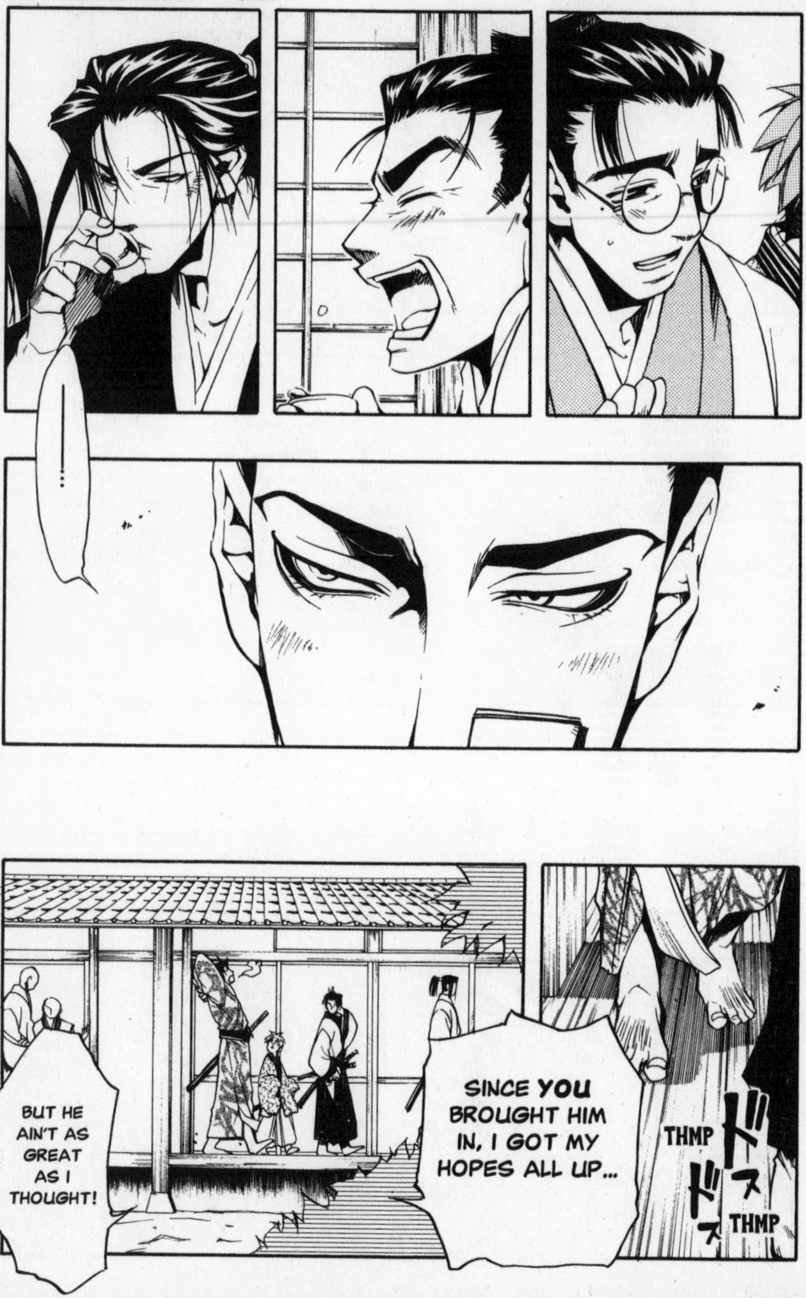
……
THMP ドス
ドス THMP
SINCE YOU BROUGHT HIM IN, I GOT MY HOPES ALL UP...
BUT HE AIN'T AS GREAT AS I THOUGHT!

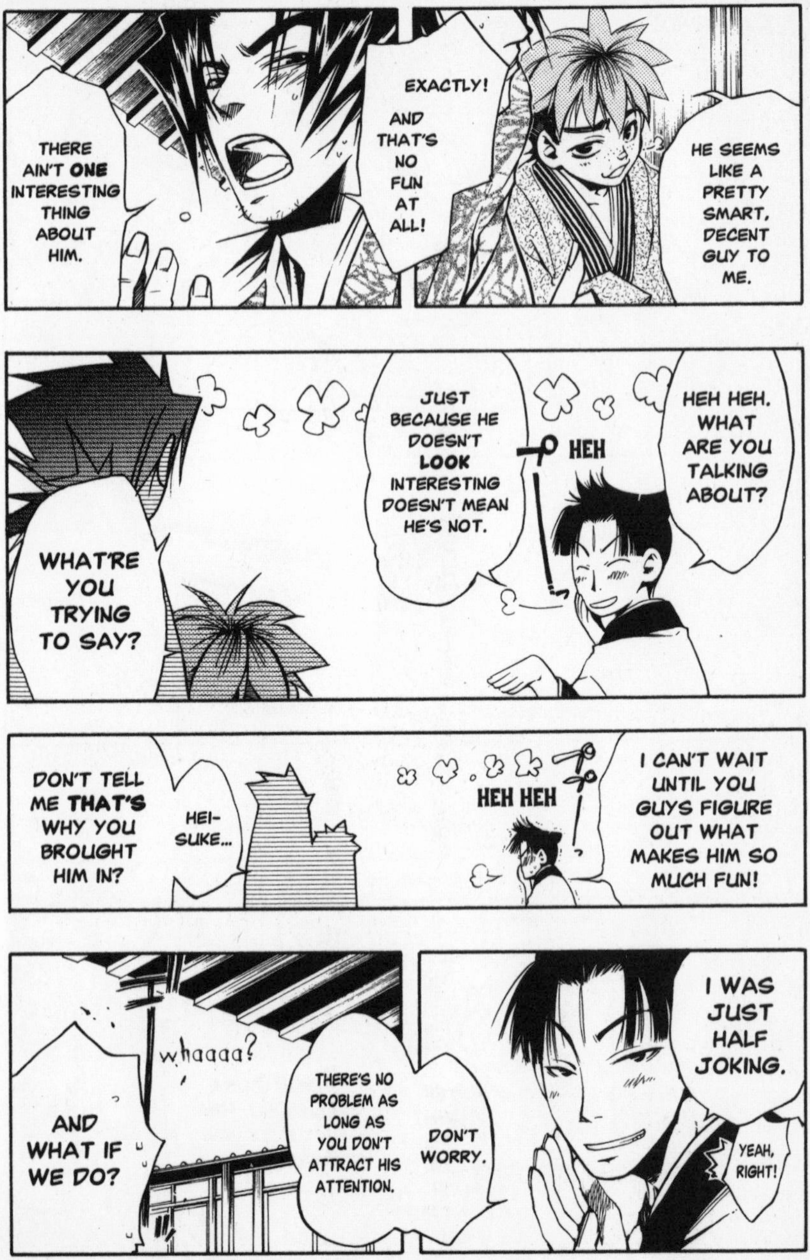
HE SEEMS LIKE A PRETTY SMART, DECENT GUY TO ME.
EXACTLY!
AND THAT'S NO FUN AT ALL!
THERE AIN'T **ONE** INTERESTING THING ABOUT HIM.
HEH HEH. WHAT ARE YOU TALKING ABOUT?
HEH
JUST BECAUSE HE DOESN'T **LOOK** INTERESTING DOESN'T MEAN HE'S NOT.
WHAT'RE YOU TRYING TO SAY?
I CAN'T WAIT UNTIL YOU GUYS FIGURE OUT WHAT MAKES HIM SO MUCH FUN!
HEH HEH
HEI-SUKE...
DON'T TELL ME **THAT'S** WHY YOU BROUGHT HIM IN?
I WAS JUST HALF JOKING.
YEAH, RIGHT!
DON'T WORRY.
THERE'S NO PROBLEM AS LONG AS YOU DON'T ATTRACT HIS ATTENTION.
whaaaa?
AND WHAT IF WE DO?

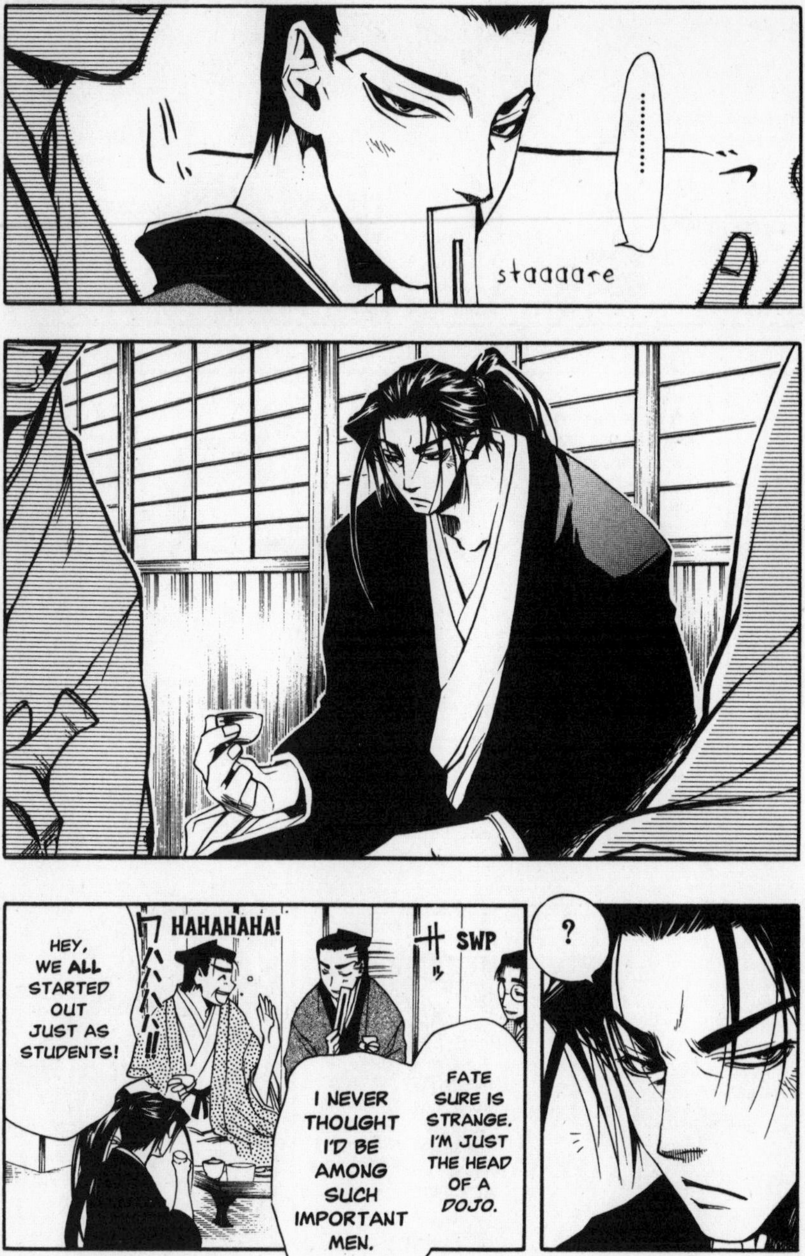
......
staaaare
?
SWP
HAHAHAHA!
HEY, WE ALL STARTED OUT JUST AS STUDENTS!
FATE SURE IS STRANGE. I'M JUST THE HEAD OF A DOJO.
I NEVER THOUGHT I'D BE AMONG SUCH IMPORTANT MEN.

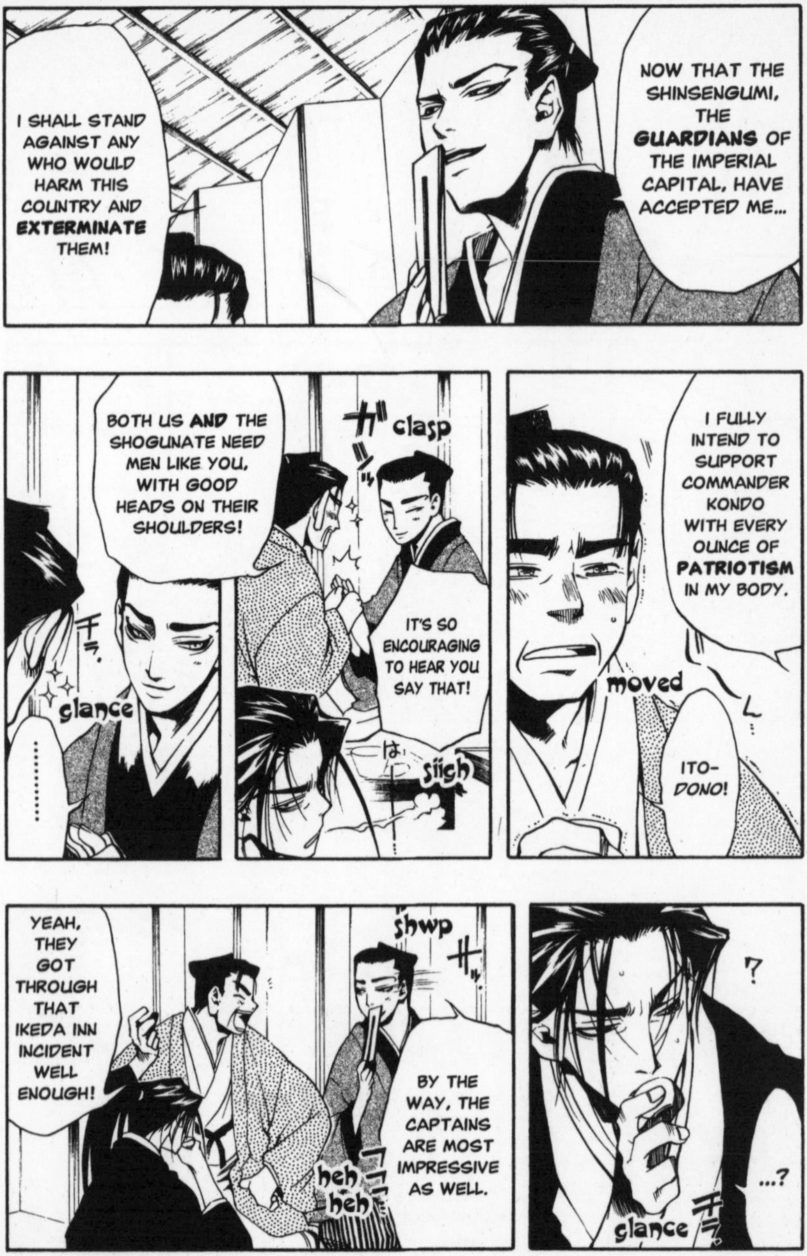

NOW THAT THE SHINSENGUMI, THE GUARDIANS OF THE IMPERIAL CAPITAL, HAVE ACCEPTED ME...
I SHALL STAND AGAINST ANY WHO WOULD HARM THIS COUNTRY AND EXTERMINATE THEM!
I FULLY INTEND TO SUPPORT COMMANDER KONDO WITH EVERY OUNCE OF PATRIOTISM IN MY BODY.
moved
ITO-DONO!
clasp
BOTH US AND THE SHOGUNATE NEED MEN LIKE YOU, WITH GOOD HEADS ON THEIR SHOULDERS!
IT'S SO ENCOURAGING TO HEAR YOU SAY THAT!
siigh
glance
....
?
...?
glance
shwp
BY THE WAY, THE CAPTAINS ARE MOST IMPRESSIVE AS WELL.
YEAH, THEY GOT THROUGH THAT IKEDA INN INCIDENT WELL ENOUGH!
heh heh

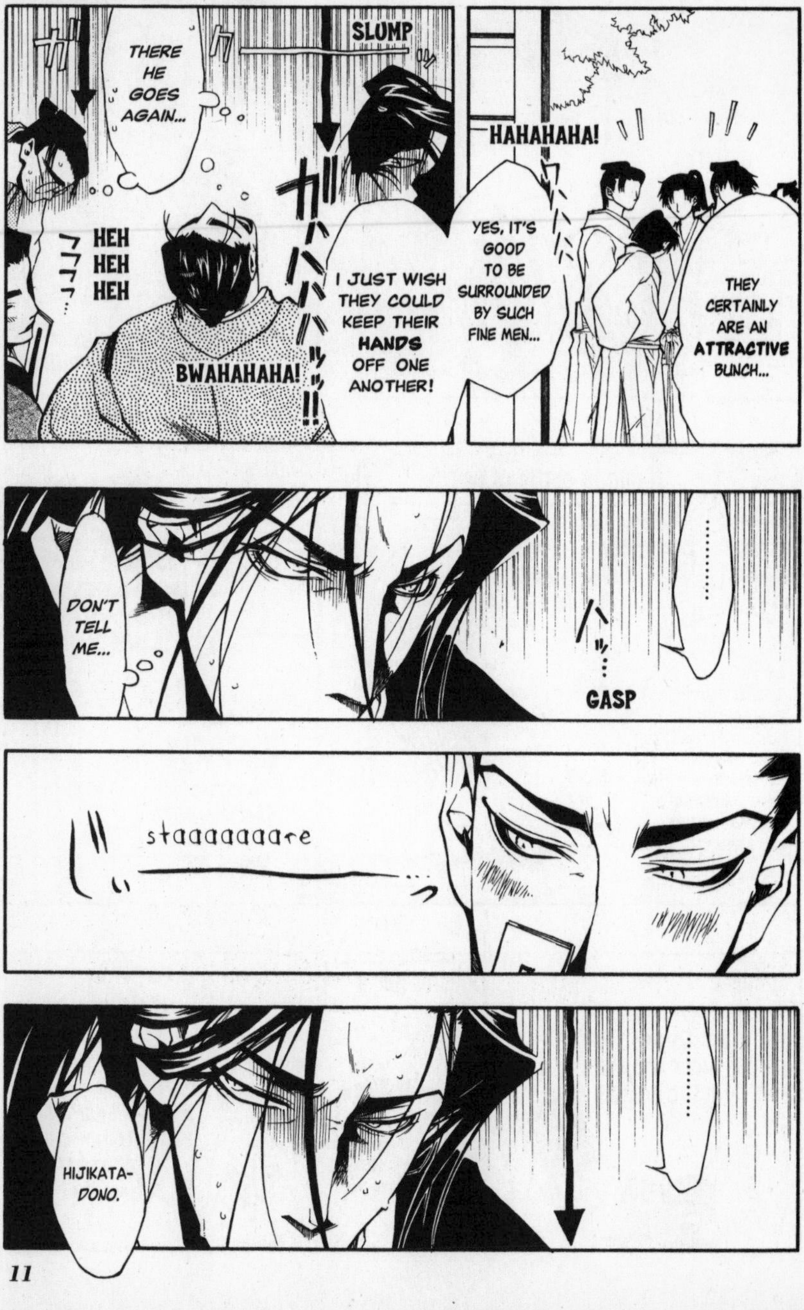
HAHAHAHA!
THEY CERTAINLY ARE AN ATTRACTIVE BUNCH...
YES, IT'S GOOD TO BE SURROUNDED BY SUCH FINE MEN...
SLUMP
I JUST WISH THEY COULD KEEP THEIR HANDS OFF ONE ANOTHER!
BWAHAHAHA!
THERE HE GOES AGAIN...
HEH HEH HEH
GASP
DON'T TELL ME...
staaaaaaaare
HIJIKATA-DONO.

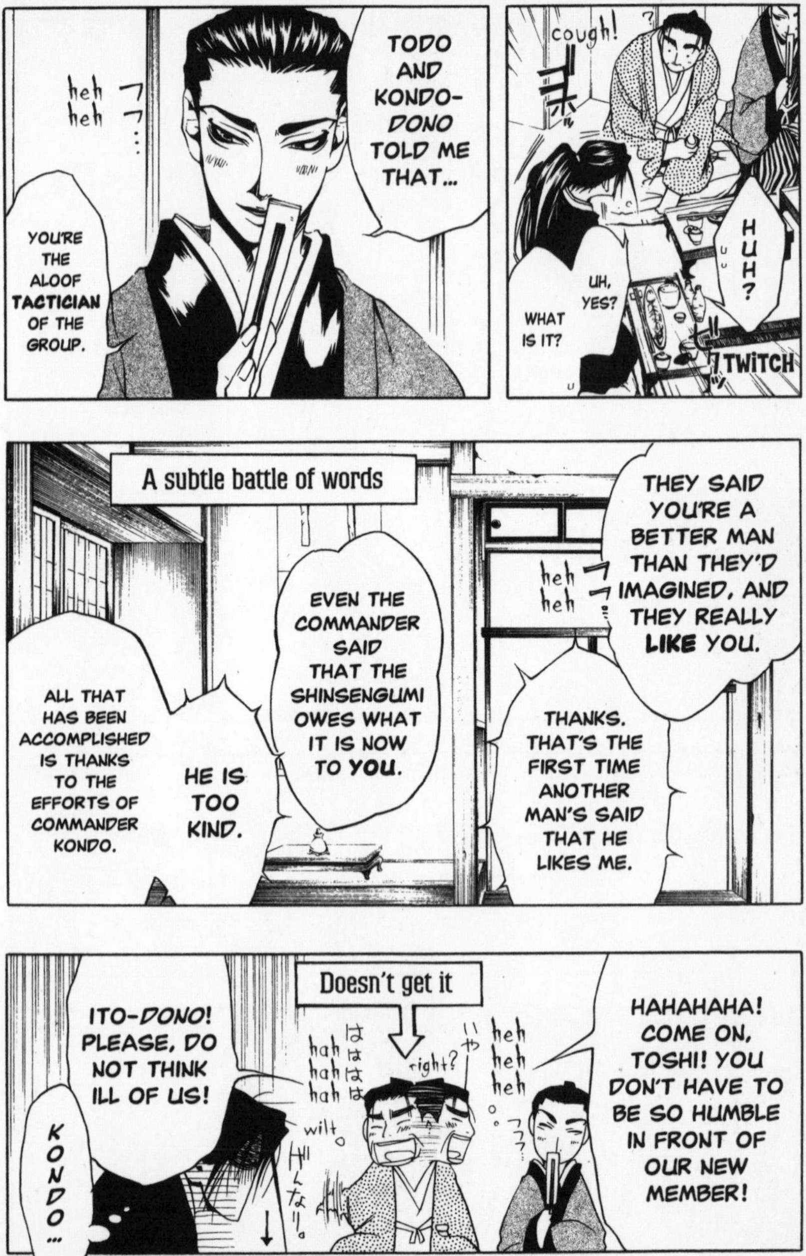
cough!
HUH?
TWITCH
UH, YES?
WHAT IS IT?
heh heh
TODO AND KONDO-DONO TOLD ME THAT...
YOU'RE THE ALOOF TACTICIAN OF THE GROUP.
A subtle battle of words
THEY SAID YOU'RE A BETTER MAN THAN THEY'D IMAGINED, AND THEY REALLY LIKE YOU.
heh heh
THANKS. THAT'S THE FIRST TIME ANOTHER MAN'S SAID THAT HE LIKES ME.
EVEN THE COMMANDER SAID THAT THE SHINSENGUMI OWES WHAT IT IS NOW TO YOU.
HE IS TOO KIND.
ALL THAT HAS BEEN ACCOMPLISHED IS THANKS TO THE EFFORTS OF COMMANDER KONDO.
Doesn't get it
HAHAHAHA! COME ON, TOSHI! YOU DON'T HAVE TO BE SO HUMBLE IN FRONT OF OUR NEW MEMBER!
heh heh heh
right?
hah hah hah
wilt
ITO-DONO! PLEASE, DO NOT THINK ILL OF US!
KONDO...

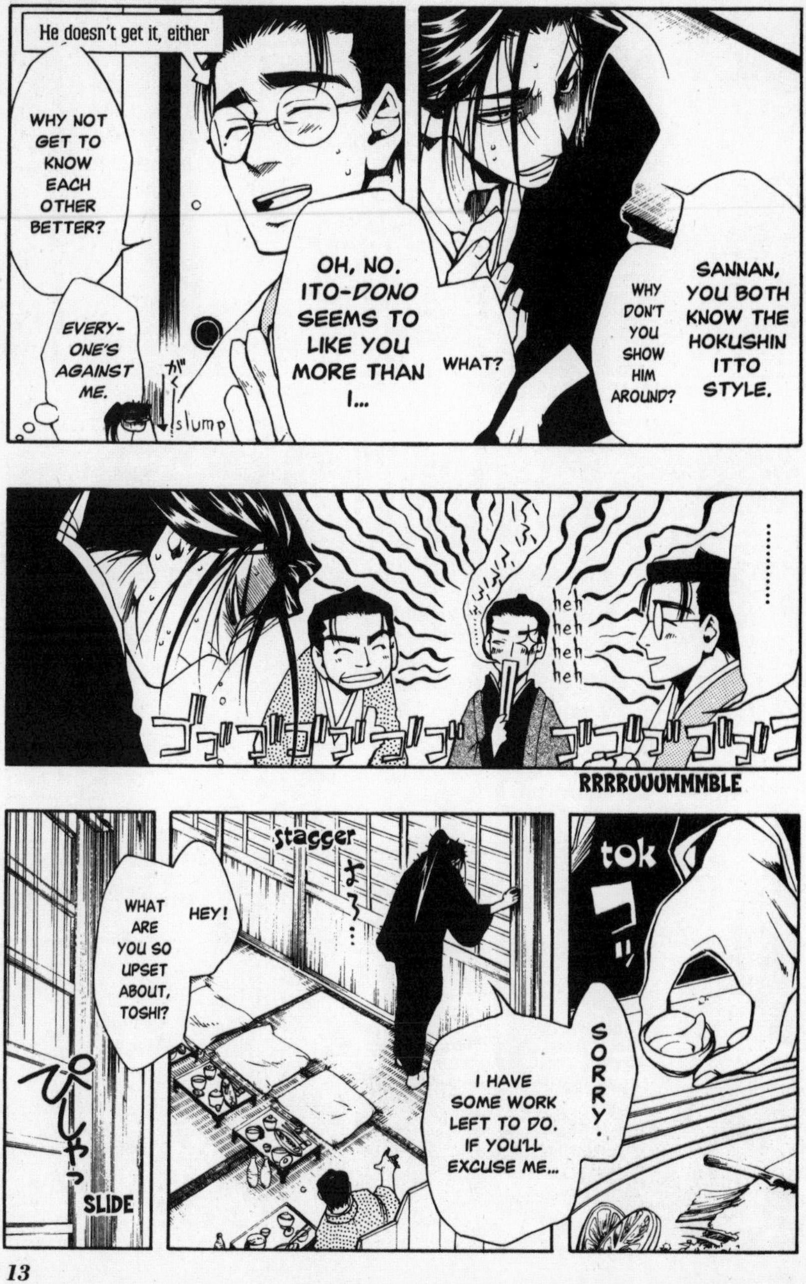
SANNAN, YOU BOTH KNOW THE HOKUSHIN ITTO STYLE.
WHY DON'T YOU SHOW HIM AROUND?
WHAT?
OH, NO. ITO-*DONO* SEEMS TO LIKE YOU MORE THAN I...
He doesn't get it, either
WHY NOT GET TO KNOW EACH OTHER BETTER?
EVERY-ONE'S AGAINST ME.
がく
slump
......
heh heh heh heh
ゴゴゴゴゴゴ ゴゴゴゴゴ
RRRRUUUMMMBLE
tok
コッ
SORRY.
I HAVE SOME WORK LEFT TO DO. IF YOU'LL EXCUSE ME...
stagger
よろ...
HEY!
WHAT ARE YOU SO UPSET ABOUT, TOSHI?
ぴしゃっ
SLIDE

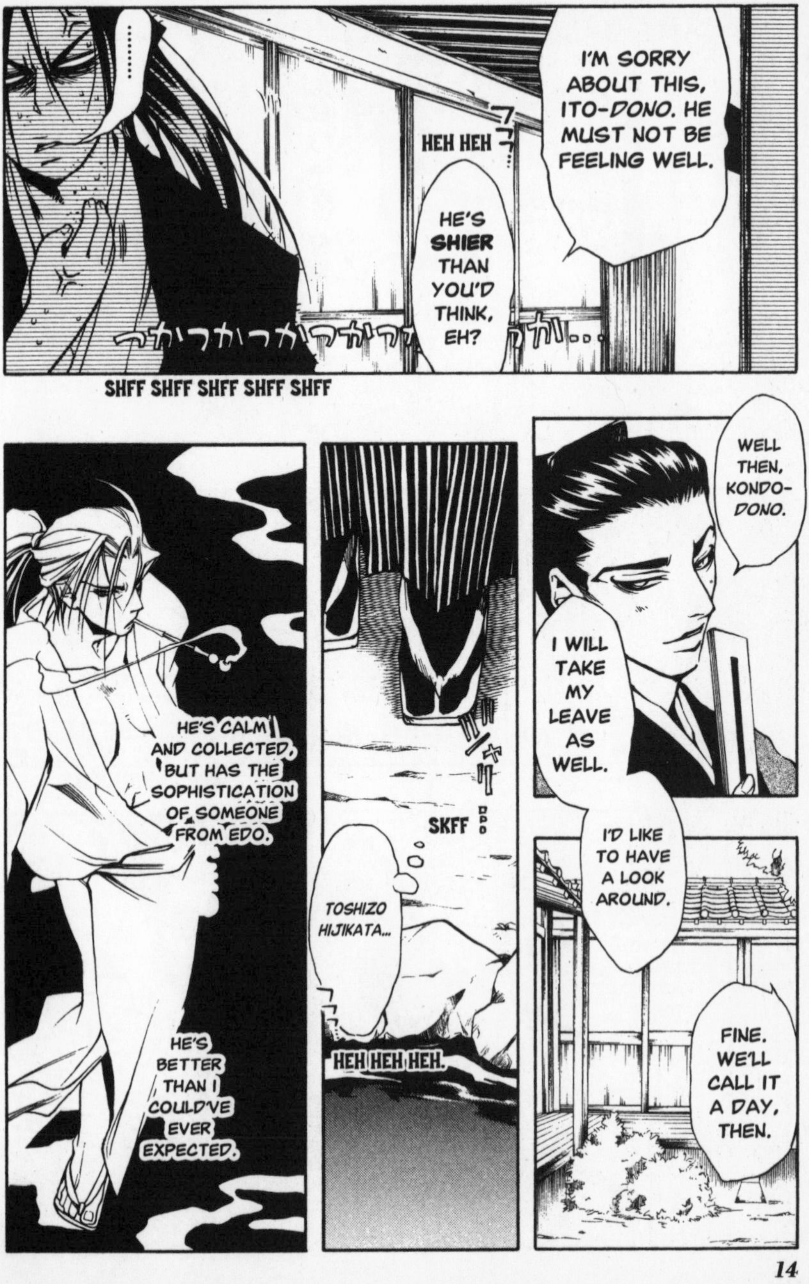
I'M SORRY ABOUT THIS, ITO-*DONO*. HE MUST NOT BE FEELING WELL.
HEH HEH
HE'S **SHIER** THAN YOU'D THINK, EH?
......
SHFF SHFF SHFF SHFF SHFF
WELL THEN, KONDO-*DONO*.
I WILL TAKE MY LEAVE AS WELL.
I'D LIKE TO HAVE A LOOK AROUND.
FINE. WE'LL CALL IT A DAY, THEN.
SKFF
TOSHIZO HIJIKATA...
HEH HEH HEH.
HE'S CALM AND COLLECTED, BUT HAS THE SOPHISTICATION OF SOMEONE FROM EDO.
HE'S BETTER THAN I COULD'VE EVER EXPECTED.

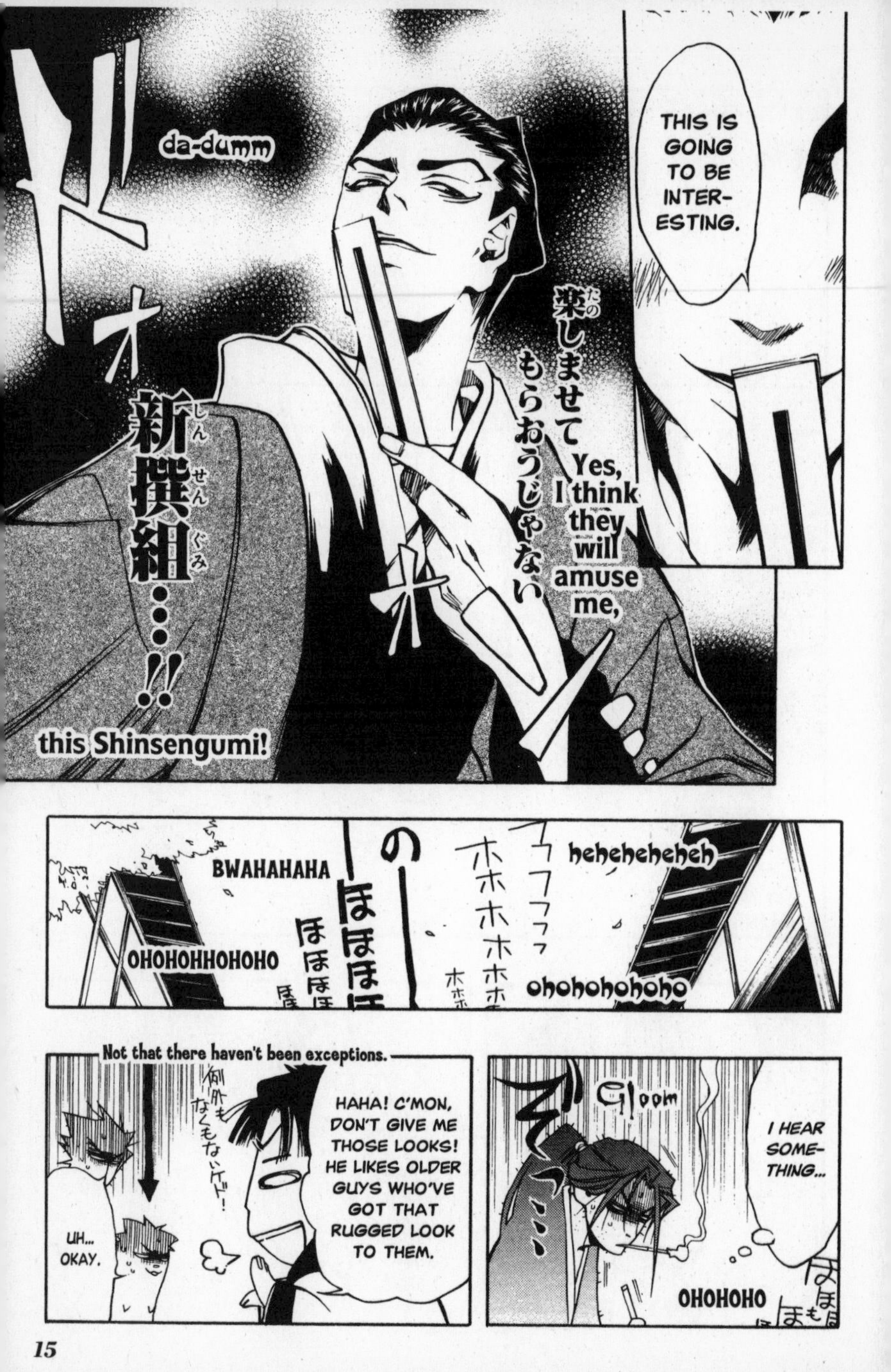
THIS IS GOING TO BE INTER-ESTING.
楽しませてもらおうじゃない
Yes, I think they will amuse me,
新撰組…!!
this Shinsengumi!
ドォ
da-dumm
フフフフフ
hehehehehehe
ホホホホホ
ohohohohoho
のーほほほ
BWAHAHAHA
OHOHOHHOHOHO
I HEAR SOME-THING...
Gloom
OHOHOHO
Not that there haven't been exceptions.
例外もなくもないケド!
HAHA! C'MON, DON'T GIVE ME THOSE LOOKS! HE LIKES OLDER GUYS WHO'VE GOT THAT RUGGED LOOK TO THEM.
UH... OKAY.

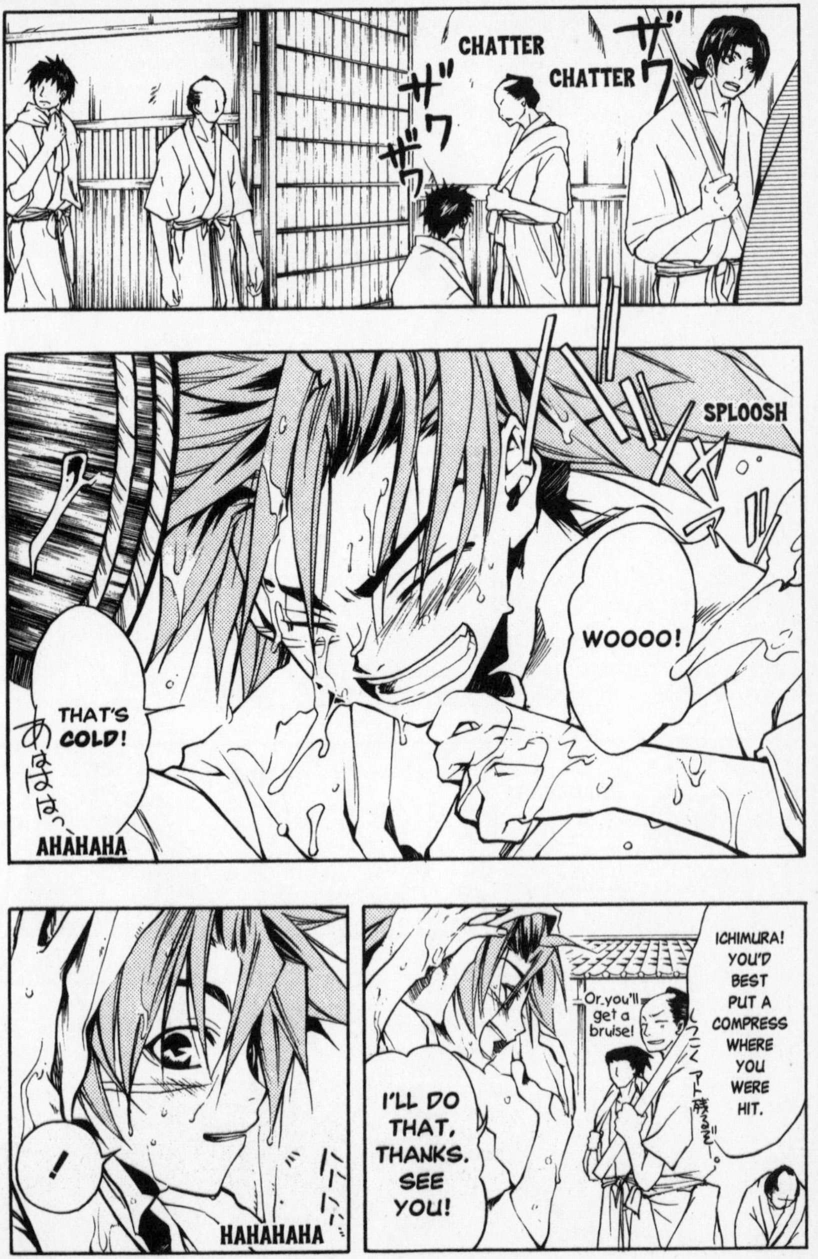
CHATTER
CHATTER
ザワ
ザワ
ザワ
SPLOOSH
WOOOO!
THAT'S COLD!
AHAHAHA
ICHIMURA! YOU'D BEST PUT A COMPRESS WHERE YOU WERE HIT.
Or you'll get a bruise!
I'LL DO THAT, THANKS. SEE YOU!
!
HAHAHAHA

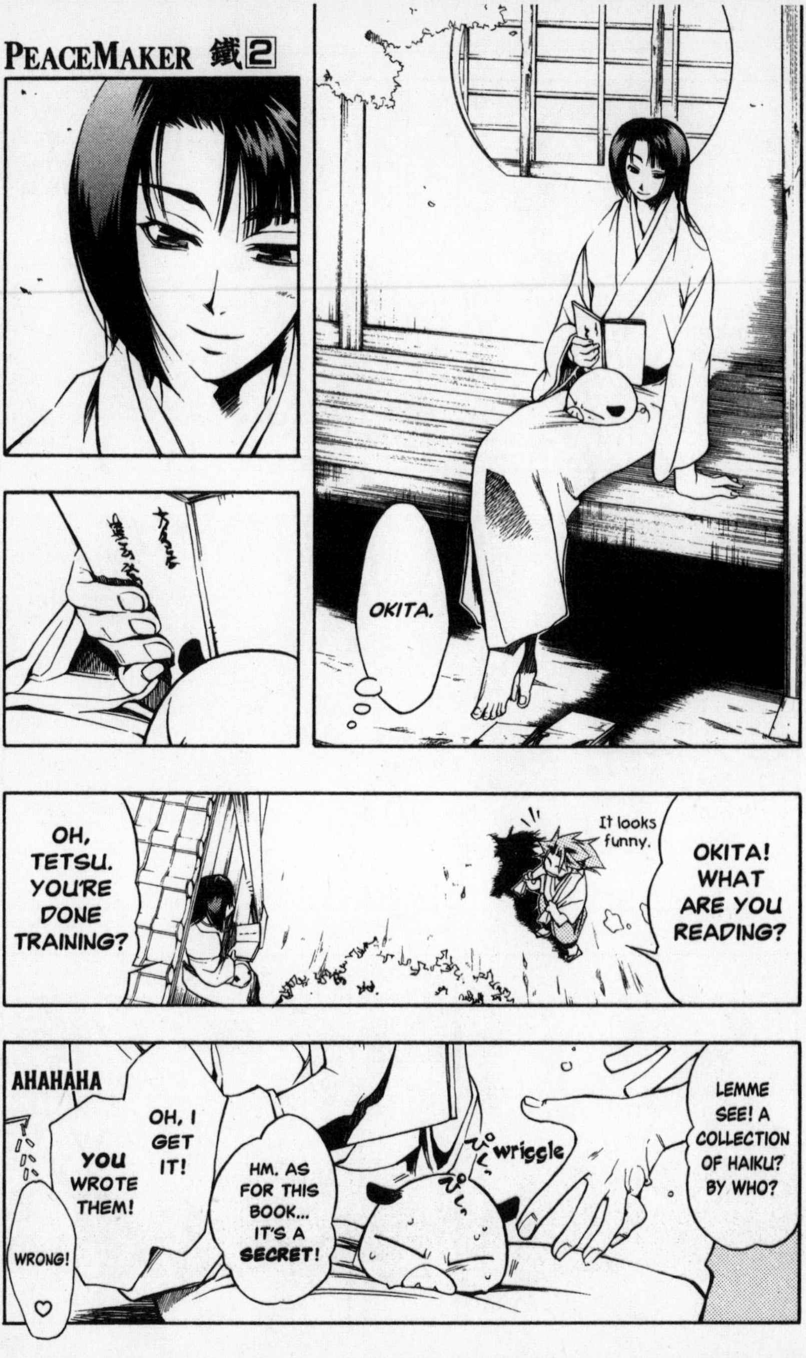
OKITA.
OKITA! WHAT ARE YOU READING?
It looks funny.
OH, TETSU. YOU'RE DONE TRAINING?
LEMME SEE! A COLLECTION OF HAIKU? BY WHO?
wriggle
HM. AS FOR THIS BOOK... IT'S A SECRET!
OH, I GET IT! YOU WROTE THEM!
WRONG! ♡
AHAHAHA

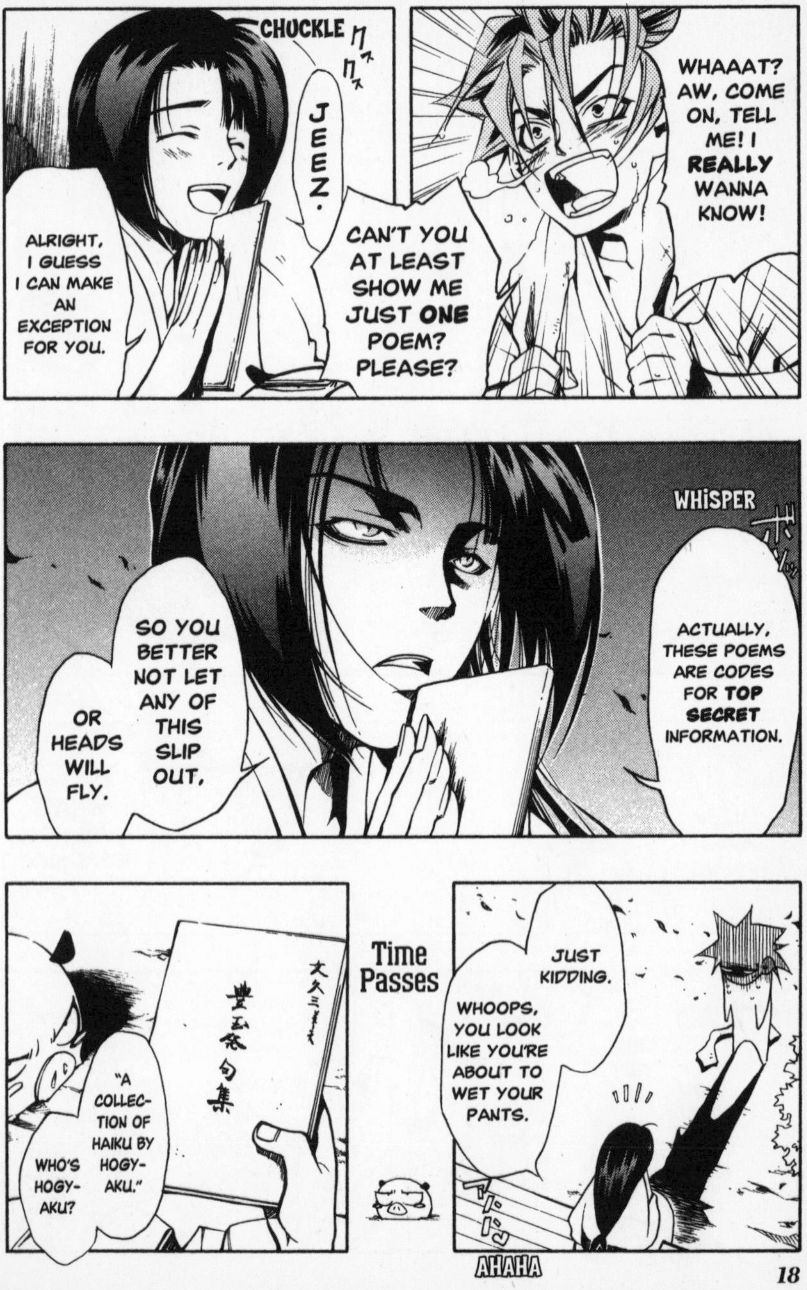
WHAAAT? AW, COME ON, TELL ME! I REALLY WANNA KNOW!
CAN'T YOU AT LEAST SHOW ME JUST ONE POEM? PLEASE?
CHUCKLE
JEEZ.
ALRIGHT, I GUESS I CAN MAKE AN EXCEPTION FOR YOU.
WHISPER
ACTUALLY, THESE POEMS ARE CODES FOR TOP SECRET INFORMATION.
SO YOU BETTER NOT LET ANY OF THIS SLIP OUT,
OR HEADS WILL FLY.
JUST KIDDING.
WHOOPS, YOU LOOK LIKE YOU'RE ABOUT TO WET YOUR PANTS.
AHAHA
Time Passes
豊玉発句集
"A COLLECTION OF HAIKU BY HOGYAKU."
WHO'S HOGYAKU?

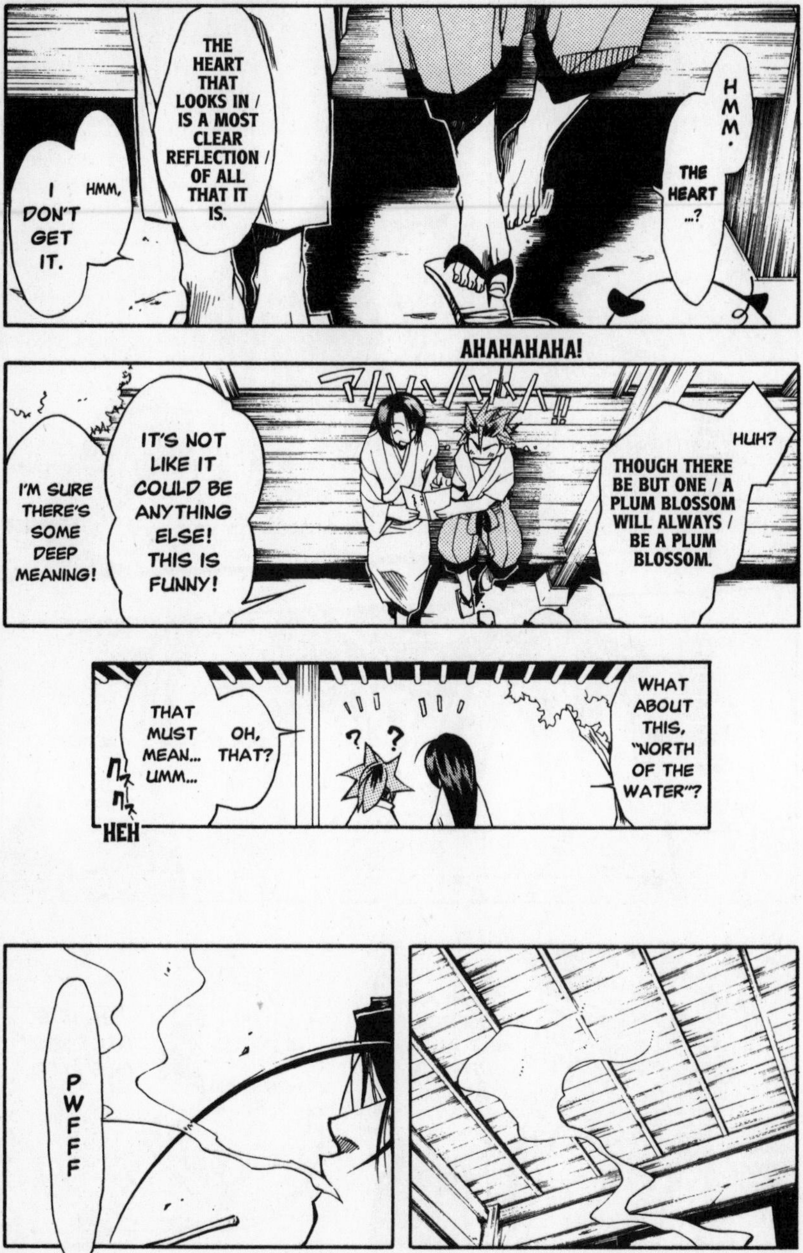
HMM.
THE HEART ...?
THE HEART THAT LOOKS IN / IS A MOST CLEAR REFLECTION / OF ALL THAT IT IS.
HMM,
I DON'T GET IT.
AHAHAHAHA!
HUH?
THOUGH THERE BE BUT ONE / A PLUM BLOSSOM WILL ALWAYS / BE A PLUM BLOSSOM.
IT'S NOT LIKE IT COULD BE ANYTHING ELSE! THIS IS FUNNY!
I'M SURE THERE'S SOME DEEP MEANING!
WHAT ABOUT THIS, "NORTH OF THE WATER"?
OH, THAT?
THAT MUST MEAN... UMM...
HEH
PWFFF

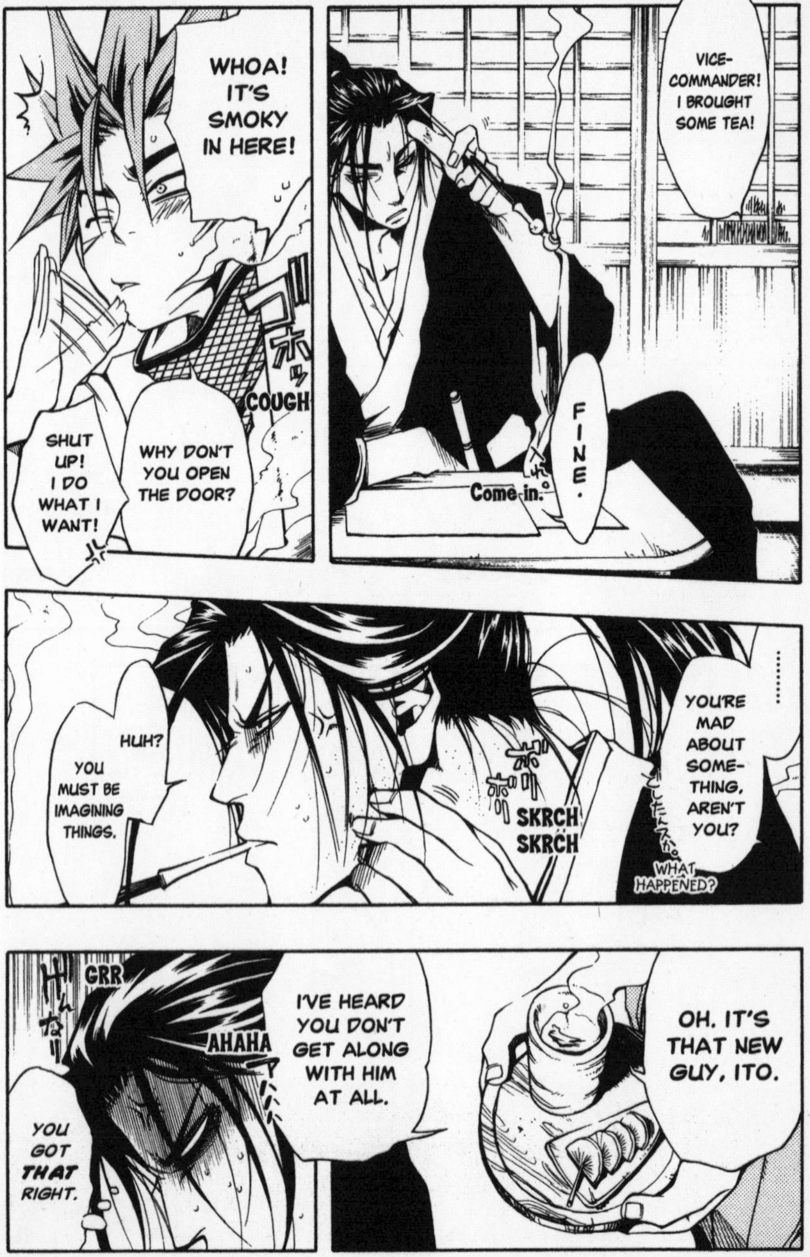
VICE-COMMANDER! I BROUGHT SOME TEA!
Come in.
FINE.
WHOA! IT'S SMOKY IN HERE!
COUGH
WHY DON'T YOU OPEN THE DOOR?
SHUT UP! I DO WHAT I WANT!
......
YOU'RE MAD ABOUT SOME-THING, AREN'T YOU?
WHAT HAPPENED?
SKRCH SKRCH
HUH?
YOU MUST BE IMAGINING THINGS.
OH. IT'S THAT NEW GUY, ITO.
I'VE HEARD YOU DON'T GET ALONG WITH HIM AT ALL.
AHAHA
GRR
YOU GOT ***THAT*** RIGHT.

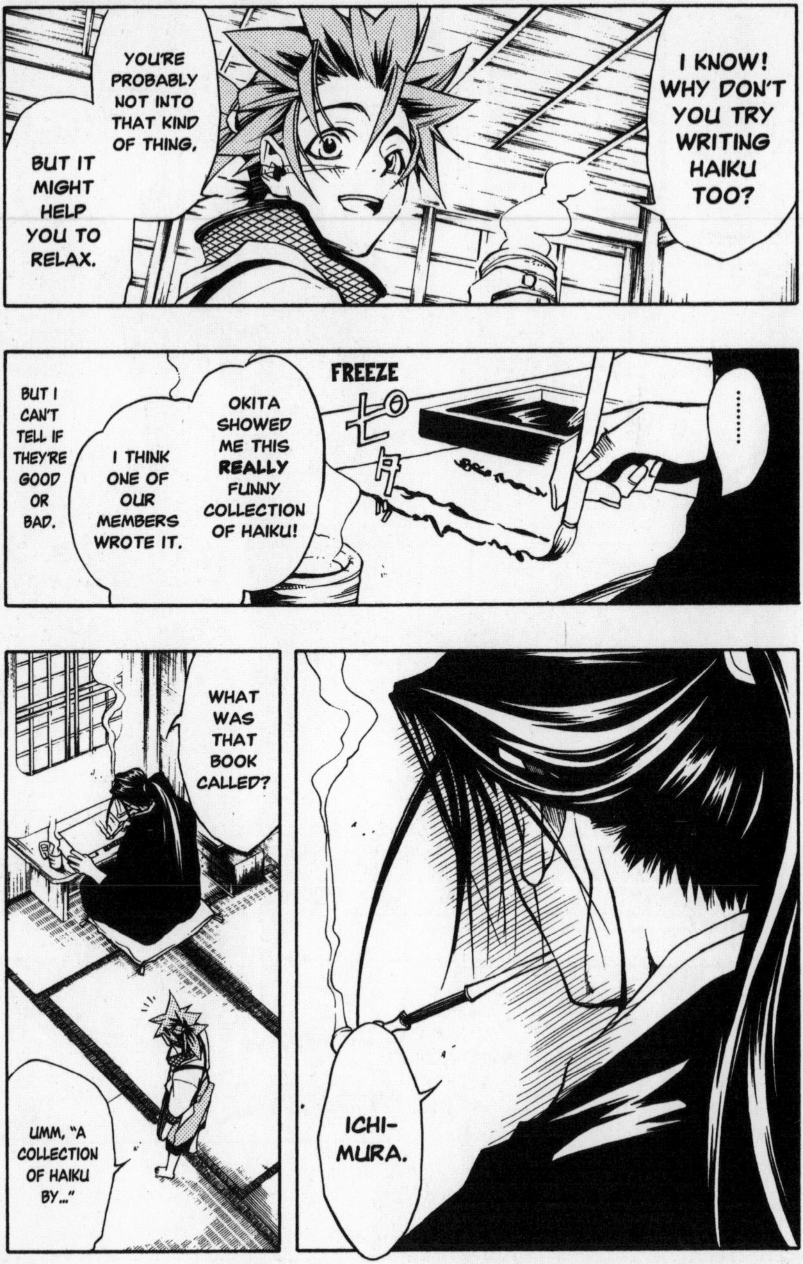
I KNOW! WHY DON'T YOU TRY WRITING HAIKU TOO?
YOU'RE PROBABLY NOT INTO THAT KIND OF THING,
BUT IT MIGHT HELP YOU TO RELAX.
......
FREEZE
OKITA SHOWED ME THIS REALLY FUNNY COLLECTION OF HAIKU!
I THINK ONE OF OUR MEMBERS WROTE IT.
BUT I CAN'T TELL IF THEY'RE GOOD OR BAD.
ICHI-MURA.
WHAT WAS THAT BOOK CALLED?
UMM, "A COLLECTION OF HAIKU BY..."

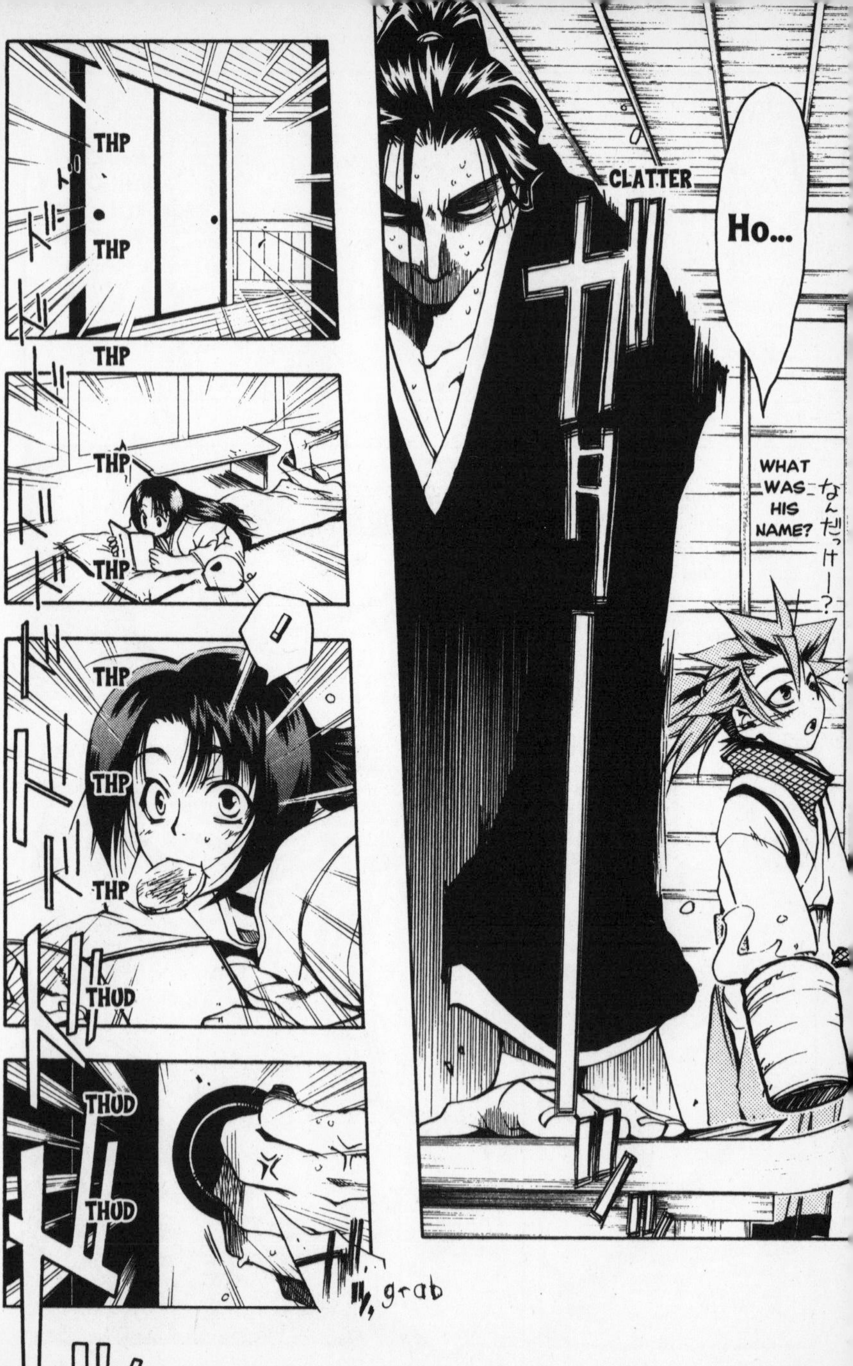

Ho...
CLATTER
WHAT WAS HIS NAME?
なんだっけー?
THP
THP
THP
THP
THP
!
THP
THP
THP
THUD
THUD
THUD
grab

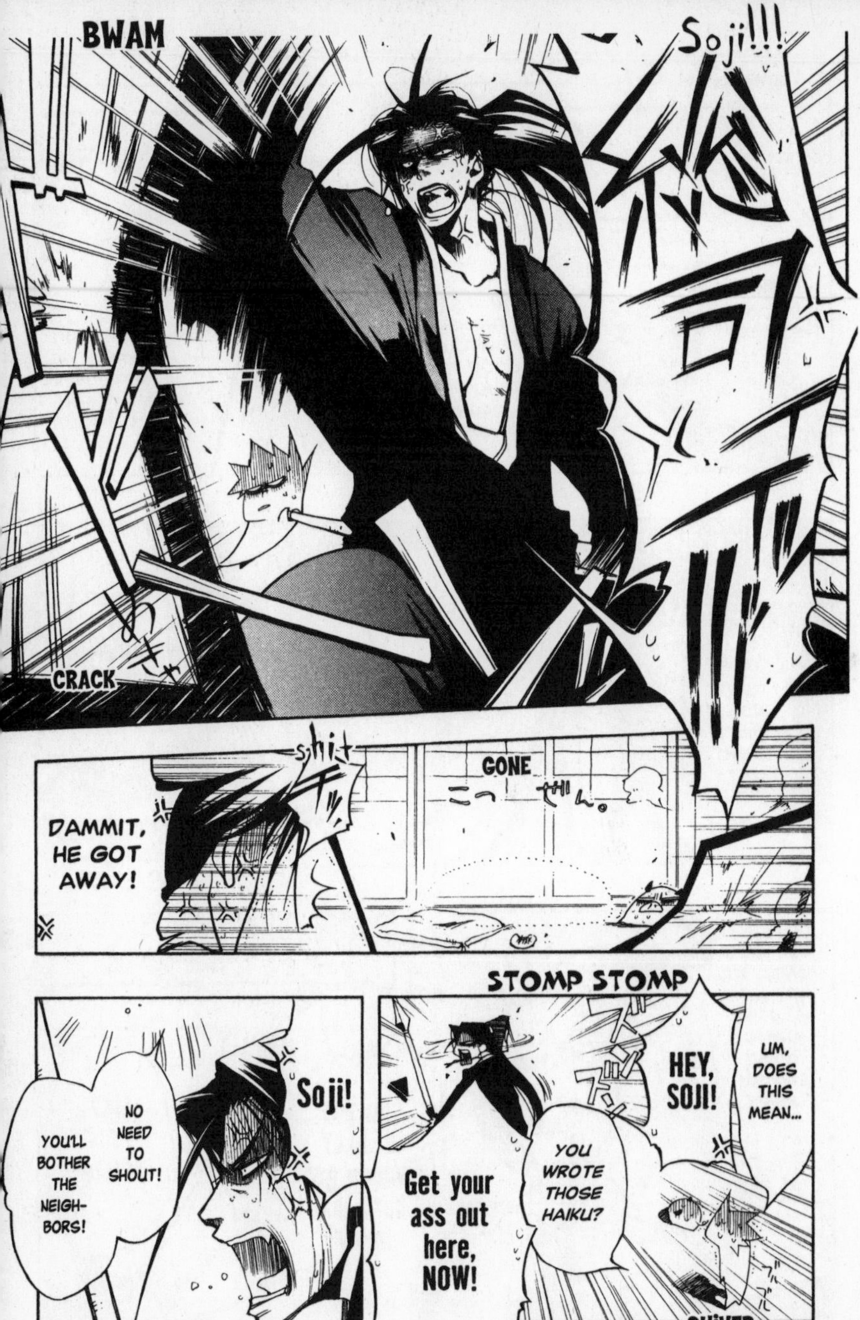
Soji!!!
BWAM
CRACK
shit
GONE
DAMMIT, HE GOT AWAY!
STOMP STOMP
UM, DOES THIS MEAN...
HEY, SOJI!
YOU WROTE THOSE HAIKU?
Get your ass out here, NOW!
SHIVER
Soji!
NO NEED TO SHOUT!
YOU'LL BOTHER THE NEIGH-BORS!

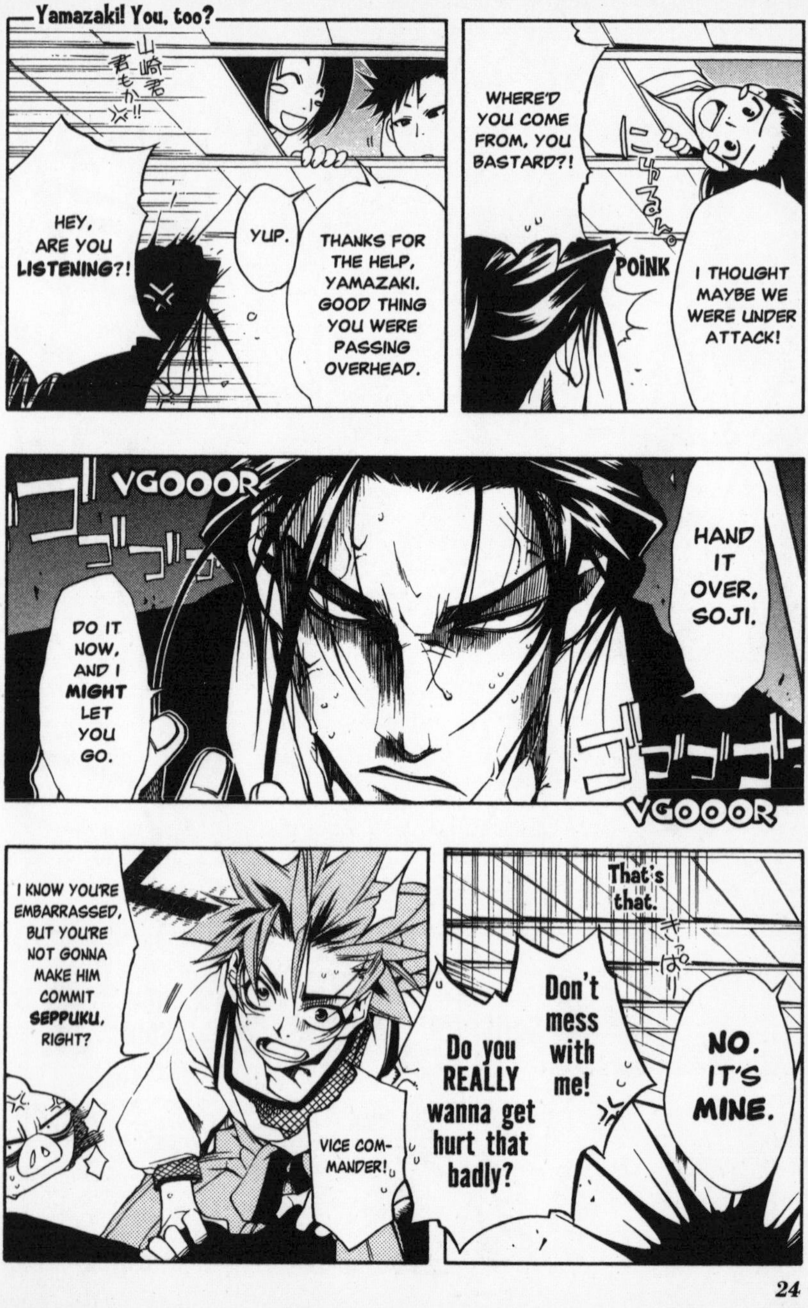
Yamazaki! You, too?
WHERE'D YOU COME FROM, YOU BASTARD?!
POINK
I THOUGHT MAYBE WE WERE UNDER ATTACK!
THANKS FOR THE HELP, YAMAZAKI. GOOD THING YOU WERE PASSING OVERHEAD.
YUP.
HEY, ARE YOU LISTENING?!
HAND IT OVER, SOJI.
VGOOOR
DO IT NOW, AND I MIGHT LET YOU GO.
VGOOOR
That's that.
NO. IT'S MINE.
Don't mess with me!
Do you REALLY wanna get hurt that badly?
VICE COMMANDER!
I KNOW YOU'RE EMBARRASSED, BUT YOU'RE NOT GONNA MAKE HIM COMMIT SEPPUKU, RIGHT?

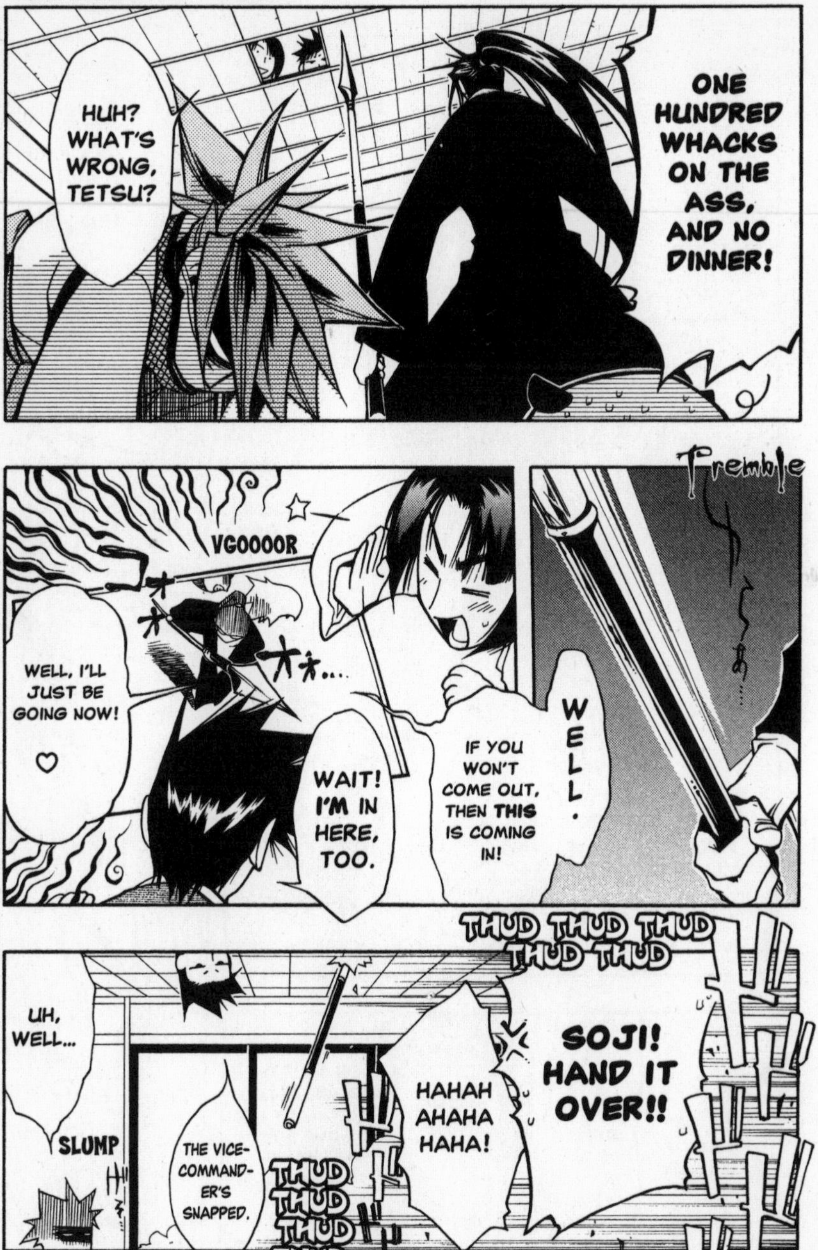
HUH? WHAT'S WRONG, TETSU?
ONE HUNDRED WHACKS ON THE ASS, AND NO DINNER!
Tremble
WELL.
IF YOU WON'T COME OUT, THEN THIS IS COMING IN!
VGOOOOR
WAIT! I'M IN HERE, TOO.
WELL, I'LL JUST BE GOING NOW! ♡
THUD THUD THUD THUD THUD
SOJI! HAND IT OVER!!
HAHAH AHAHA HAHA!
THE VICE-COMMANDER'S SNAPPED.
THUD THUD THUD THUD
UH, WELL...
SLUMP

「"A Collection of Haiku by Hogyoku"」

This collection was written by Toshizo Hijikata before he came to Kyoto. "Hogyoku" was Hijikata's pen name.

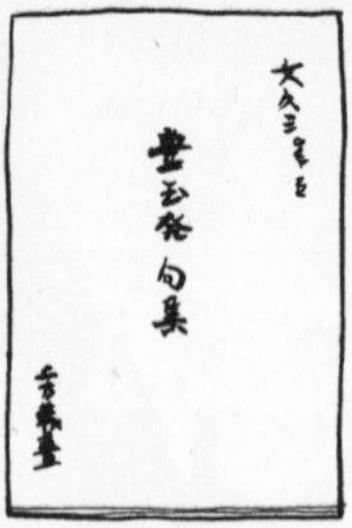

It is currently being held for safekeeping and display at his birthplace in Hino, which is now a memorial museum.

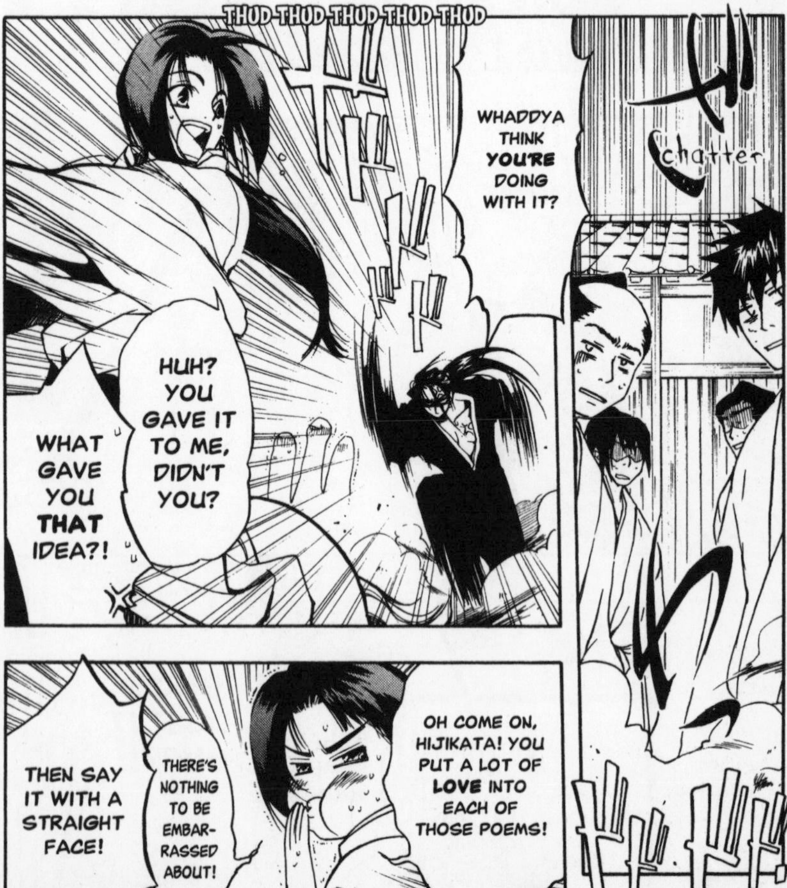
THUD THUD THUD THUD THUD
chatter
WHADDYA THINK YOU'RE DOING WITH IT?
HUH? YOU GAVE IT TO ME, DIDN'T YOU?
WHAT GAVE YOU THAT IDEA?!
OH COME ON, HIJIKATA! YOU PUT A LOT OF LOVE INTO EACH OF THOSE POEMS!
THERE'S NOTHING TO BE EMBARRASSED ABOUT!
THEN SAY IT WITH A STRAIGHT FACE!
THUD THUD THUD THUD

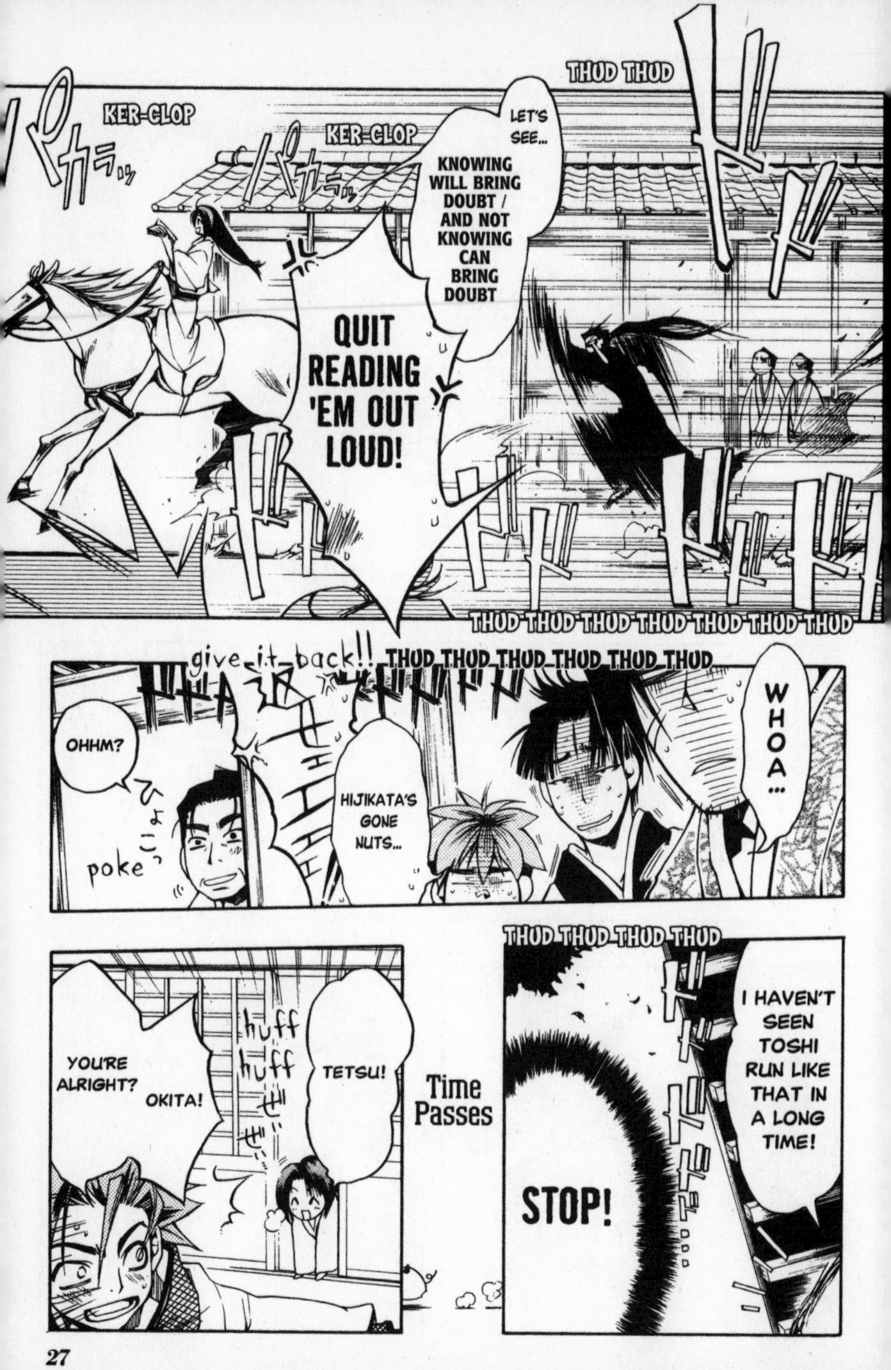
THUD THUD
LET'S SEE...
KNOWING WILL BRING DOUBT / AND NOT KNOWING CAN BRING DOUBT
QUIT READING 'EM OUT LOUD!
KER-CLOP
KER-CLOP
THUD THUD THUD THUD THUD THUD THUD
THUD THUD THUD THUD THUD THUD
give it back!!
WHOA...
HIJIKATA'S GONE NUTS...
OHHM?
poke
THUD THUD THUD THUD
I HAVEN'T SEEN TOSHI RUN LIKE THAT IN A LONG TIME!
STOP!
Time Passes
TETSU!
huff huff
OKITA!
YOU'RE ALRIGHT?

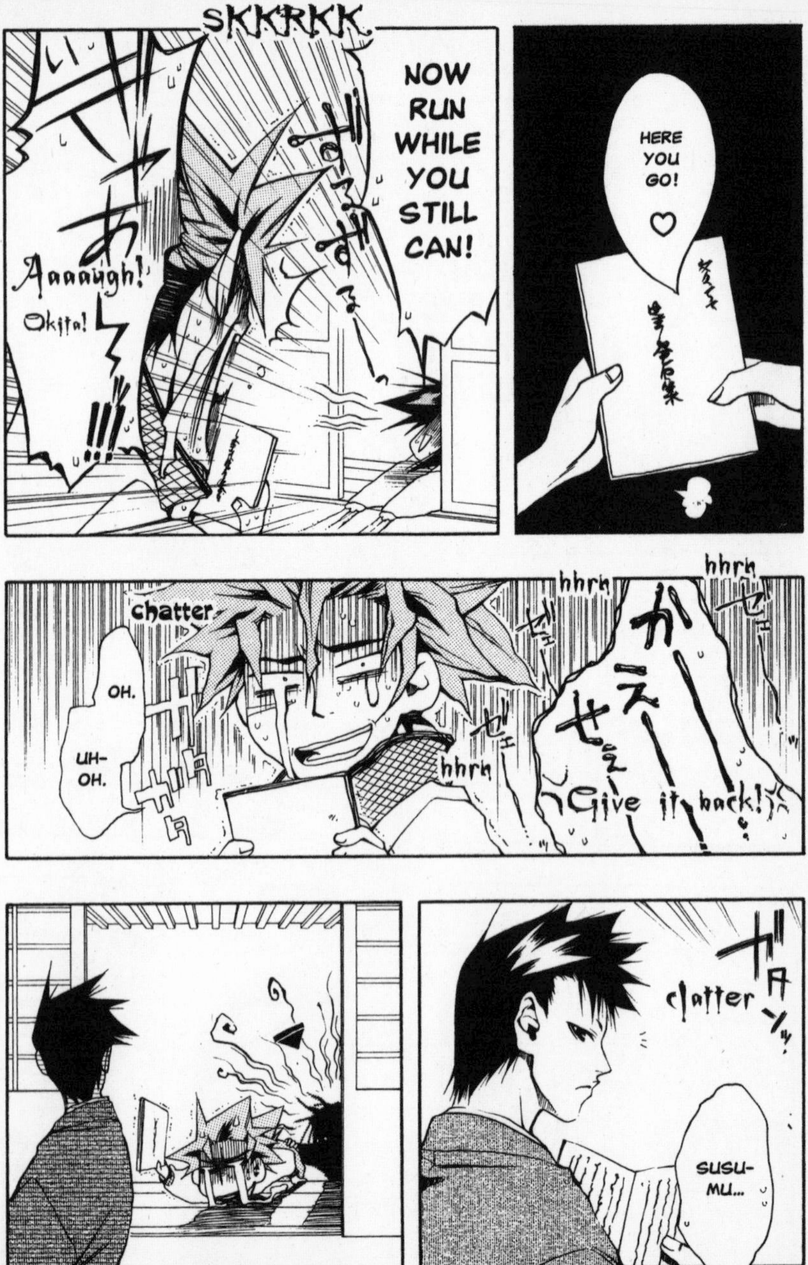

HERE YOU GO! ♡
SKKRKK
NOW RUN WHILE YOU STILL CAN!
Aaaaugh!
Okita!
hhrn
Give it back!
hhrn
hhrn
chatter
OH.
UH-OH.
clatter
SUSU-MU...

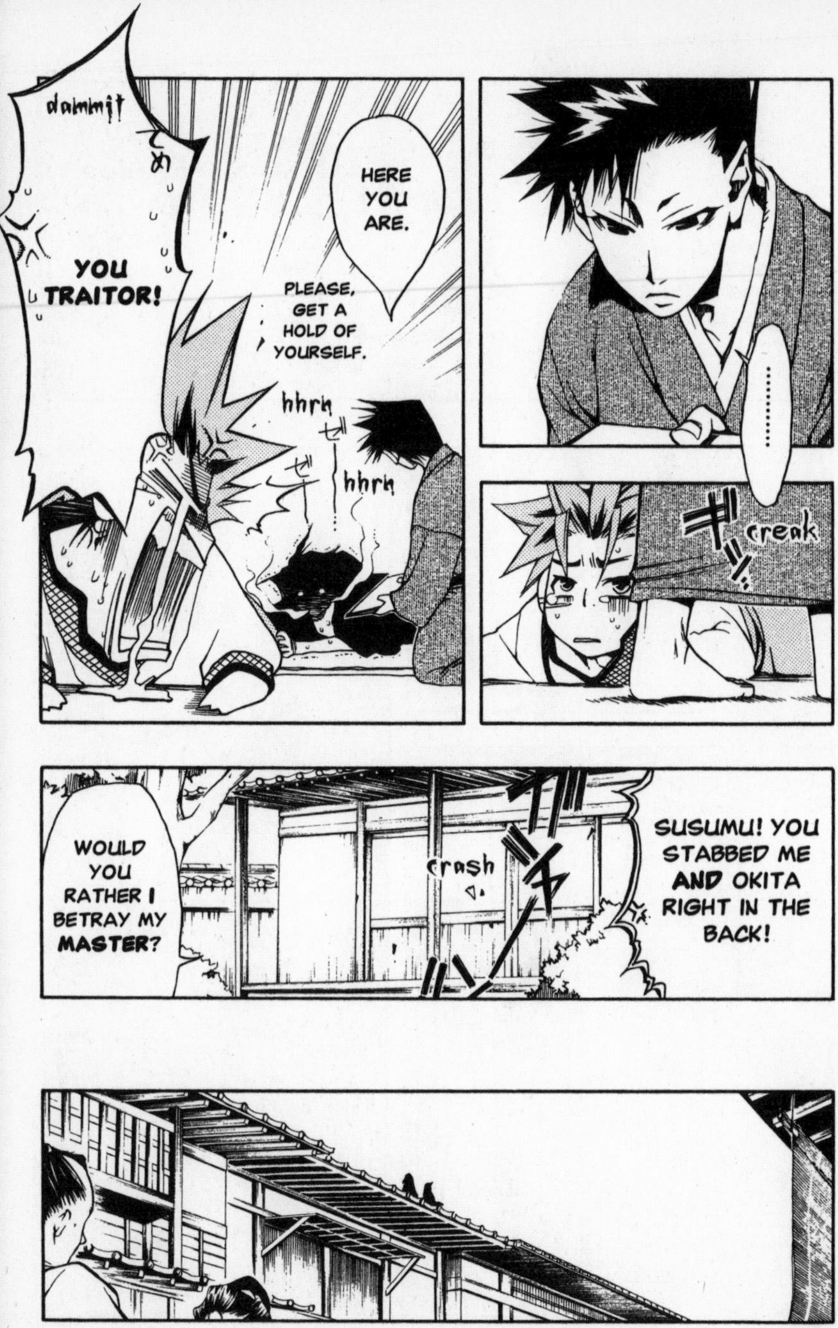
......
creak
HERE YOU ARE.
PLEASE, GET A HOLD OF YOURSELF.
hhrh
hhrh
dammit
YOU TRAITOR!
SUSUMU! YOU STABBED ME AND OKITA RIGHT IN THE BACK!
crash
WOULD YOU RATHER I BETRAY MY MASTER?

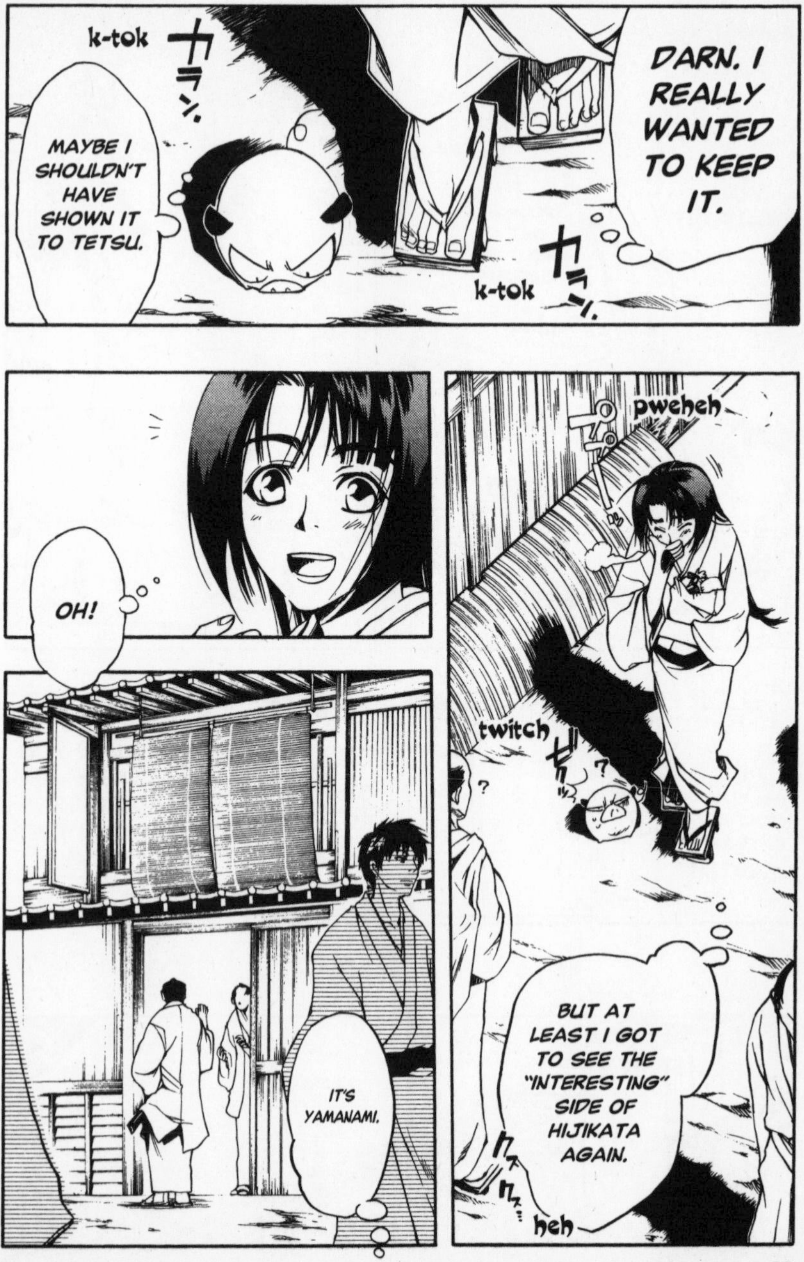
DARN. I REALLY WANTED TO KEEP IT.
k-tok
MAYBE I SHOULDN'T HAVE SHOWN IT TO TETSU.
k-tok
pweheh
twitch
BUT AT LEAST I GOT TO SEE THE "INTERESTING" SIDE OF HIJIKATA AGAIN.
heh
OH!
IT'S YAMANAMI.

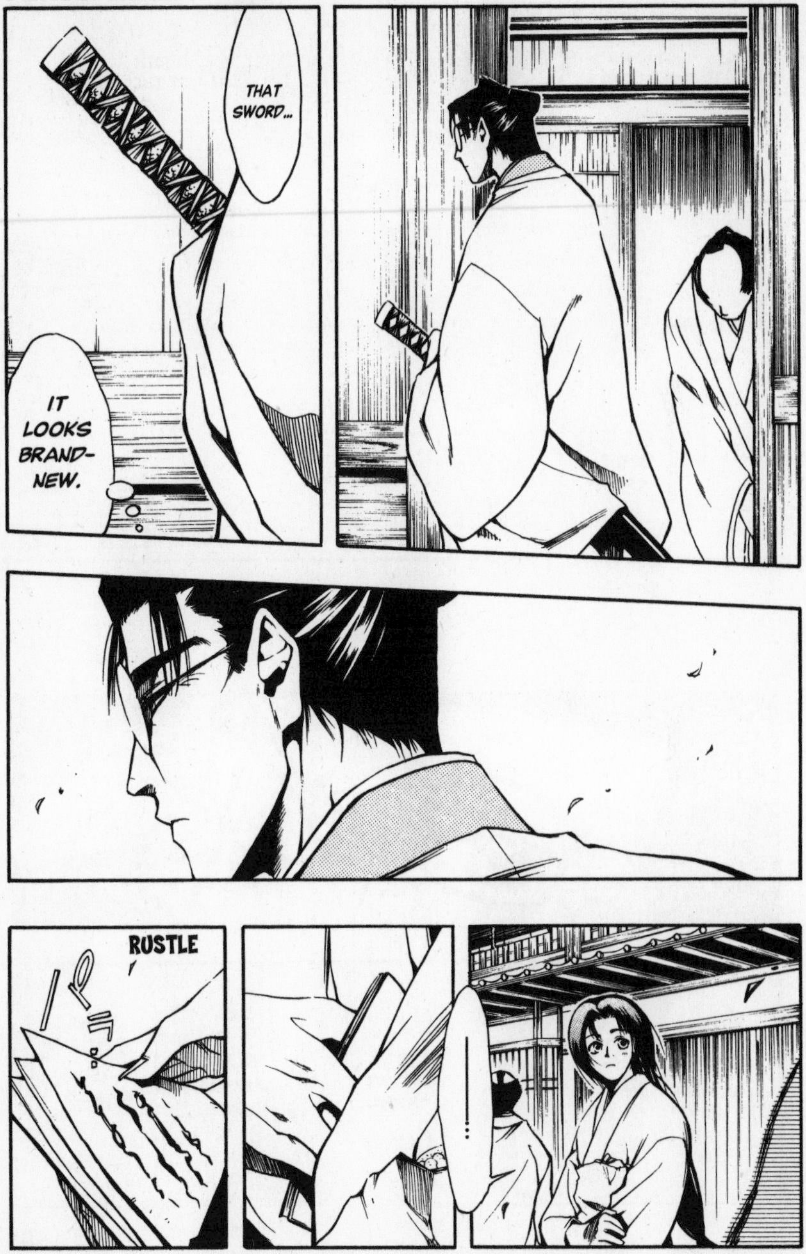
THAT SWORD...
IT LOOKS BRAND-NEW.
...
RUSTLE

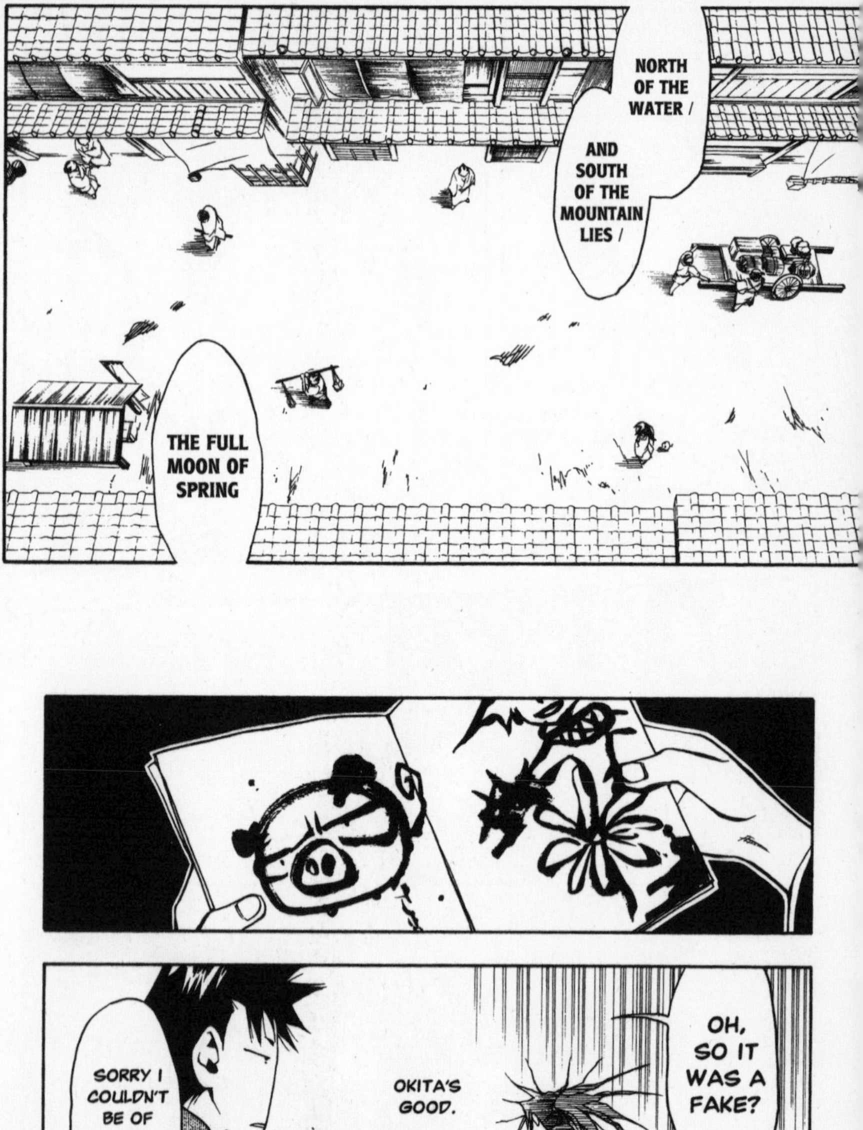
NORTH OF THE WATER /
AND SOUTH OF THE MOUNTAIN LIES /
THE FULL MOON OF SPRING
OH, SO IT WAS A FAKE?
OKITA'S GOOD.
SORRY I COULDN'T BE OF ANY HELP.

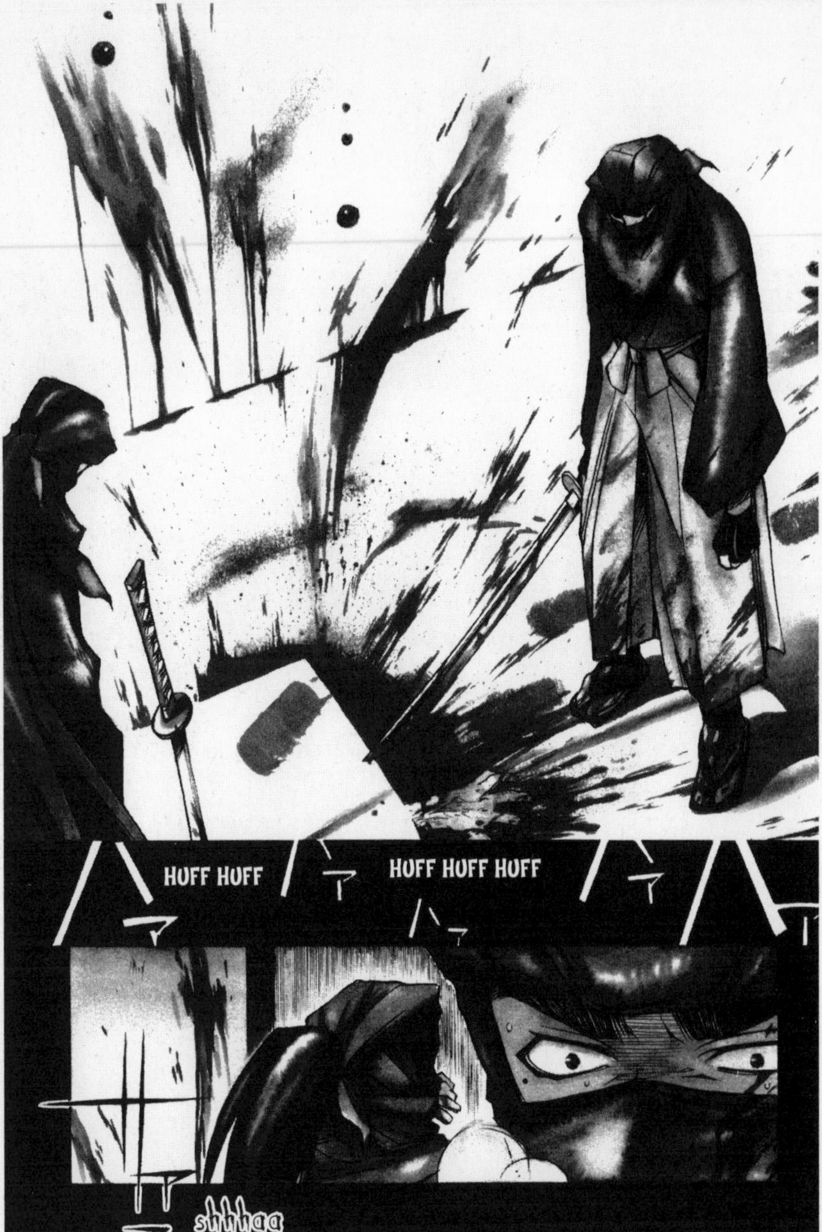

HOFF HOFF
HOFF HOFF HOFF
shhhaa

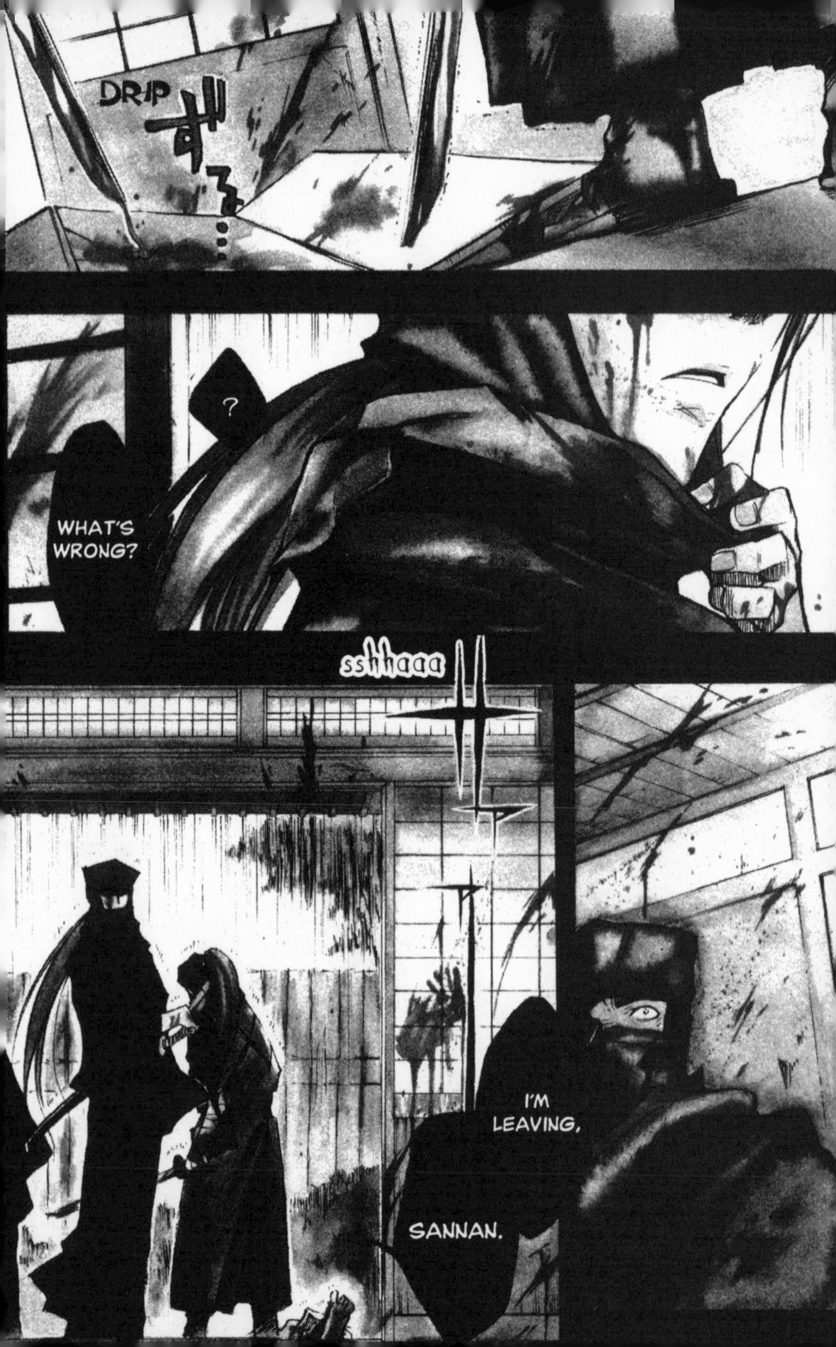
DRIP
?
WHAT'S WRONG?
sshhaaa
I'M LEAVING,
SANNAN.

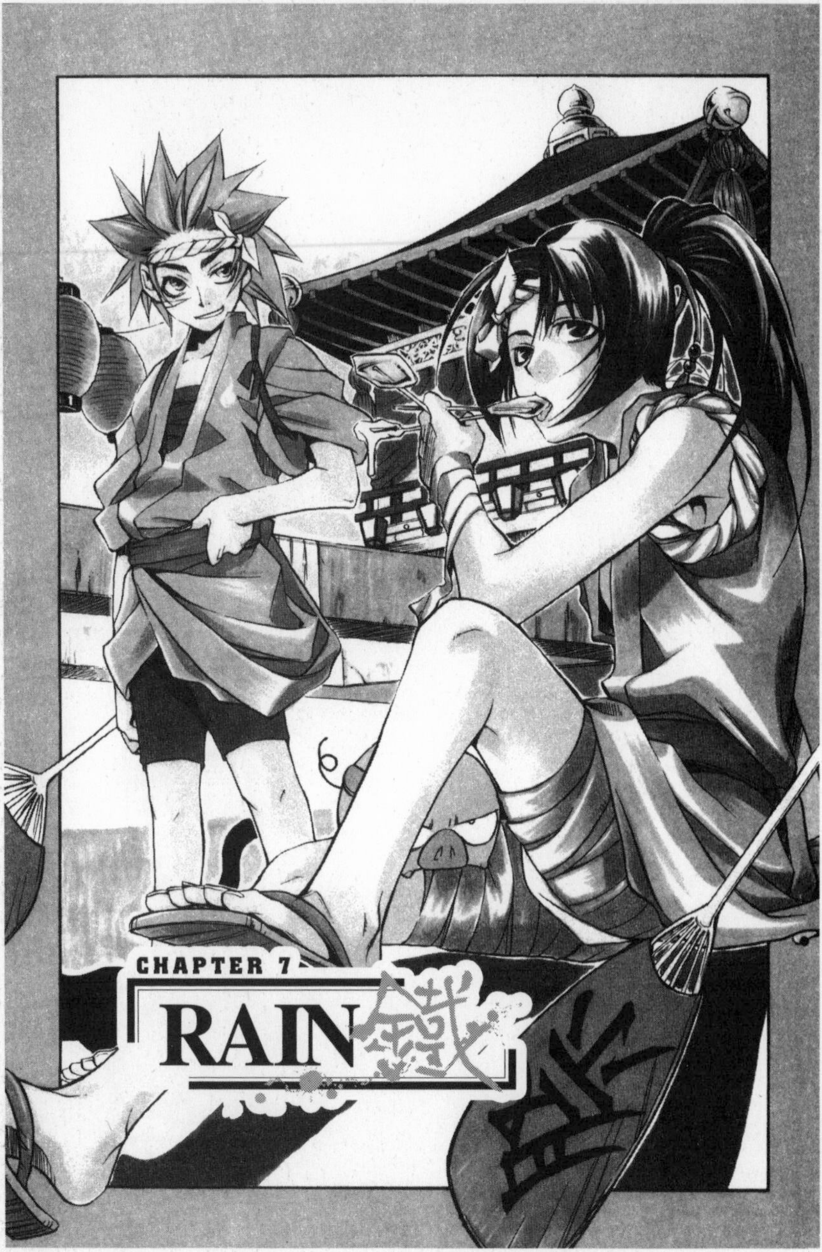
CHAPTER 7
RAIN

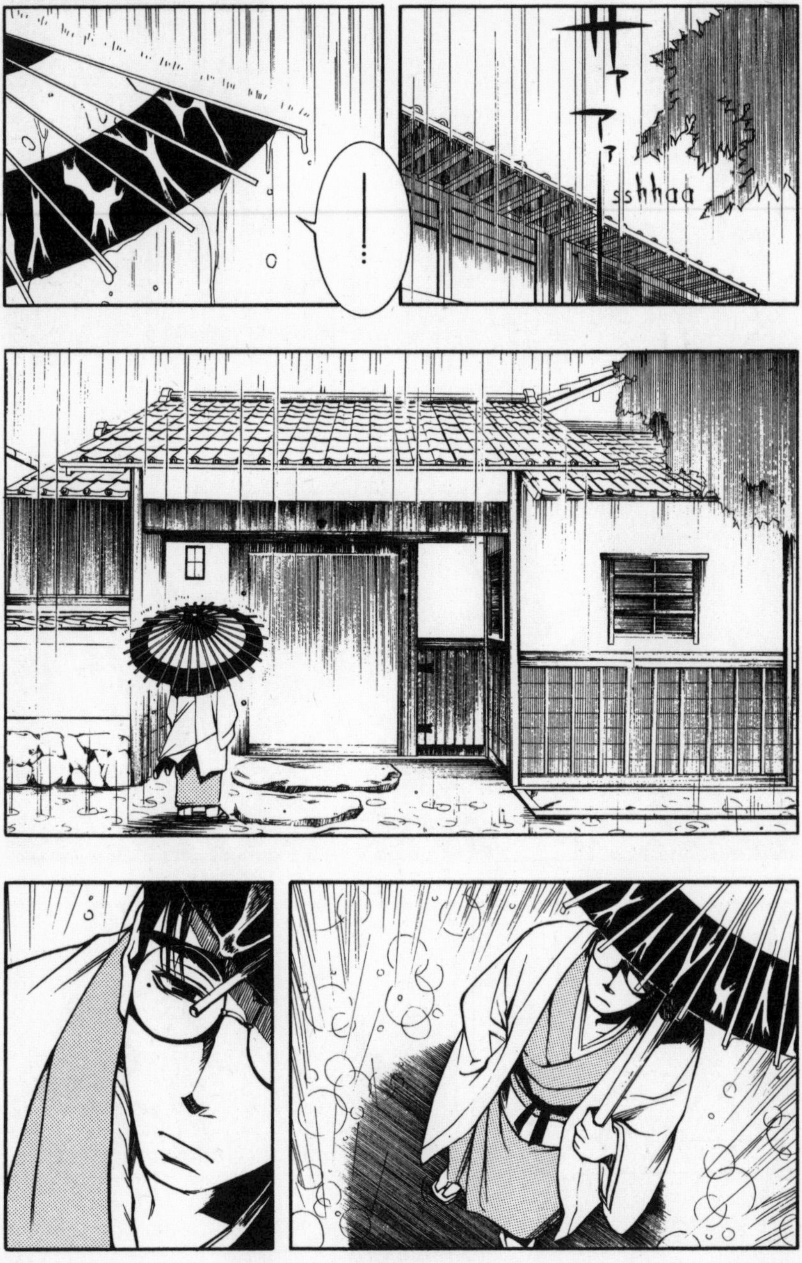
サァァァ
sshhaa
—…

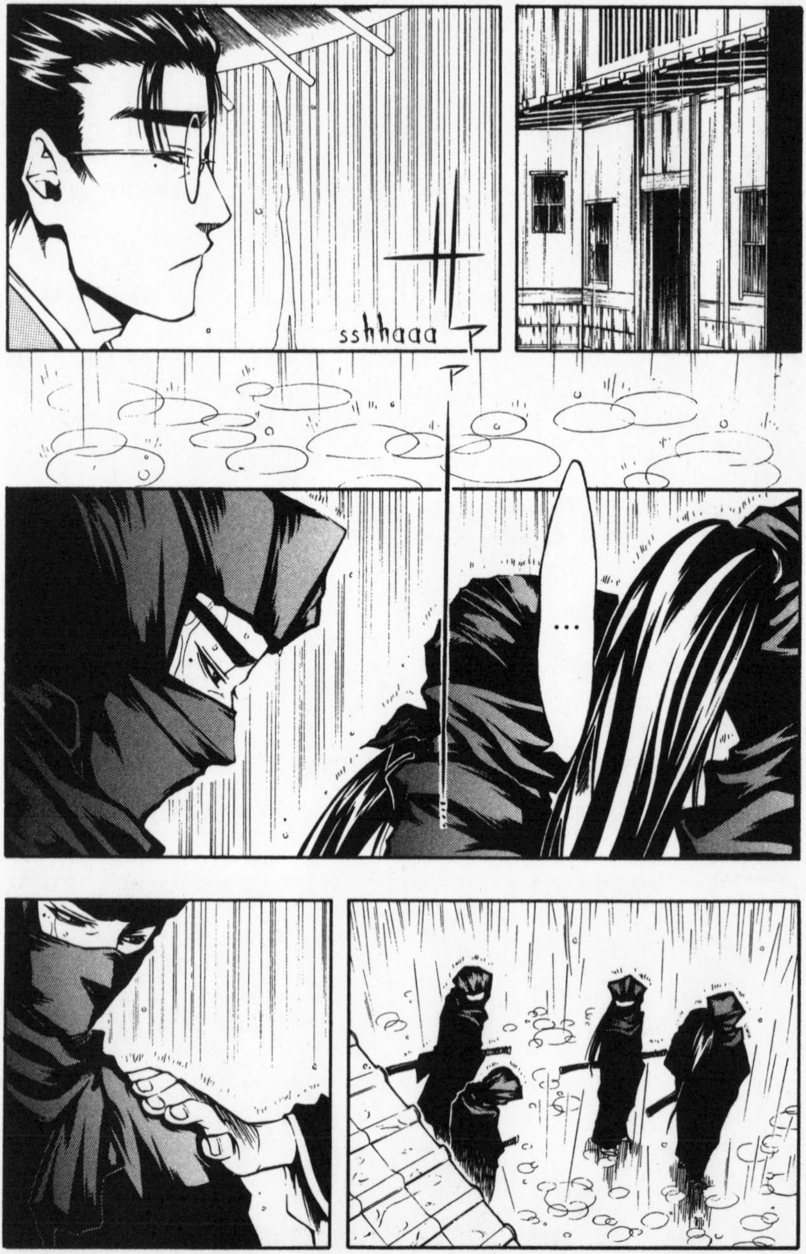

sshhaaa
...

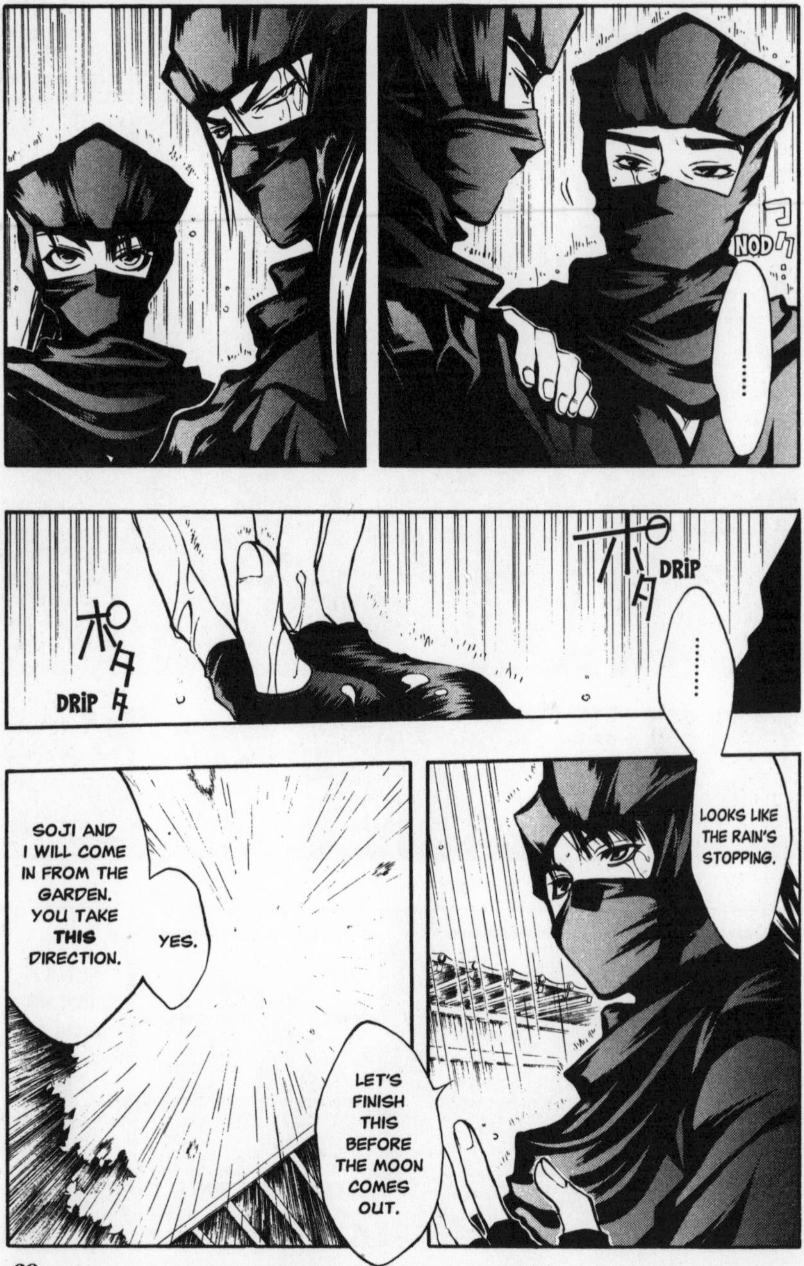
コク
NOD
......
ポタ
DRIP
ポタタ
DRIP
......
LOOKS LIKE THE RAIN'S STOPPING.
LET'S FINISH THIS BEFORE THE MOON COMES OUT.
SOJI AND I WILL COME IN FROM THE GARDEN. YOU TAKE THIS DIRECTION.
YES.

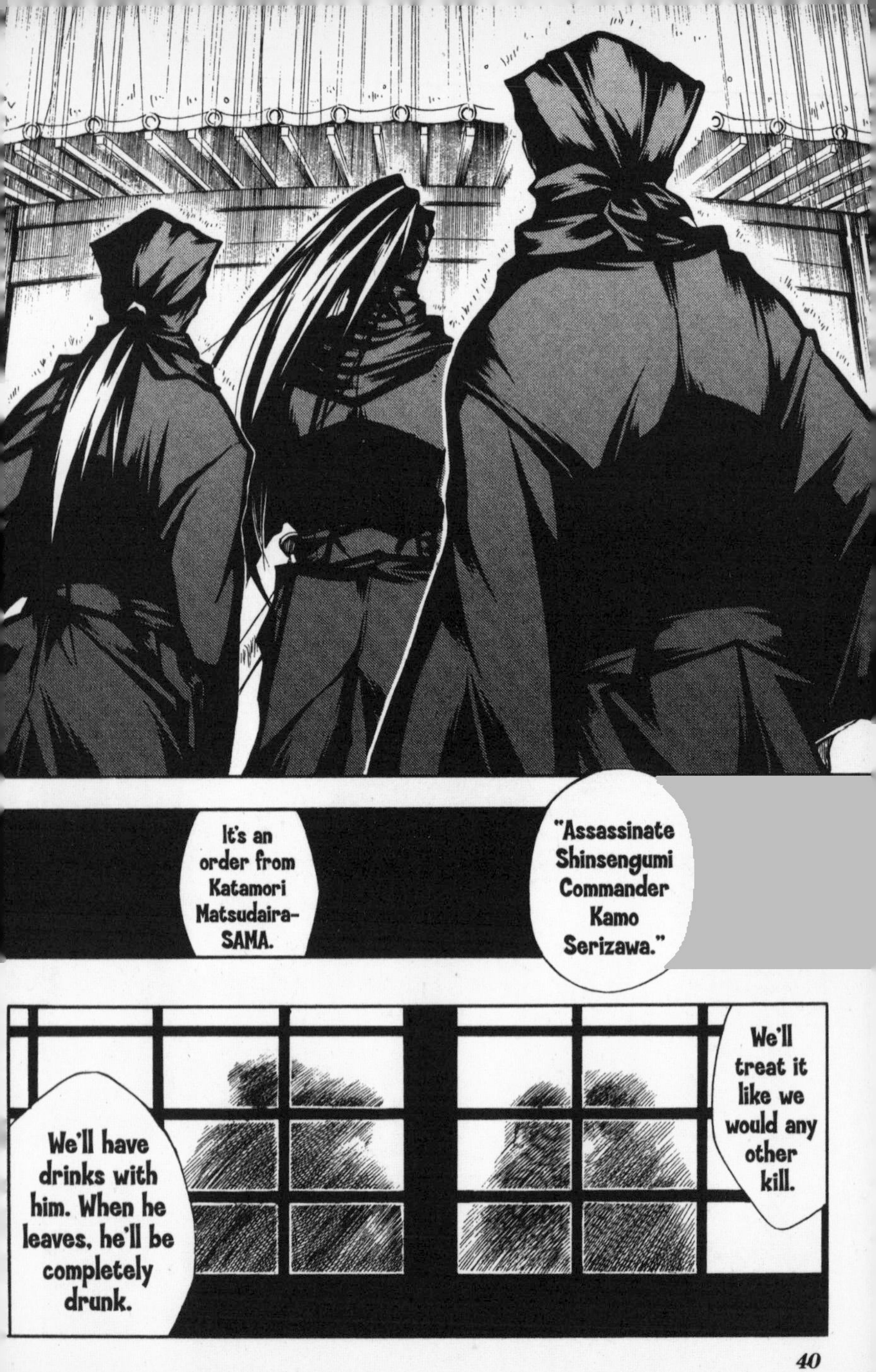
"Assassinate Shinsengumi Commander Kamo Serizawa."
It's an order from Katamori Matsudaira-SAMA.
We'll treat it like we would any other kill.
We'll have drinks with him. When he leaves, he'll be completely drunk.

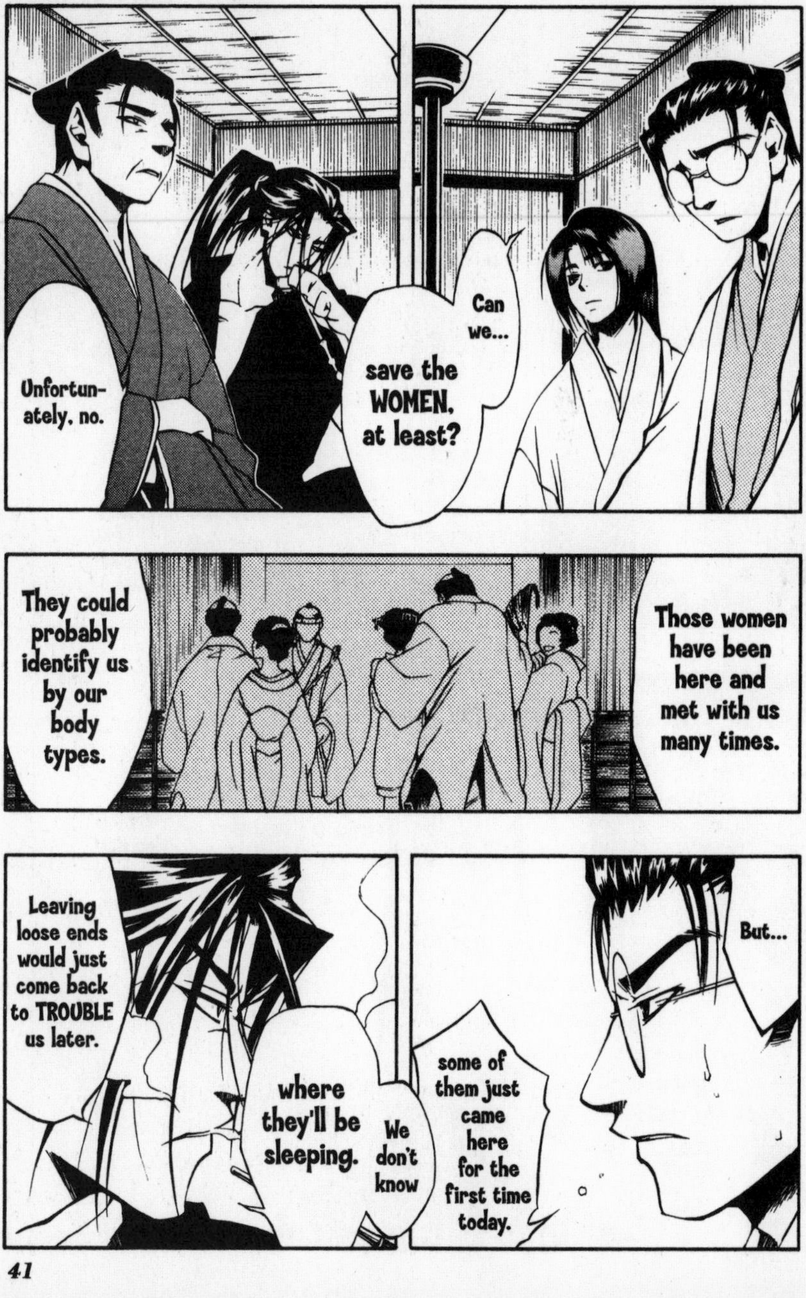
Can we...
save the WOMEN, at least?
Unfortunately, no.
Those women have been here and met with us many times.
They could probably identify us by our body types.
But...
some of them just came here for the first time today.
We don't know
where they'll be sleeping.
Leaving loose ends would just come back to TROUBLE us later.

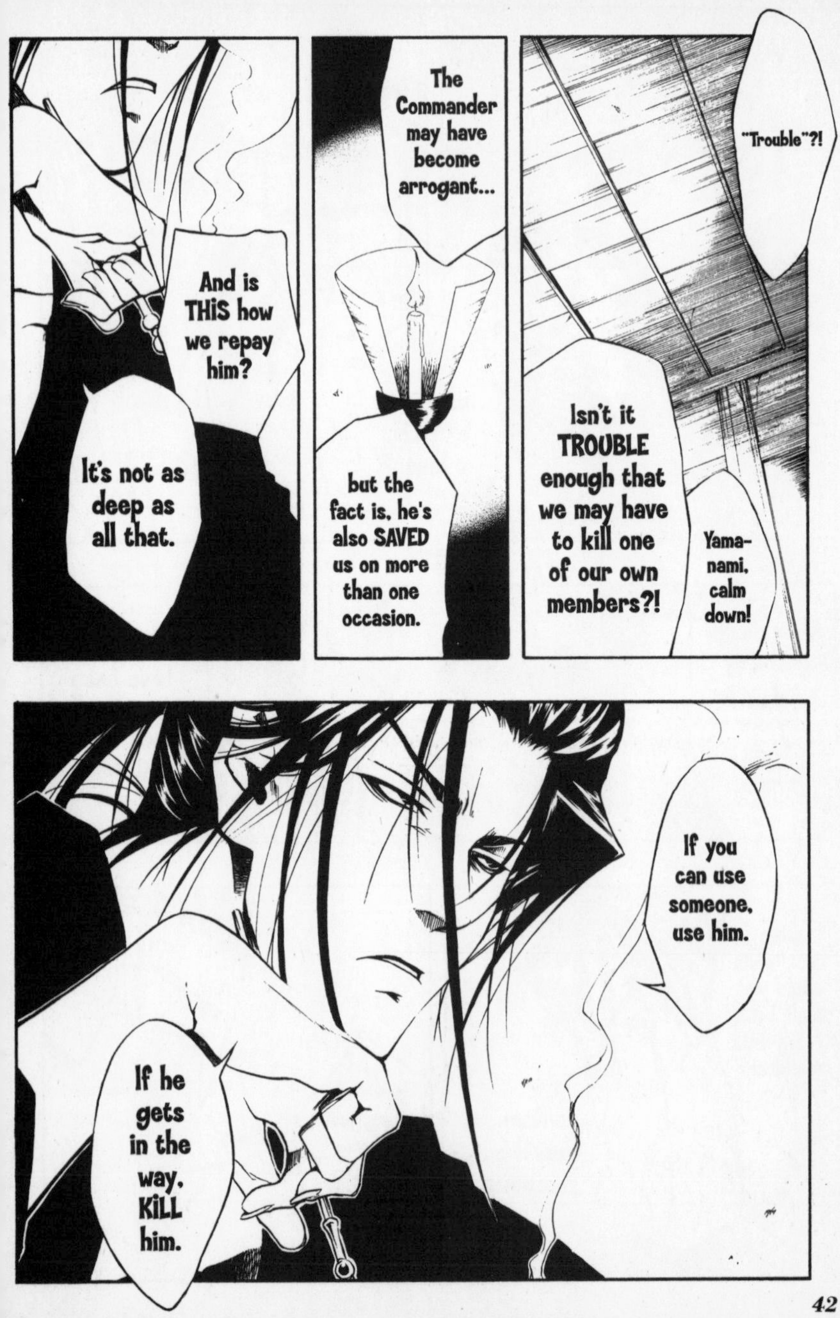
"Trouble"?!
Isn't it TROUBLE enough that we may have to kill one of our own members?!
Yamanami, calm down!
The Commander may have become arrogant...
but the fact is, he's also SAVED us on more than one occasion.
And is THIS how we repay him?
It's not as deep as all that.
If you can use someone, use him.
If he gets in the way, KILL him.

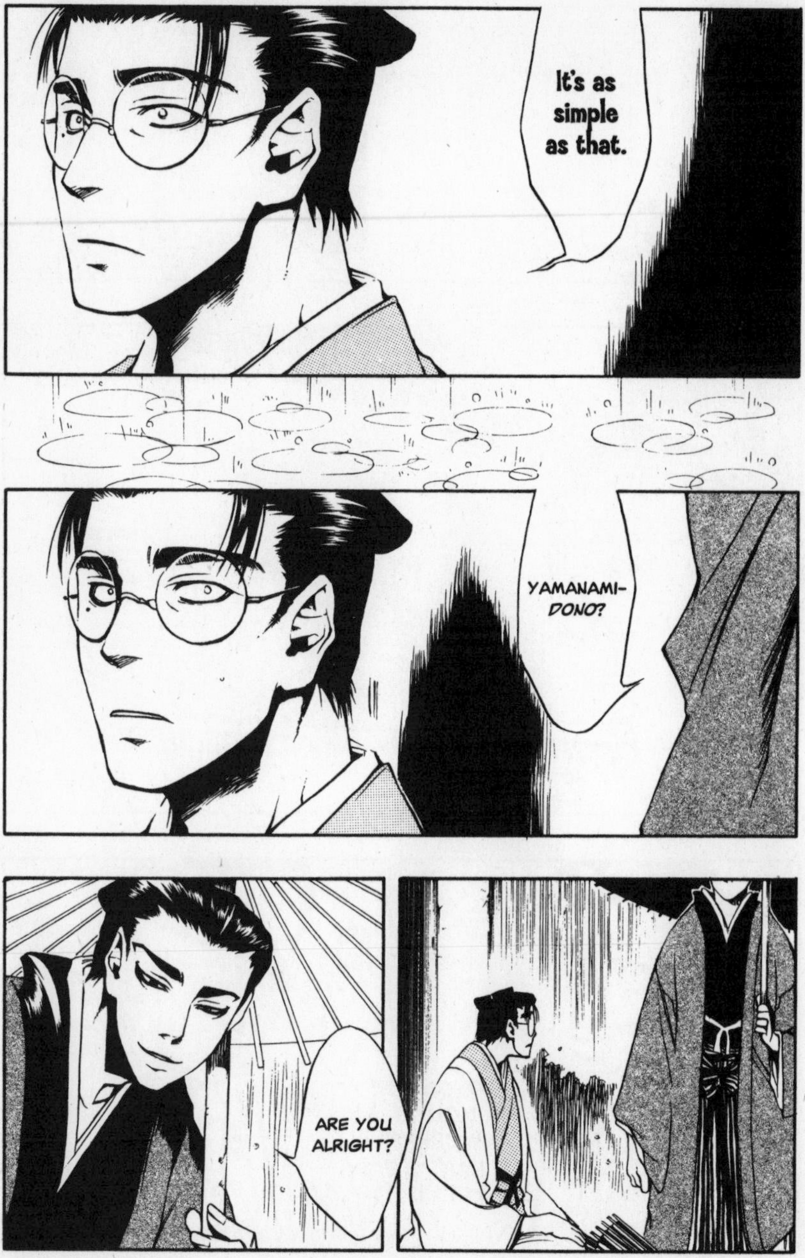
It's as simple as that.
YAMANAMI-DONO?
ARE YOU ALRIGHT?

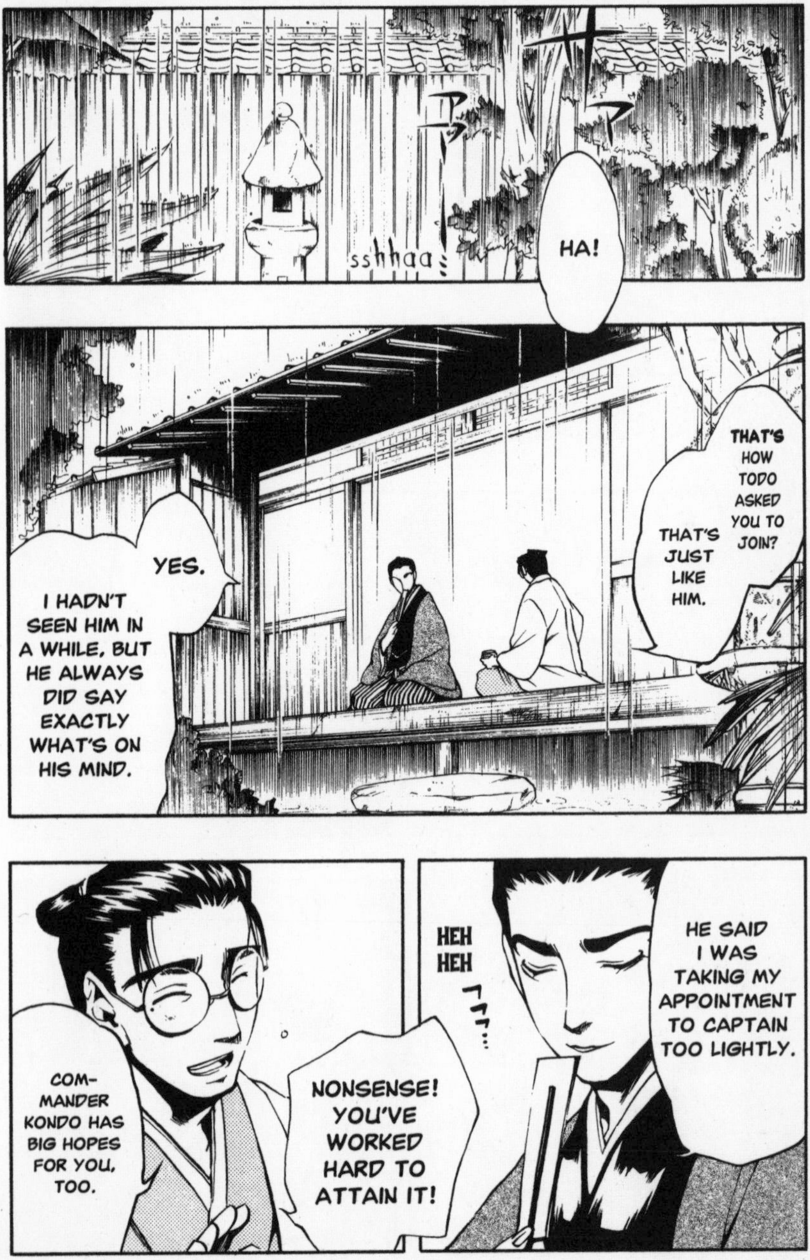
sshhaa
HA!
THAT'S HOW TODO ASKED YOU TO JOIN?
THAT'S JUST LIKE HIM.
YES.
I HADN'T SEEN HIM IN A WHILE, BUT HE ALWAYS DID SAY EXACTLY WHAT'S ON HIS MIND.
HE SAID I WAS TAKING MY APPOINTMENT TO CAPTAIN TOO LIGHTLY.
HEH HEH
NONSENSE! YOU'VE WORKED HARD TO ATTAIN IT!
COM-MANDER KONDO HAS BIG HOPES FOR YOU, TOO.

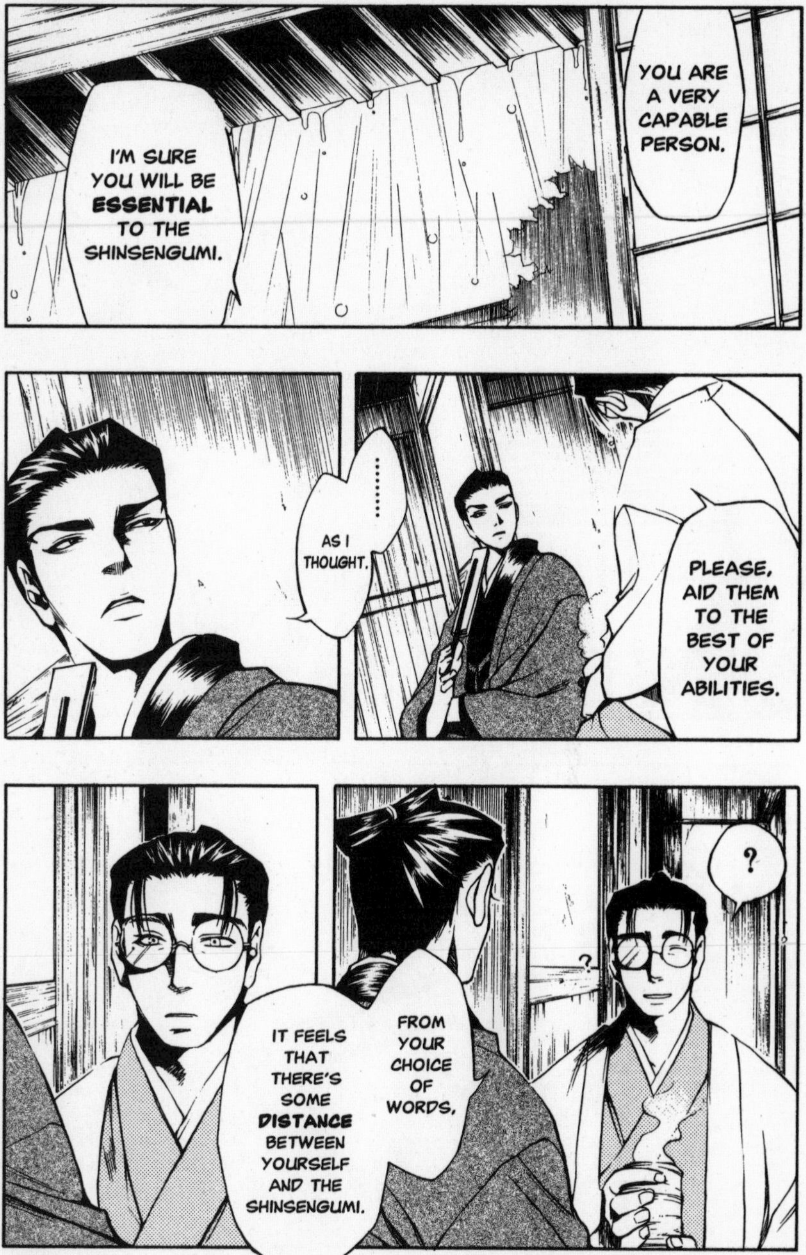
YOU ARE A VERY CAPABLE PERSON.
I'M SURE YOU WILL BE ESSENTIAL TO THE SHINSENGUMI.
PLEASE, AID THEM TO THE BEST OF YOUR ABILITIES.
......
AS I THOUGHT.
?
?
FROM YOUR CHOICE OF WORDS,
IT FEELS THAT THERE'S SOME DISTANCE BETWEEN YOURSELF AND THE SHINSENGUMI.

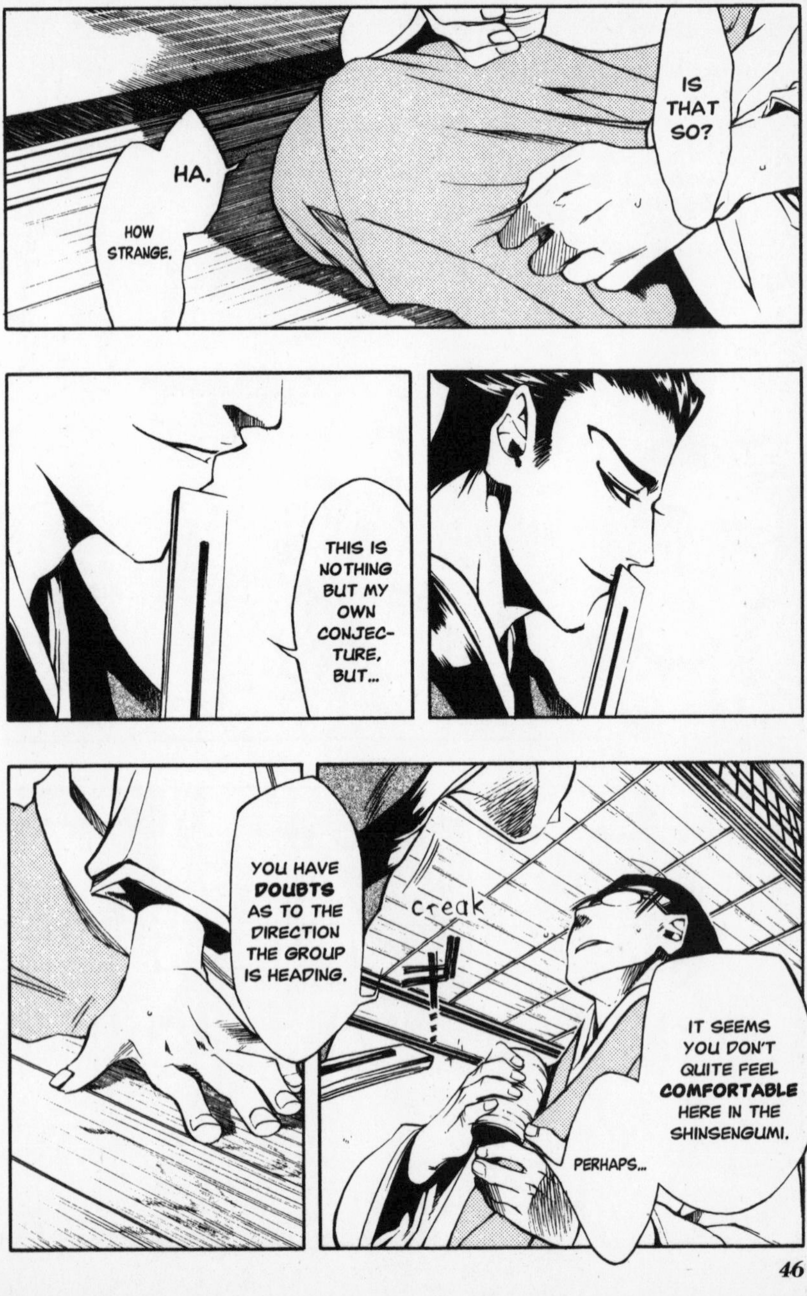
IS THAT SO?
HA.
HOW STRANGE.
THIS IS NOTHING BUT MY OWN CONJECTURE, BUT...
IT SEEMS YOU DON'T QUITE FEEL **COMFORTABLE** HERE IN THE SHINSENGUMI.
creak
PERHAPS...
YOU HAVE **DOUBTS** AS TO THE DIRECTION THE GROUP IS HEADING.

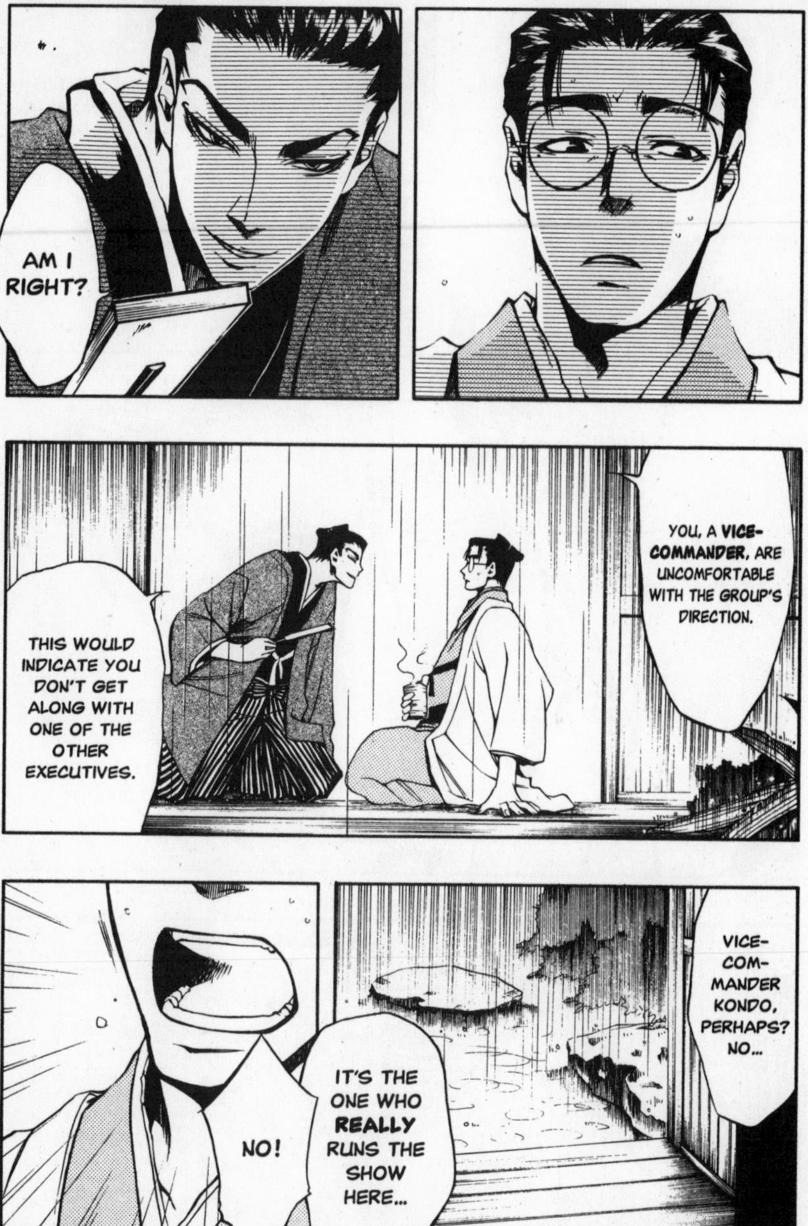
AM I RIGHT?
YOU, A VICE-COMMANDER, ARE UNCOMFORTABLE WITH THE GROUP'S DIRECTION.
THIS WOULD INDICATE YOU DON'T GET ALONG WITH ONE OF THE OTHER EXECUTIVES.
VICE-COMMANDER KONDO, PERHAPS? NO...
IT'S THE ONE WHO REALLY RUNS THE SHOW HERE...
NO!

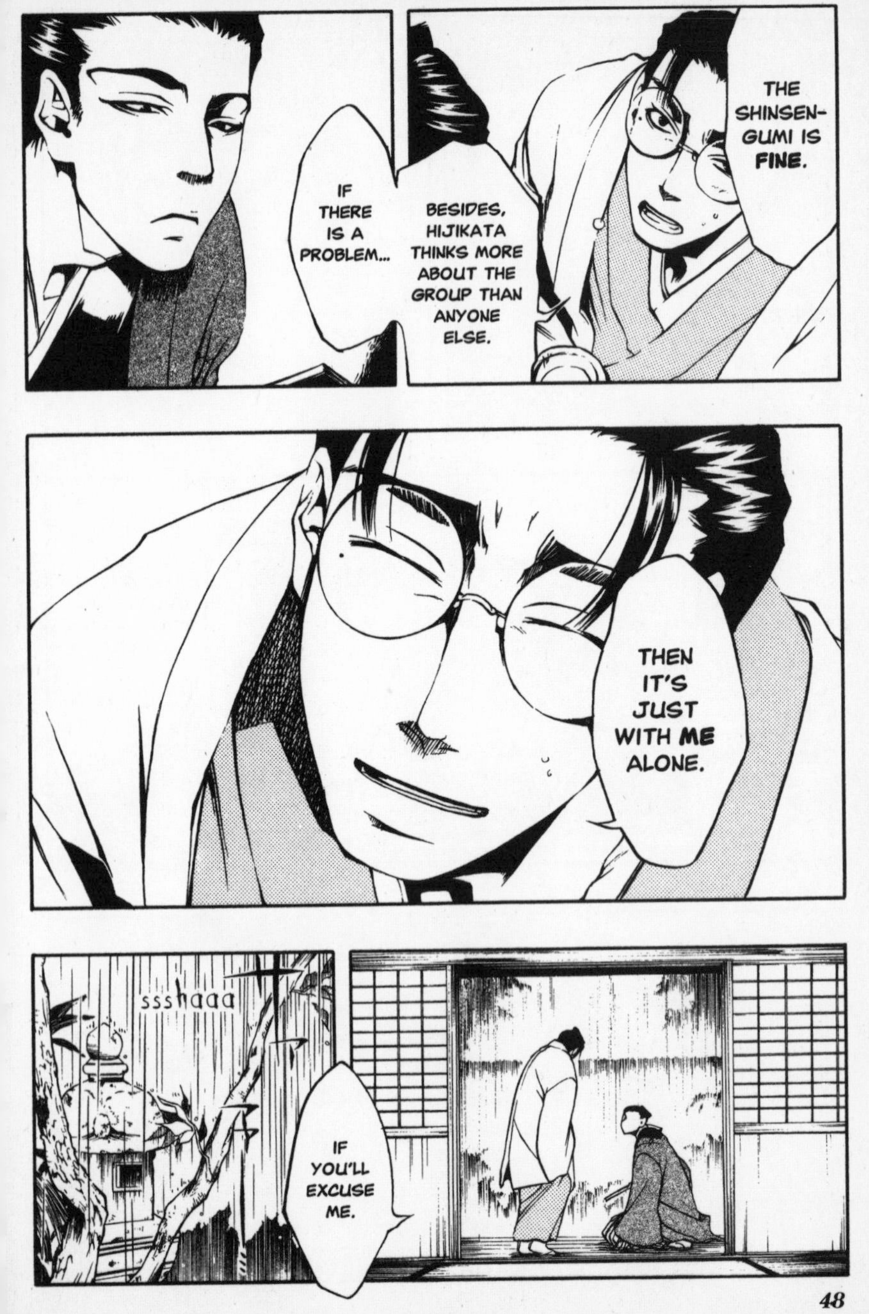
THE SHINSEN-GUMI IS FINE.
BESIDES, HIJIKATA THINKS MORE ABOUT THE GROUP THAN ANYONE ELSE.
IF THERE IS A PROBLEM...
THEN IT'S JUST WITH ME ALONE.
IF YOU'LL EXCUSE ME.
ssshaaa

PERHAPS HIS STATE OF MIND

IS MORE COMPLEX THAN I THOUGHT.

HMM.

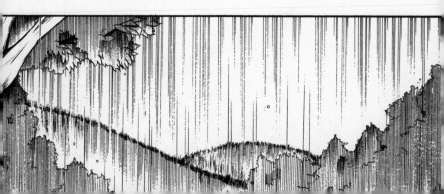

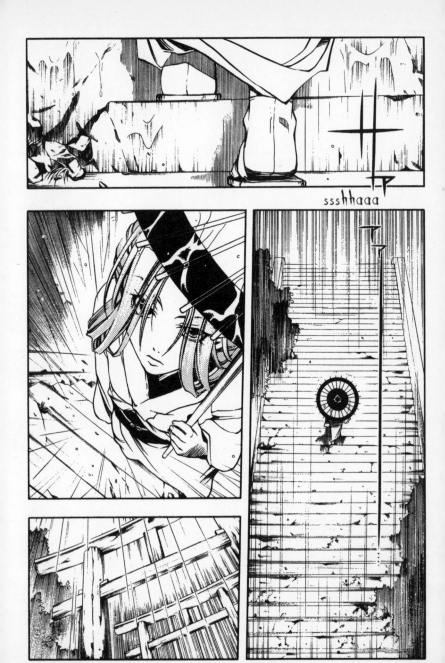

ssshhaaa

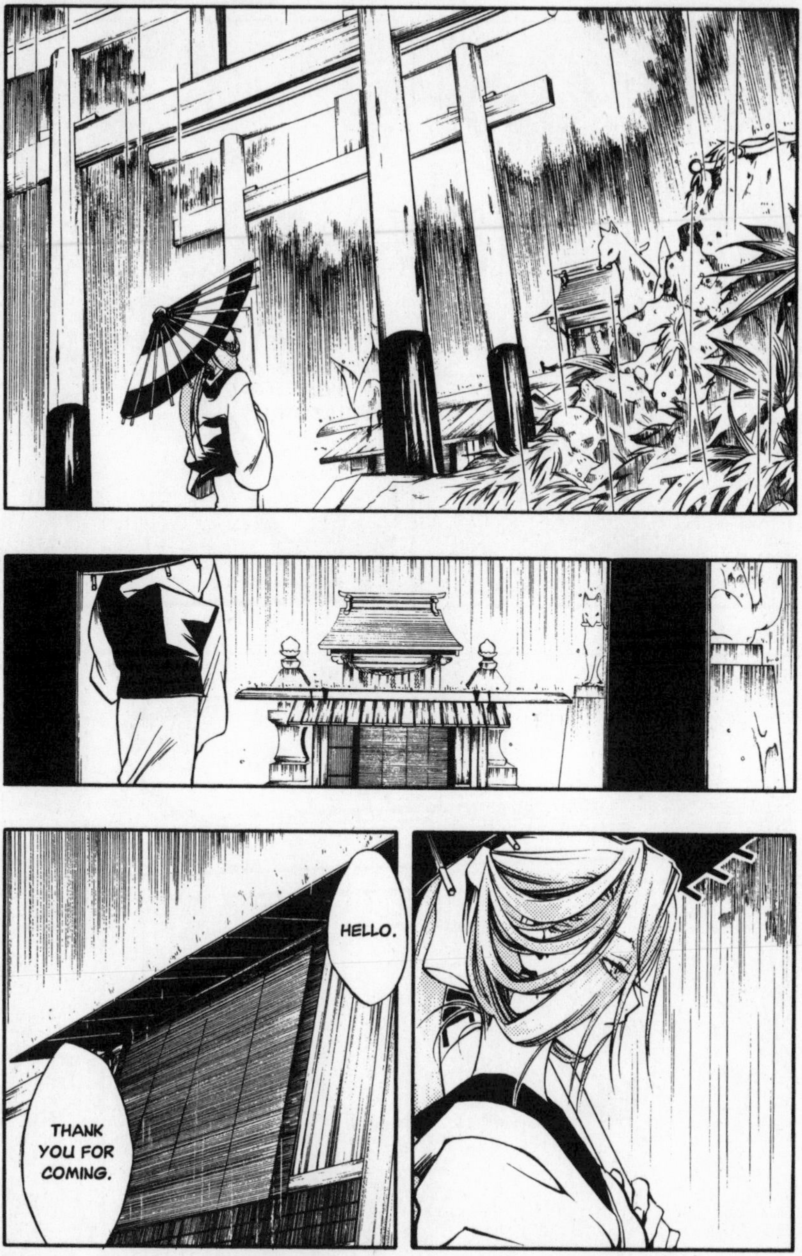
HELLO.
THANK YOU FOR COMING.

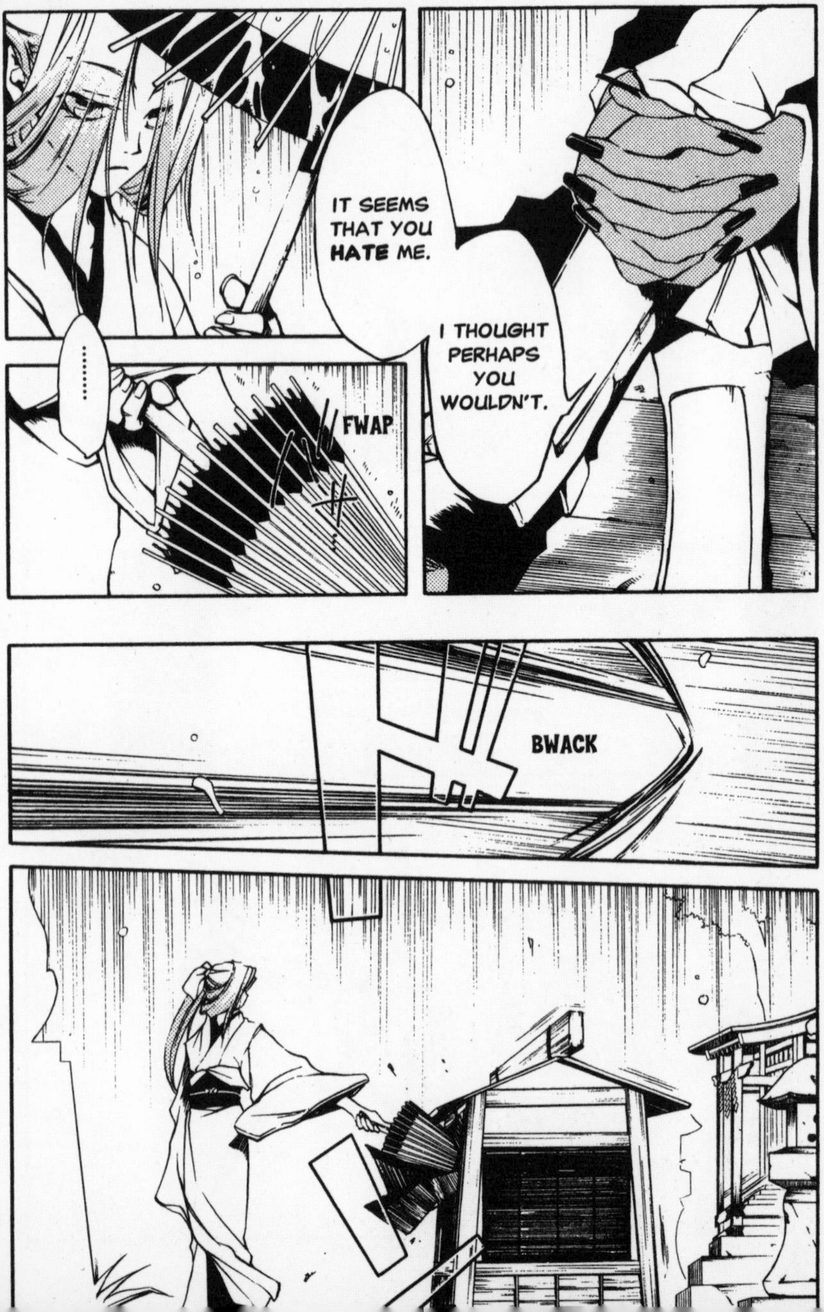
IT SEEMS THAT YOU HATE ME.
I THOUGHT PERHAPS YOU WOULDN'T.
....
FWAP
BWACK

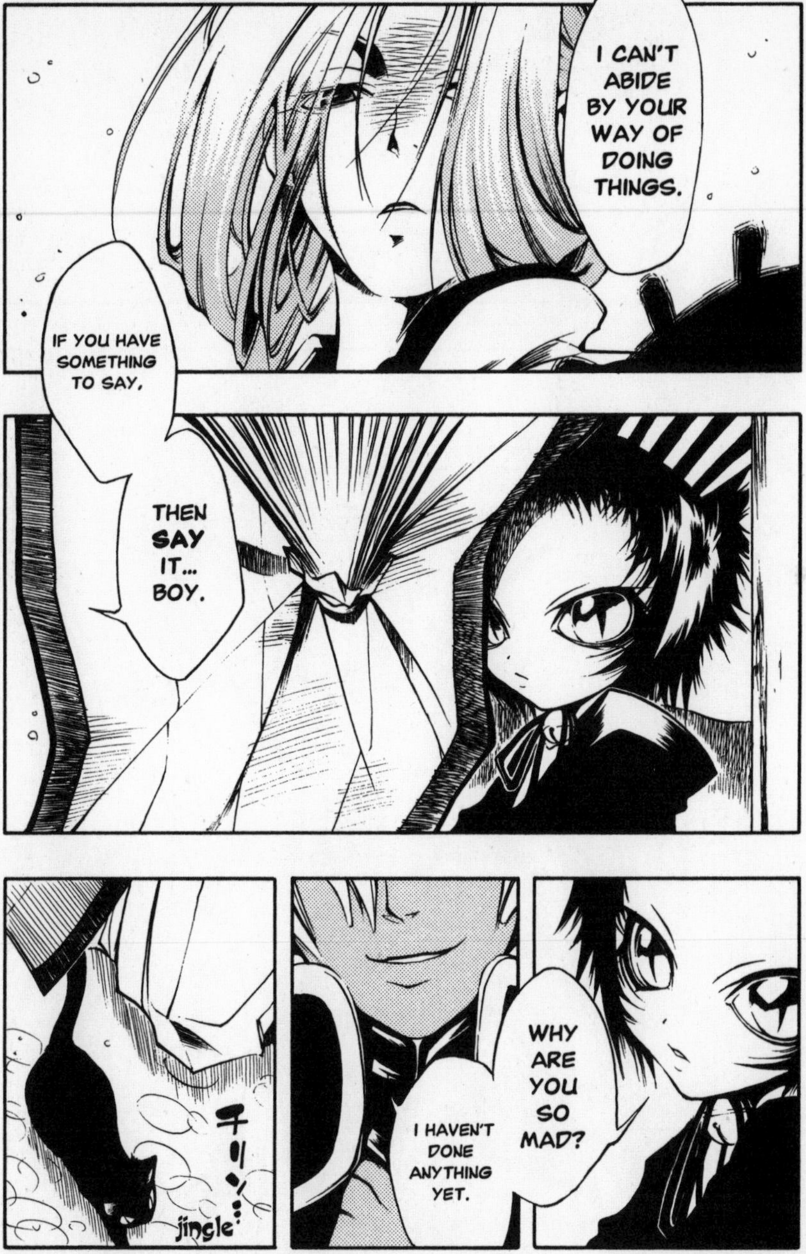
I CAN'T ABIDE BY YOUR WAY OF DOING THINGS.
IF YOU HAVE SOMETHING TO SAY,
THEN SAY IT... BOY.
WHY ARE YOU SO MAD?
I HAVEN'T DONE ANYTHING YET.
jingle

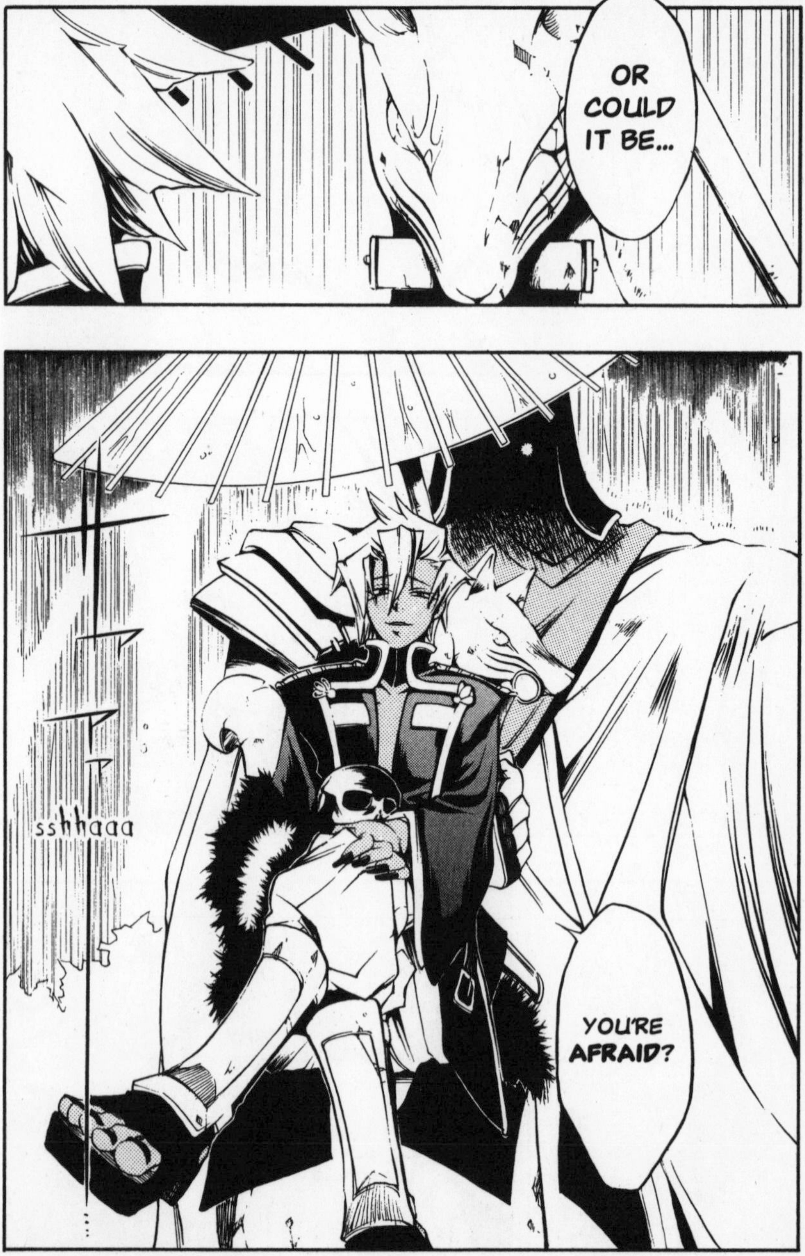
OR COULD IT BE...
sshhaaa
YOU'RE AFRAID?

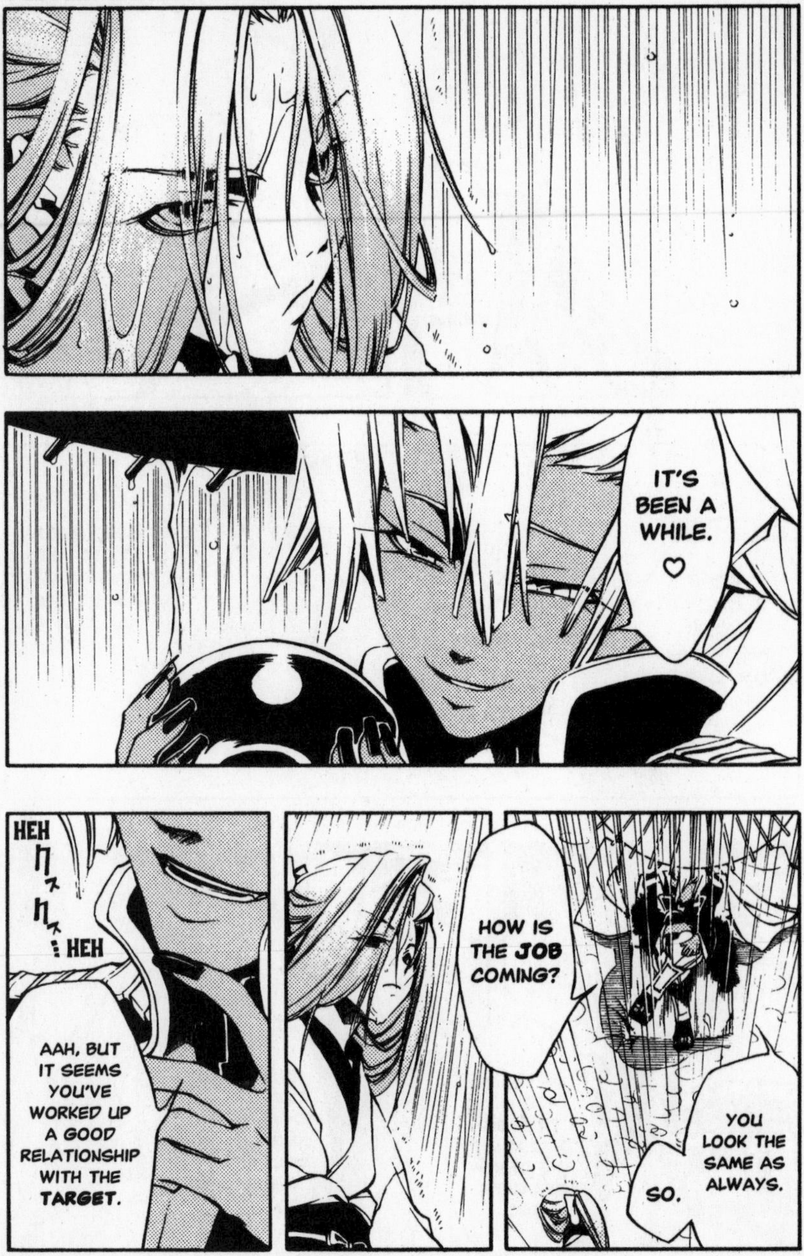
IT'S BEEN A WHILE. ♡
YOU LOOK THE SAME AS ALWAYS.
SO.
HOW IS THE **JOB** COMING?
HEH クス クス HEH
AAH, BUT IT SEEMS YOU'VE WORKED UP A GOOD RELATIONSHIP WITH THE **TARGET**.

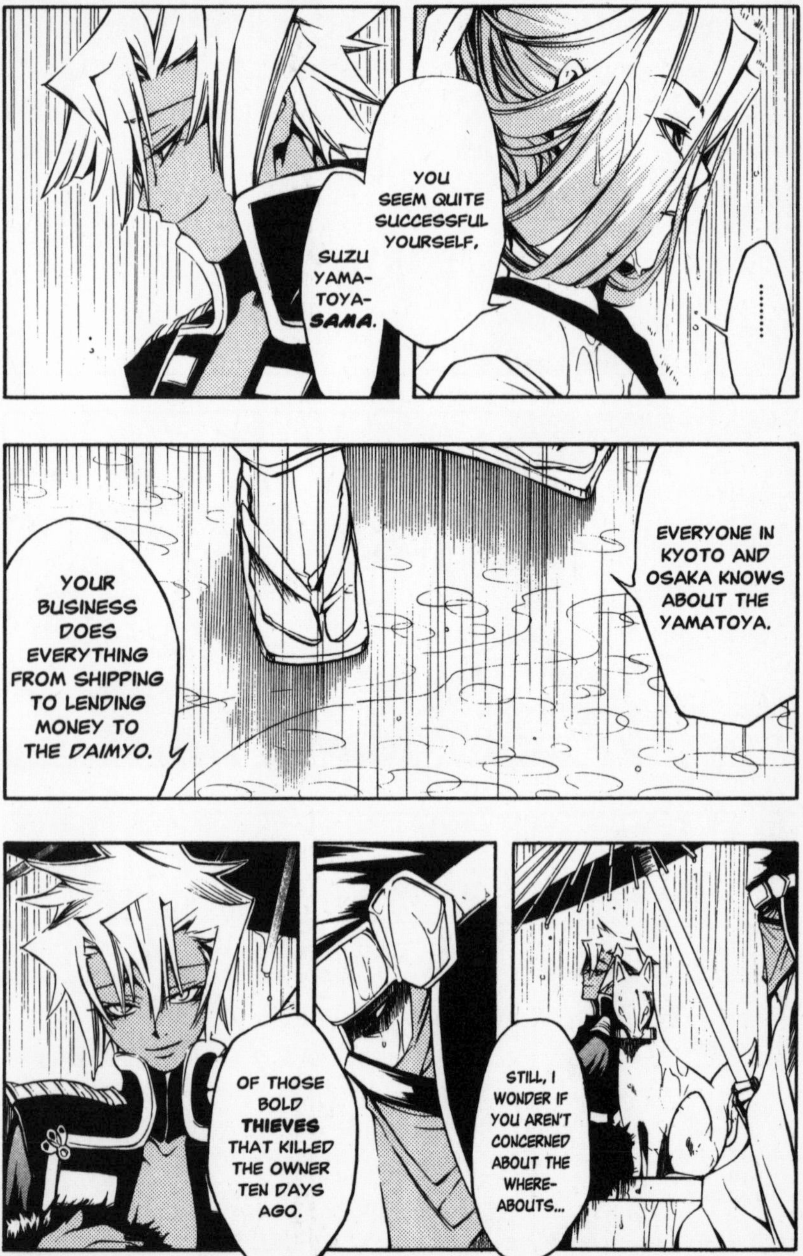
......
YOU SEEM QUITE SUCCESSFUL YOURSELF,
SUZU YAMATOYA-SAMA.
EVERYONE IN KYOTO AND OSAKA KNOWS ABOUT THE YAMATOYA.
YOUR BUSINESS DOES EVERYTHING FROM SHIPPING TO LENDING MONEY TO THE DAIMYO.
STILL, I WONDER IF YOU AREN'T CONCERNED ABOUT THE WHERE-ABOUTS...
OF THOSE BOLD THIEVES THAT KILLED THE OWNER TEN DAYS AGO.

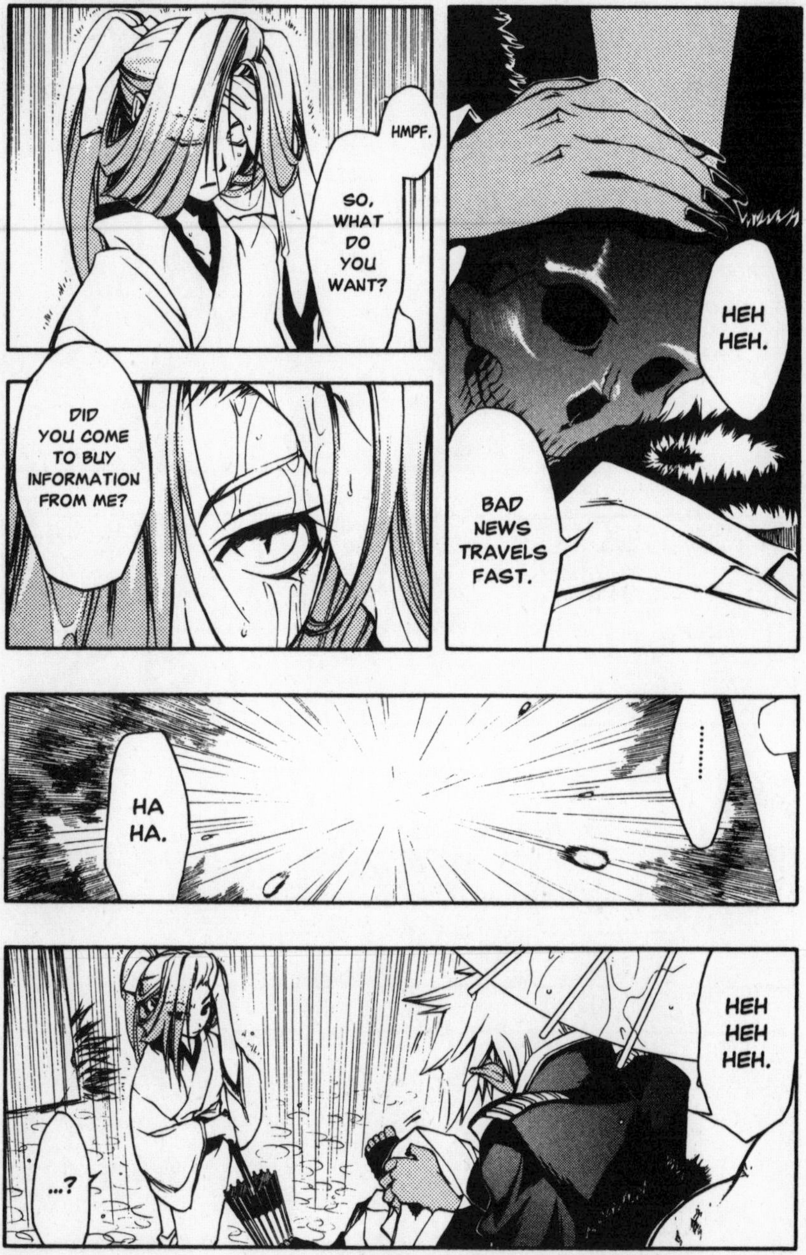
HEH HEH.
BAD NEWS TRAVELS FAST.
HMPF.
SO, WHAT DO YOU WANT?
DID YOU COME TO BUY INFORMATION FROM ME?
......
HA HA.
HEH HEH HEH.
...?

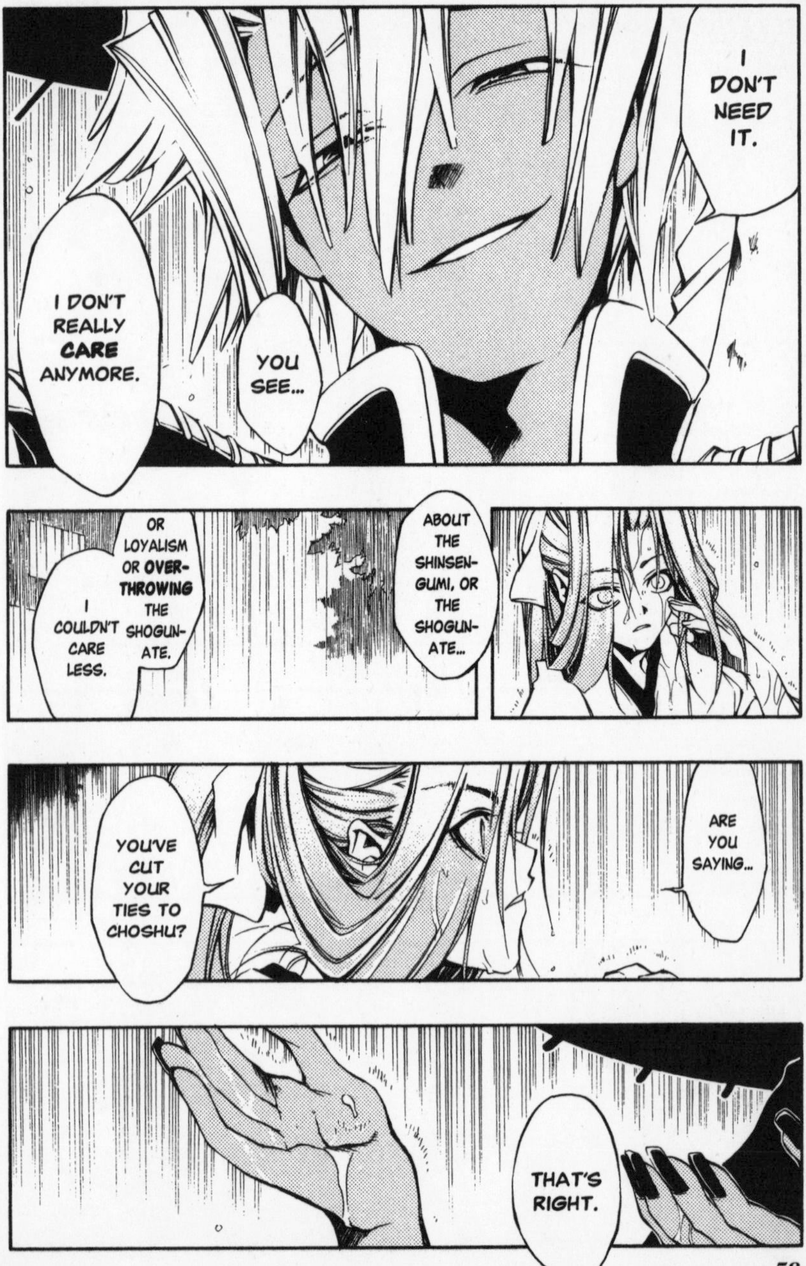
I DON'T NEED IT.
YOU SEE...
I DON'T REALLY CARE ANYMORE.
ABOUT THE SHINSEN-GUMI, OR THE SHOGUN-ATE...
OR LOYALISM OR OVER-THROWING THE SHOGUN-ATE.
I COULDN'T CARE LESS.
ARE YOU SAYING...
YOU'VE CUT YOUR TIES TO CHOSHU?
THAT'S RIGHT.

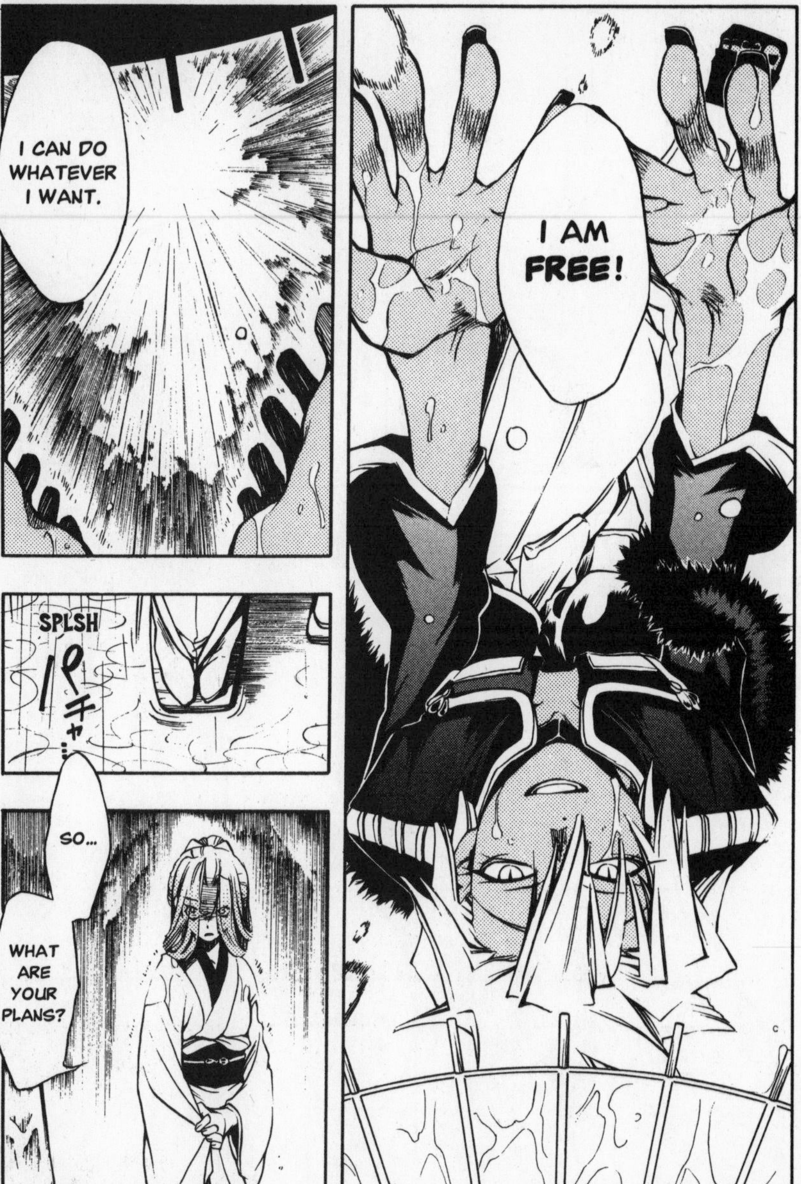
I AM FREE!
I CAN DO WHATEVER I WANT.
SPLSH
パチャ…
SO...
WHAT ARE YOUR PLANS?

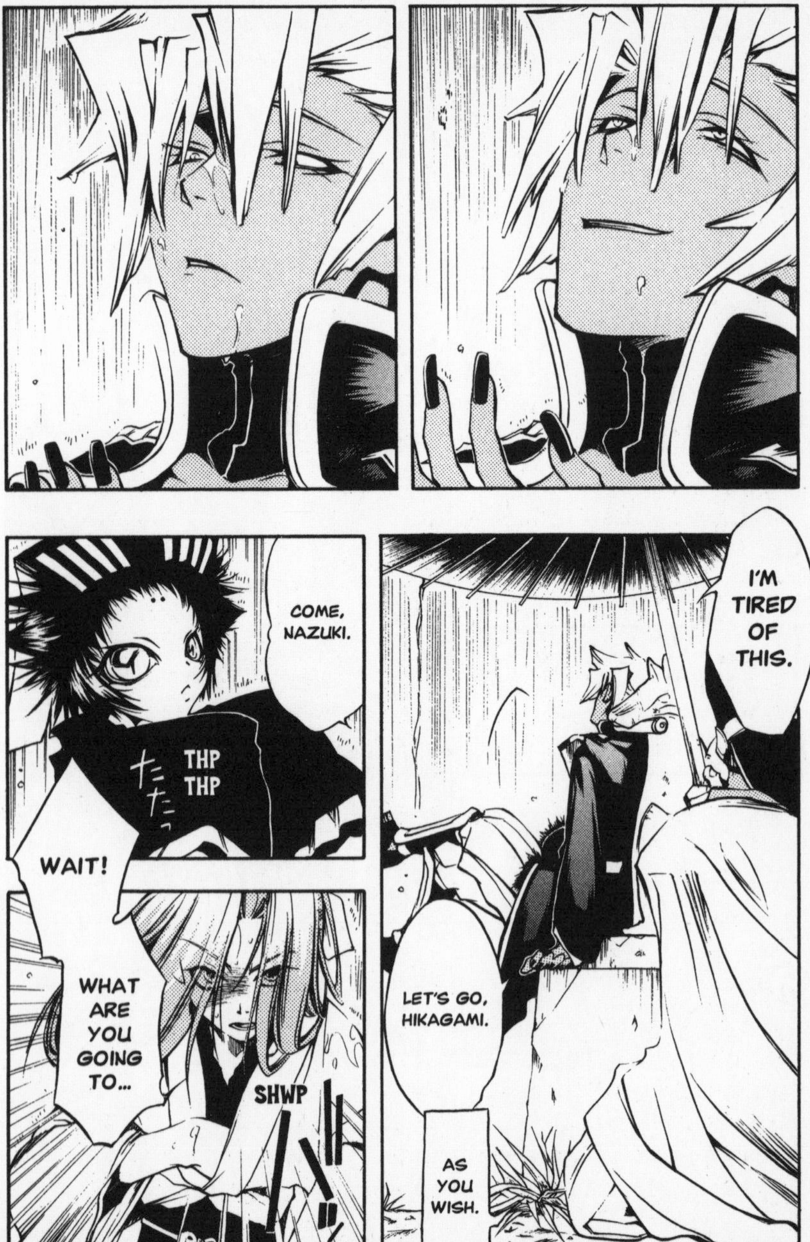
I'M TIRED OF THIS.
COME, NAZUKI.
THP THP
LET'S GO, HIKAGAMI.
AS YOU WISH.
WAIT!
WHAT ARE YOU GOING TO...
SHWP

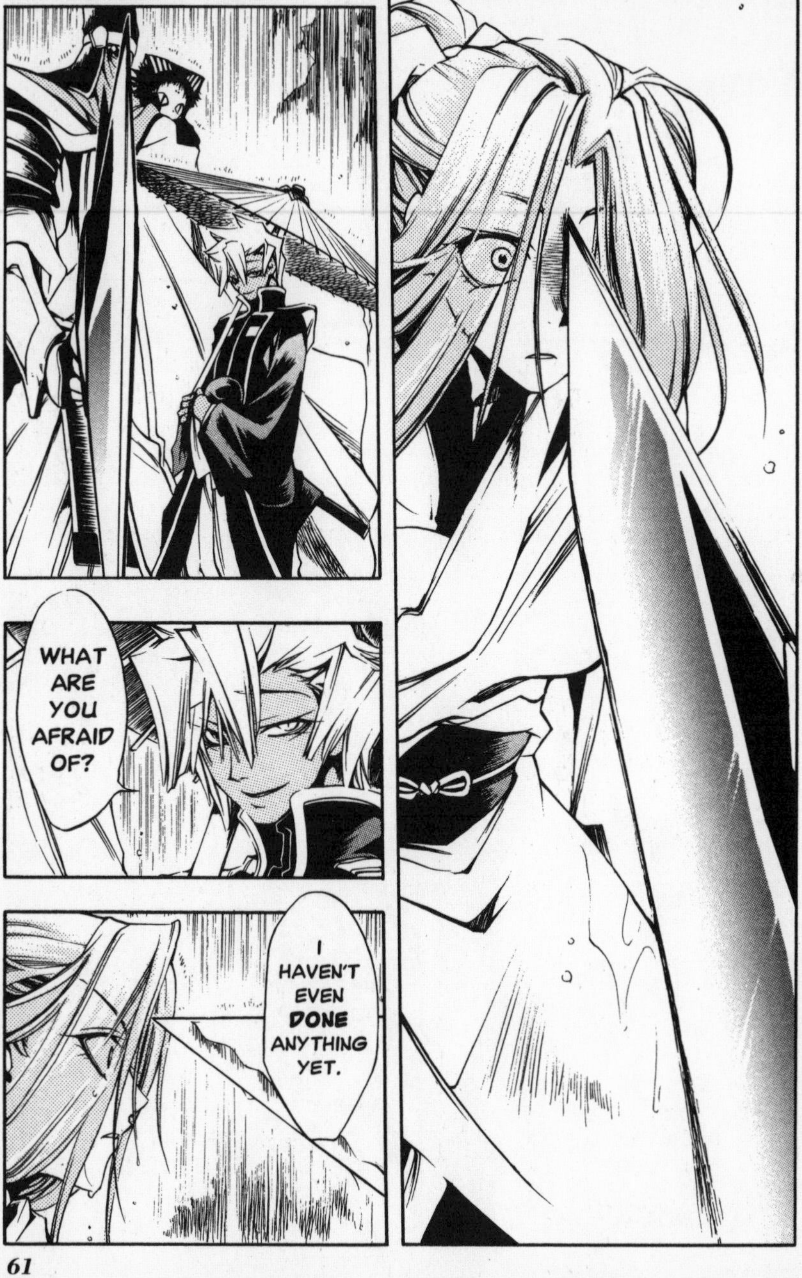
WHAT ARE YOU AFRAID OF?
I HAVEN'T EVEN **DONE** ANYTHING YET.

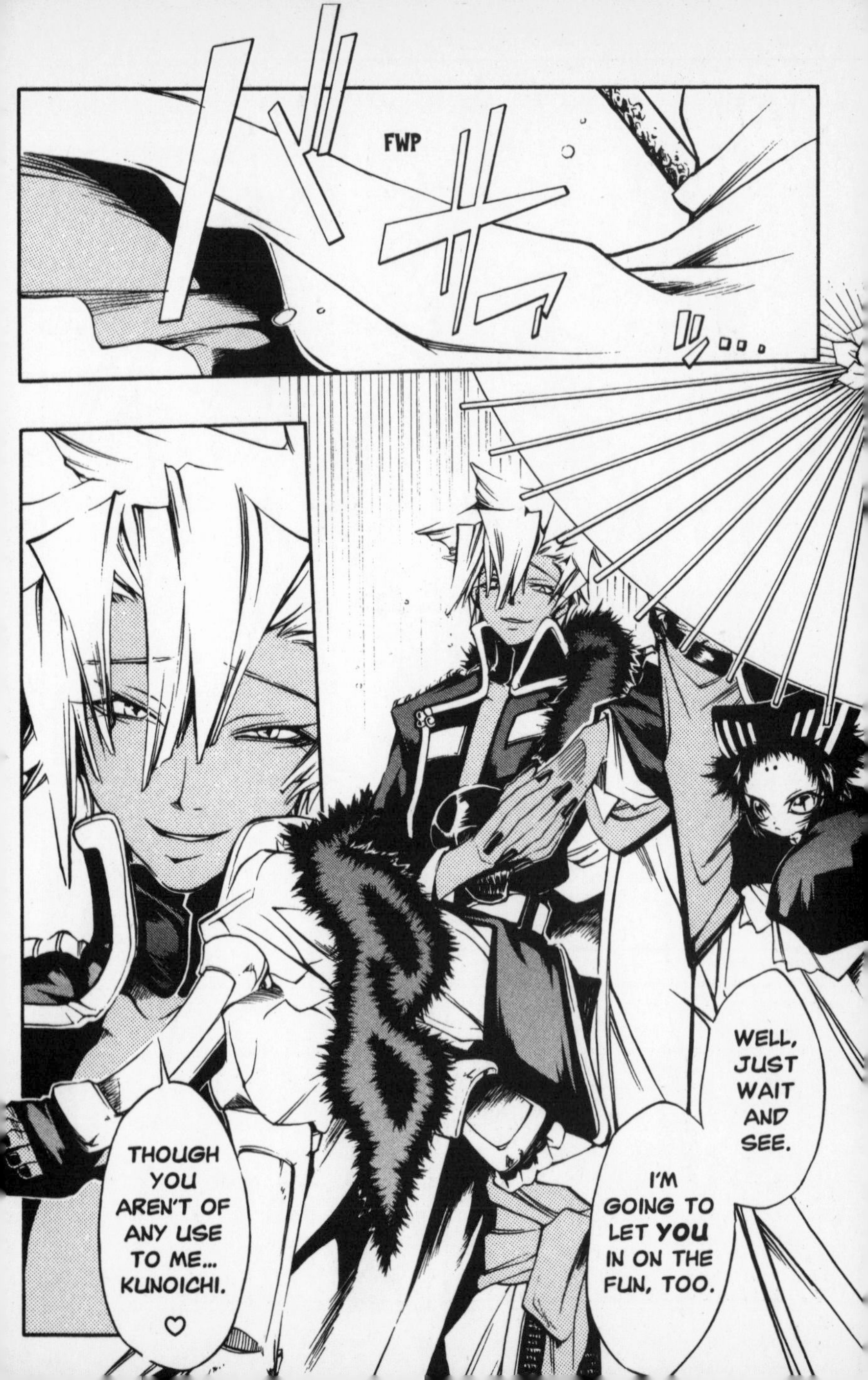
FWP
WELL, JUST WAIT AND SEE.
I'M GOING TO LET YOU IN ON THE FUN, TOO.
THOUGH YOU AREN'T OF ANY USE TO ME... KUNOICHI. ♡

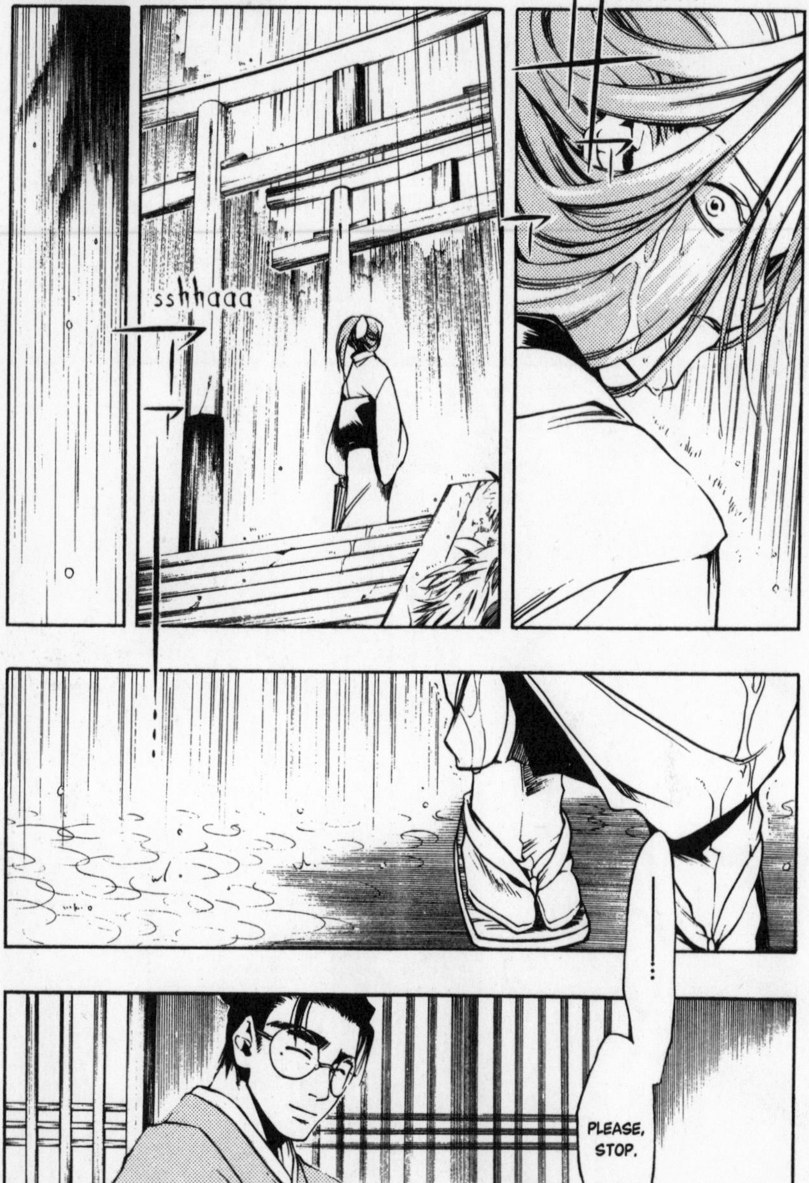
sshhaa
sshhaaa
PLEASE, STOP.

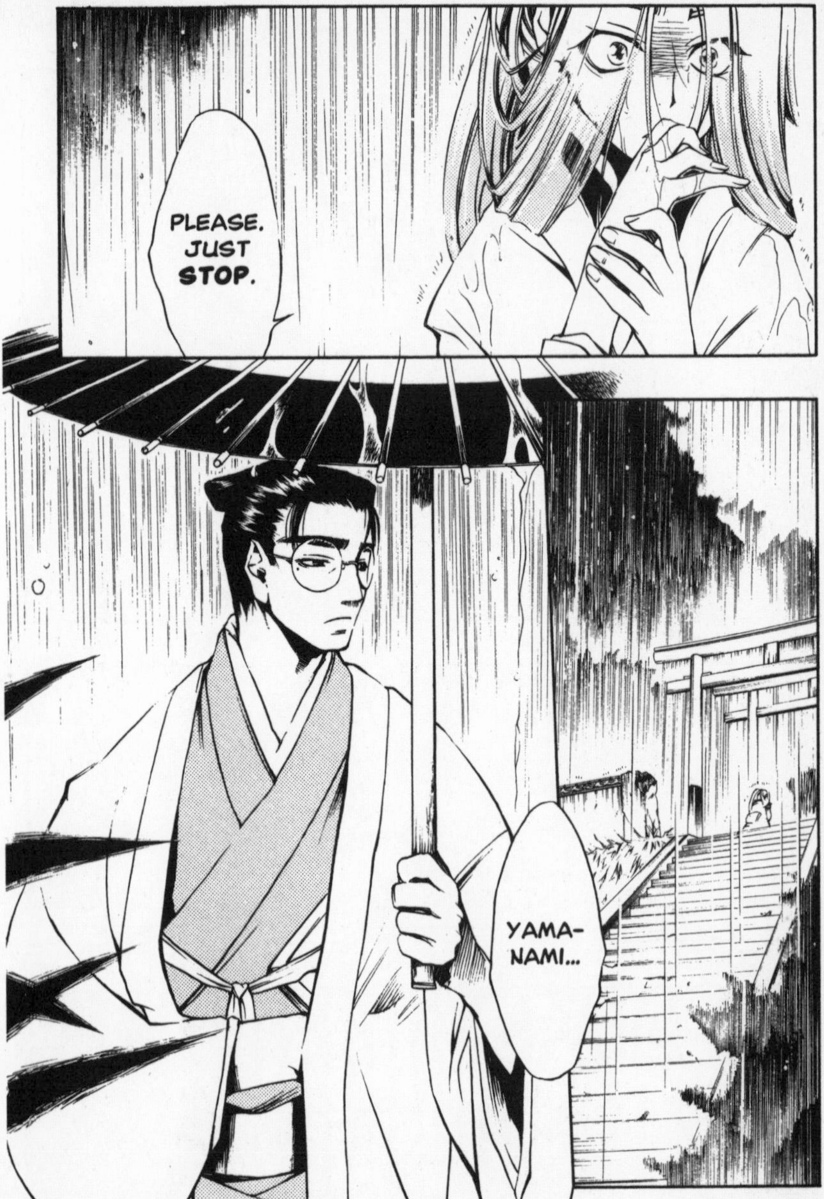
PLEASE. JUST STOP.
YAMA-NAMI...

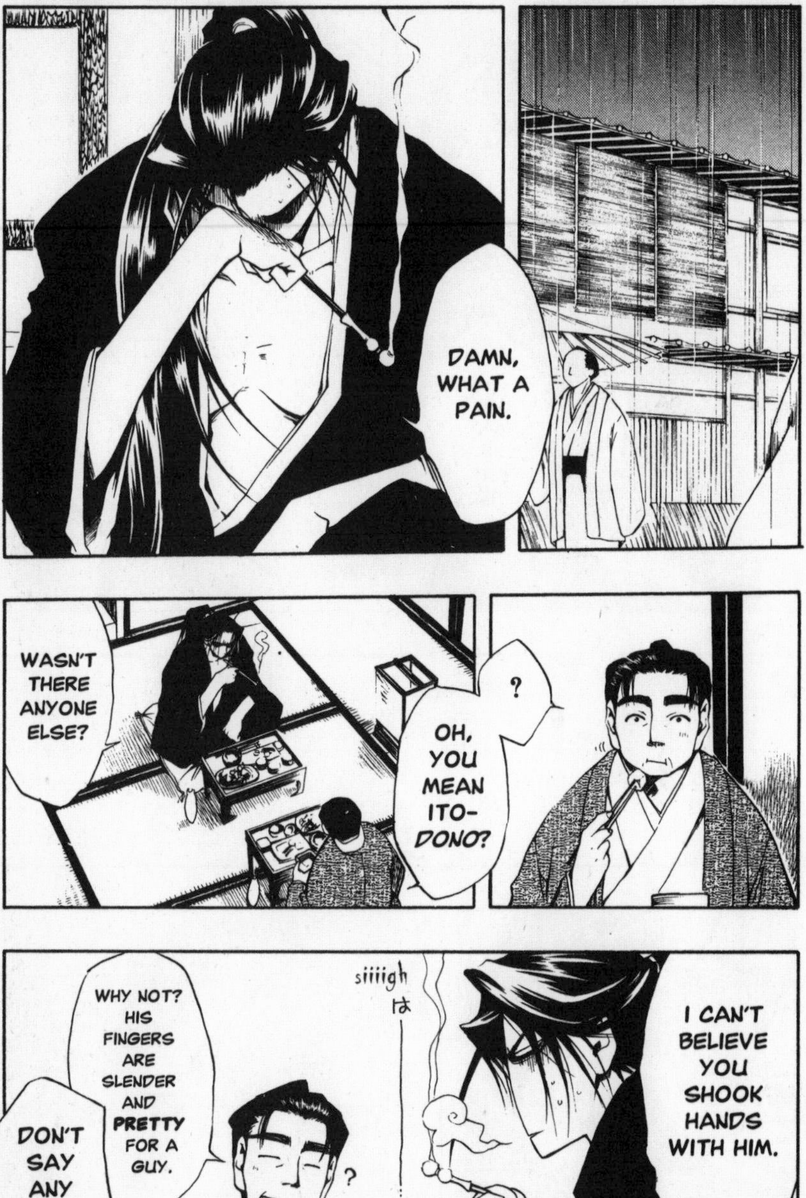
DAMN, WHAT A PAIN.
WASN'T THERE ANYONE ELSE?
?
OH, YOU MEAN ITO-DONO?
I CAN'T BELIEVE YOU SHOOK HANDS WITH HIM.
siiiigh
は
WHY NOT? HIS FINGERS ARE SLENDER AND PRETTY FOR A GUY.
?
DON'T SAY ANY MORE!

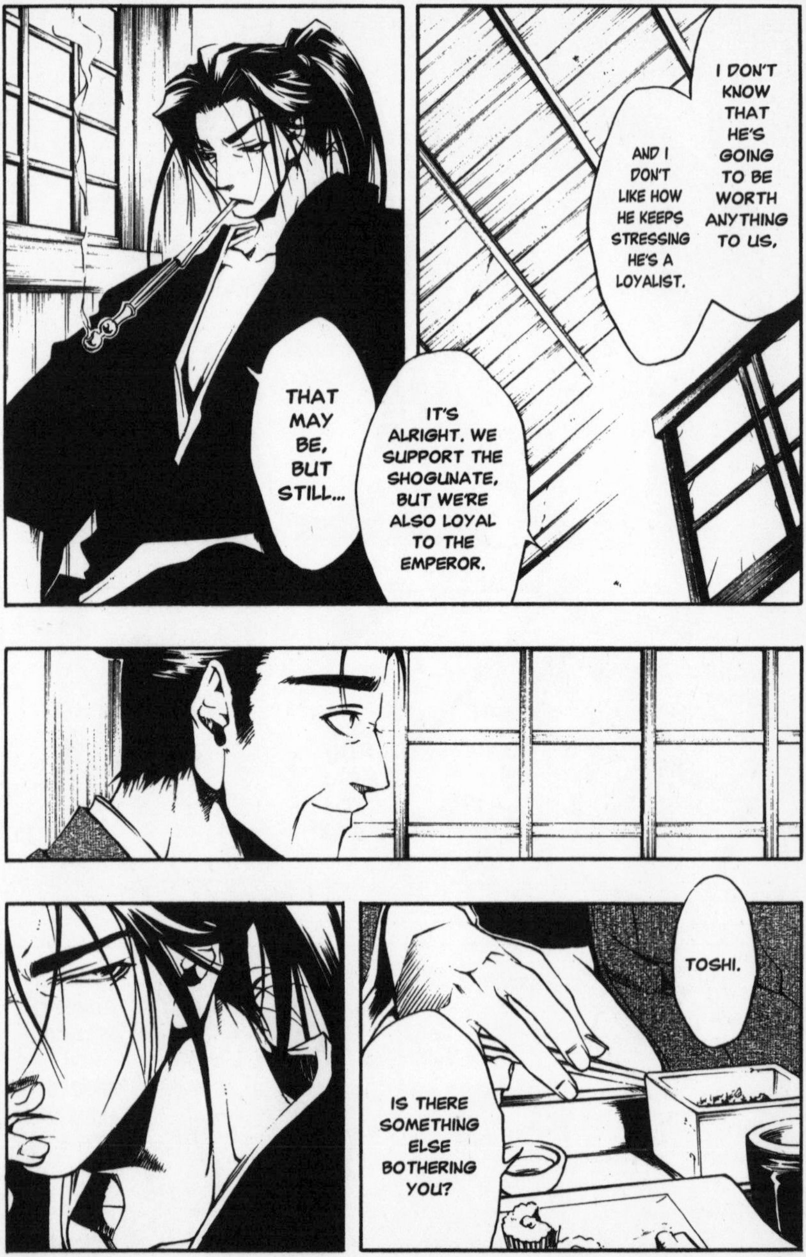
I DON'T KNOW THAT HE'S GOING TO BE WORTH ANYTHING TO US,
AND I DON'T LIKE HOW HE KEEPS STRESSING HE'S A LOYALIST.
IT'S ALRIGHT. WE SUPPORT THE SHOGUNATE, BUT WE'RE ALSO LOYAL TO THE EMPEROR.
THAT MAY BE, BUT STILL...
TOSHI.
IS THERE SOMETHING ELSE BOTHERING YOU?

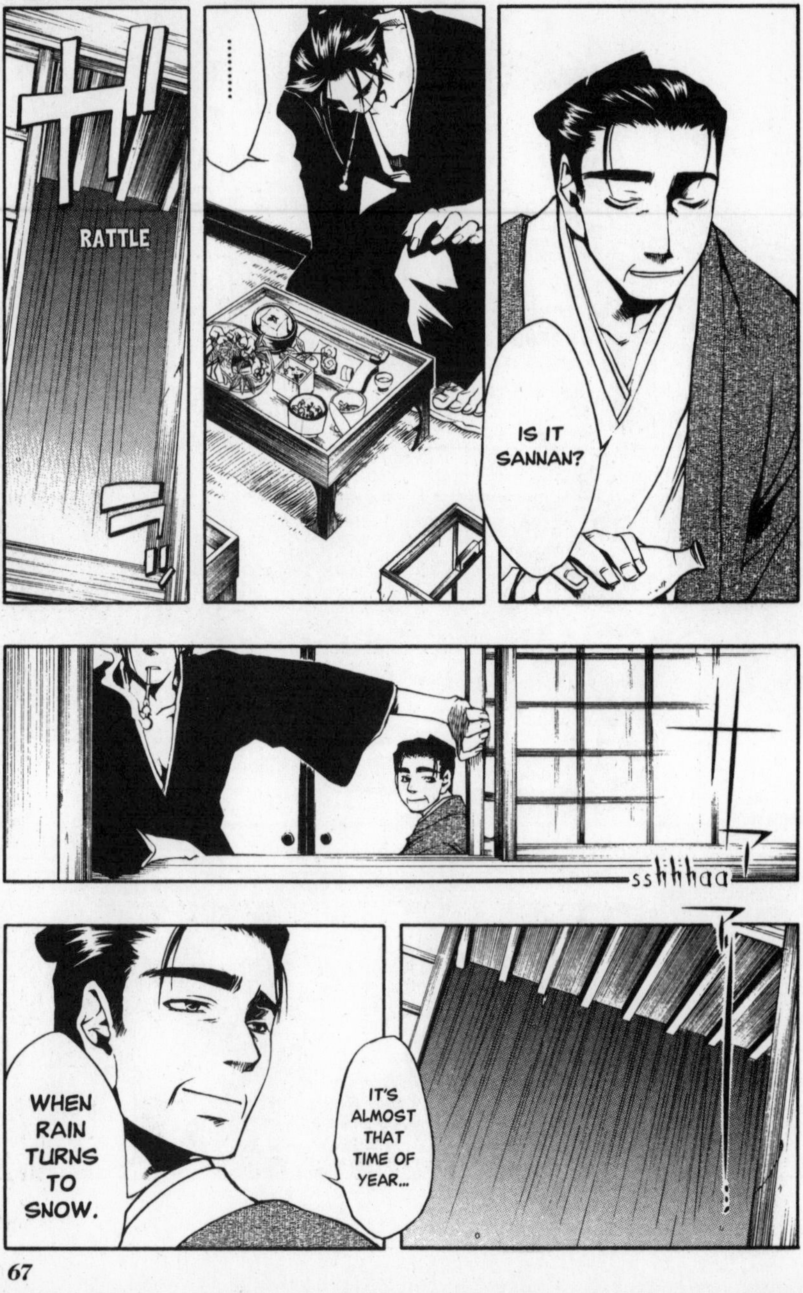
IS IT SANNAN?
......
RATTLE
sshhhaa
IT'S ALMOST THAT TIME OF YEAR...
WHEN RAIN TURNS TO SNOW.

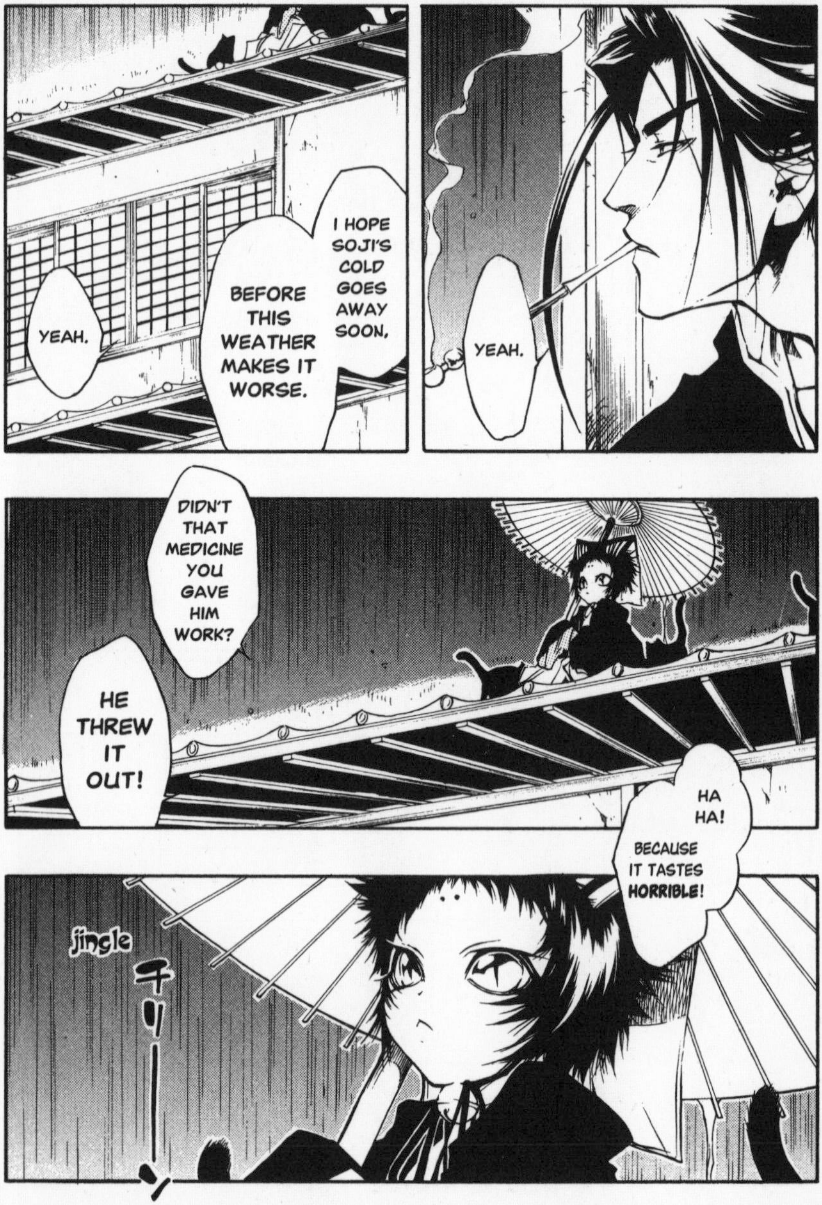
YEAH.
I HOPE SOJI'S COLD GOES AWAY SOON,
BEFORE THIS WEATHER MAKES IT WORSE.
YEAH.
DIDN'T THAT MEDICINE YOU GAVE HIM WORK?
HE THREW IT OUT!
HA HA!
BECAUSE IT TASTES **HORRIBLE!**
jingle
チリーン…

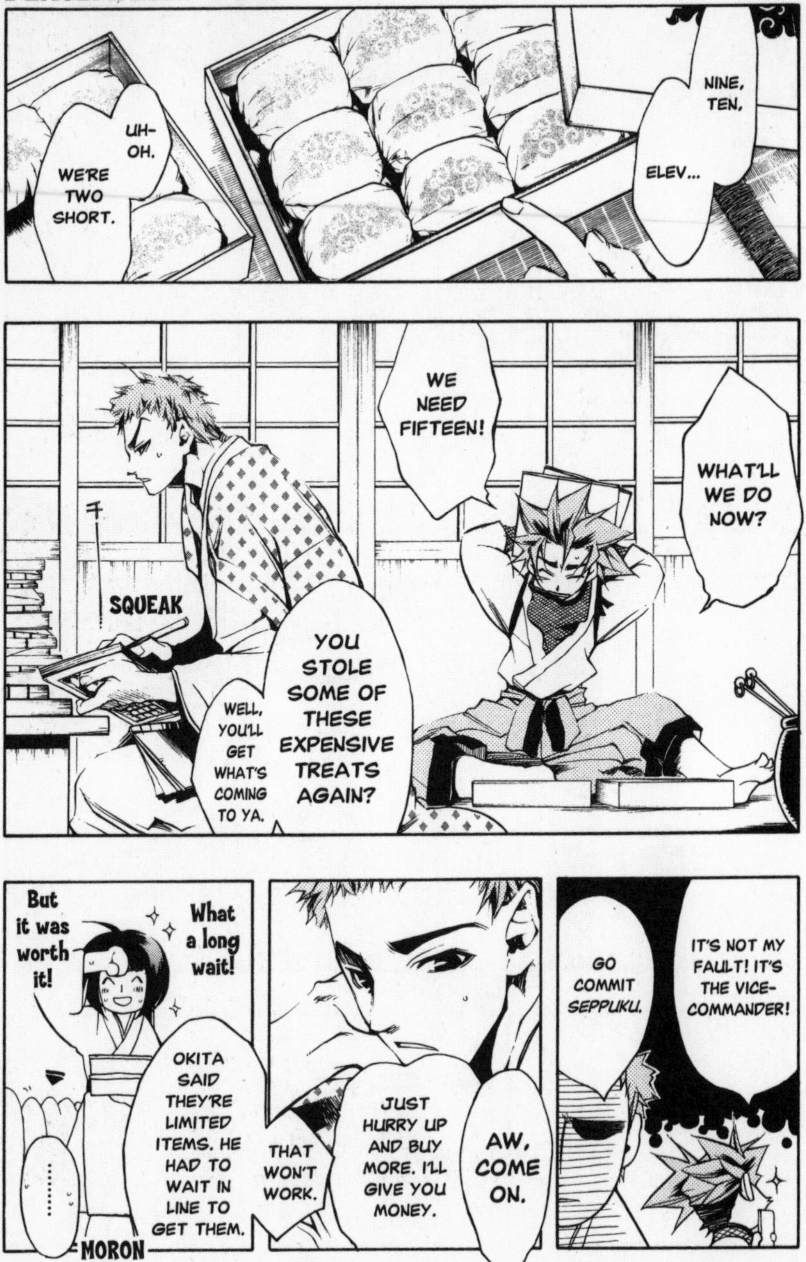
NINE, TEN,
ELEV...
UH-OH.
WE'RE TWO SHORT.
WHAT'LL WE DO NOW?
WE NEED FIFTEEN!
YOU STOLE SOME OF THESE EXPENSIVE TREATS AGAIN?
WELL, YOU'LL GET WHAT'S COMING TO YA.
SQUEAK
IT'S NOT MY FAULT! IT'S THE VICE-COMMANDER!
GO COMMIT SEPPUKU.
AW, COME ON.
JUST HURRY UP AND BUY MORE. I'LL GIVE YOU MONEY.
THAT WON'T WORK.
OKITA SAID THEY'RE LIMITED ITEMS. HE HAD TO WAIT IN LINE TO GET THEM.
What a long wait!
But it was worth it!
....
MORON

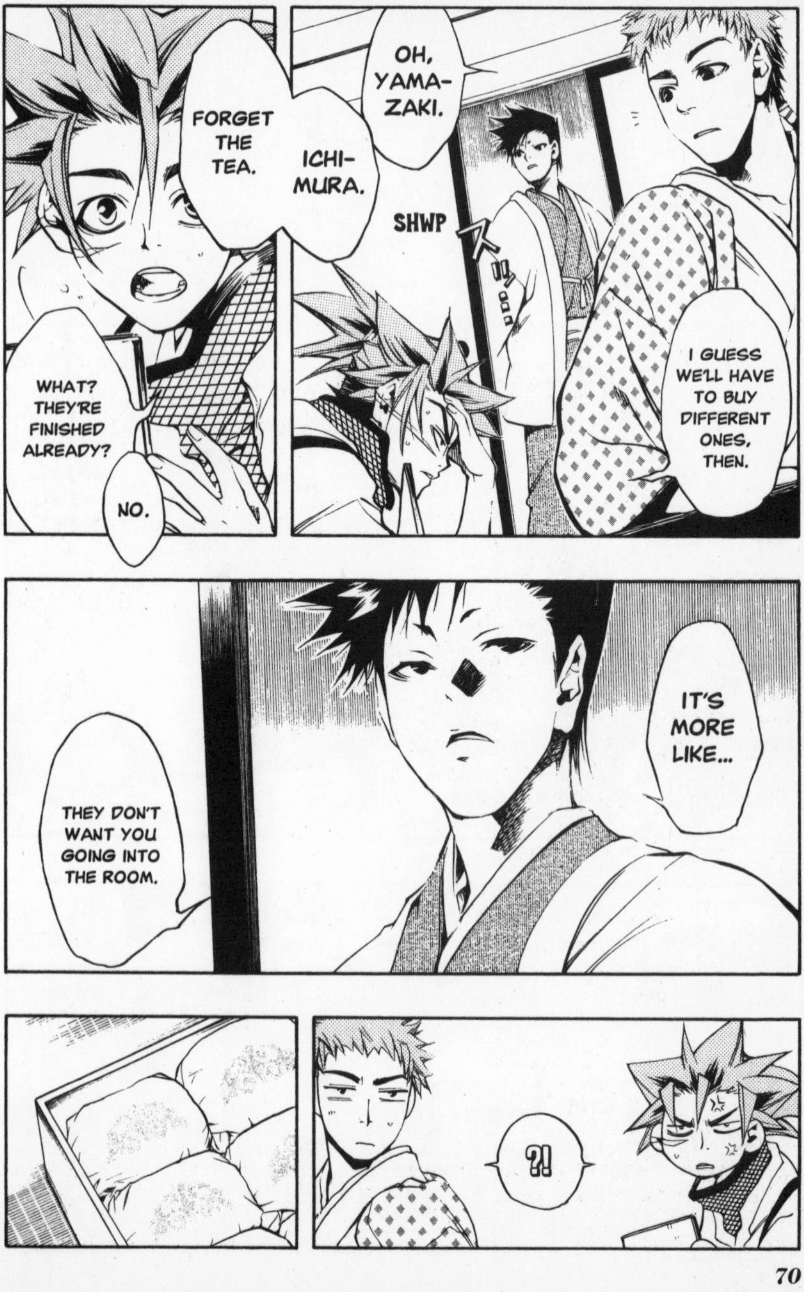
I GUESS WE'LL HAVE TO BUY DIFFERENT ONES, THEN.
OH, YAMA-ZAKI.
ICHI-MURA.
SHWP
FORGET THE TEA.
WHAT? THEY'RE FINISHED ALREADY?
NO.
IT'S MORE LIKE...
THEY DON'T WANT YOU GOING INTO THE ROOM.
?!

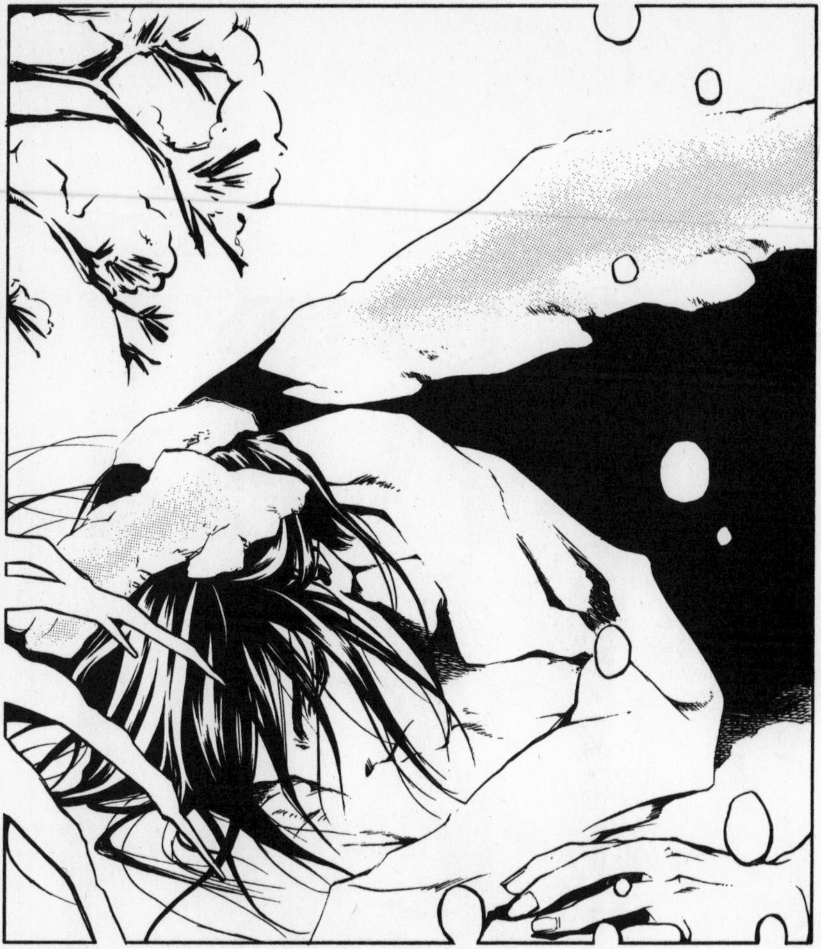

CHAPTER 8

SNOW 鐵

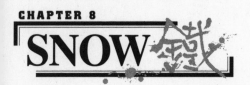

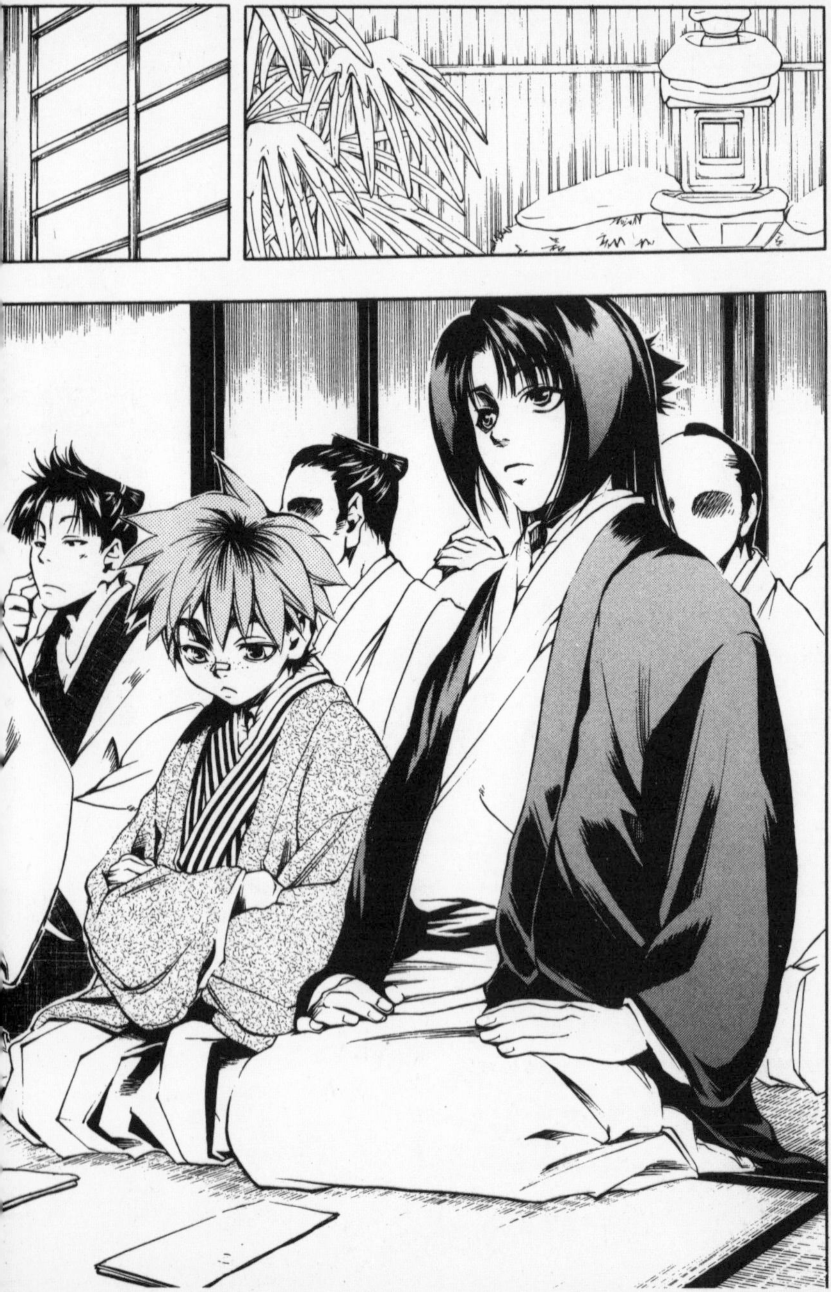

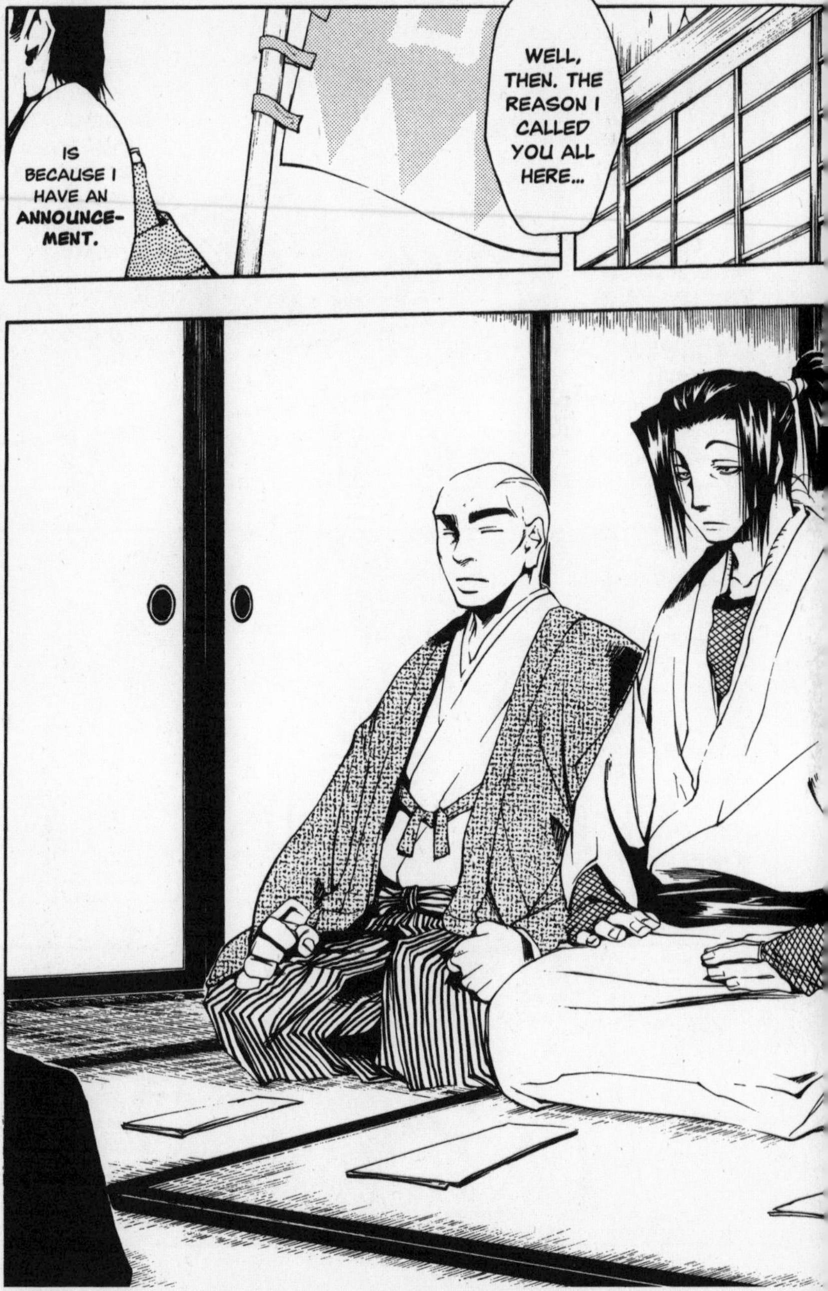
WELL, THEN. THE REASON I CALLED YOU ALL HERE...
IS BECAUSE I HAVE AN ANNOUNCEMENT.

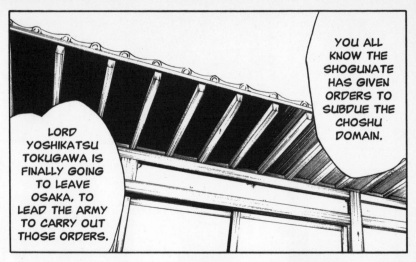

YOU ALL KNOW THE SHOGUNATE HAS GIVEN ORDERS TO SUBDUE THE CHOSHU DOMAIN.

LORD YOSHIKATSU TOKUGAWA IS FINALLY GOING TO LEAVE OSAKA, TO LEAD THE ARMY TO CARRY OUT THOSE ORDERS.

IT'S ONLY MY GUESS,

BUT IT LOOKS LIKE THE SHOGUNATE WANTS TO COMPLETELY DESTROY CHOSHU THIS TIME.

AND OF COURSE, WE'RE GOING TO JOIN THE FIGHT.

THUS...

UNFORTUNATELY, WE HAVE NO EXPERIENCE ON CAMPAIGNS LIKE THIS, AND THERE'S A CHANCE OUR GUARD MAY BECOME **LOOSE**.

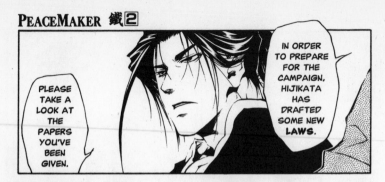

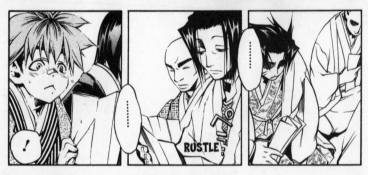

IN ORDER TO PREPARE FOR THE CAMPAIGN, HIJIKATA HAS DRAFTED SOME NEW **LAWS.**
PLEASE TAKE A LOOK AT THE PAPERS YOU'VE BEEN GIVEN.
......
......
RUSTLE
!

Laws of the Shinsengumi

1. Always be aware of your position, and do not fall out of line. Move according to your captain's orders.

2. Never criticize the strength of friend or foe. And never talk about ghosts or other strange creatures.

3. Do not eat rich foods during battle.

4. A battle can take a sudden turn at any time of day or night, but do not let it frighten you. Stay calm, and obey orders.

5. Do not fight or argue over a personal grudge during battle.

6. Before going out to battle, eat, and prepare your armor and weapons.

7. If the leader of a unit is mortally wounded, all other members of the unit must stay and fight to the death. Any who give in to fear and try to flee will be caught and duly punished. Be prepared, and enter the battlefield without regret.

8. Even in a battle where the death toll is high, it is not allowed to retrieve the bodies of the dead, except for the corpse of the leader of the unit. Do not retreat; see the battle through to the end.

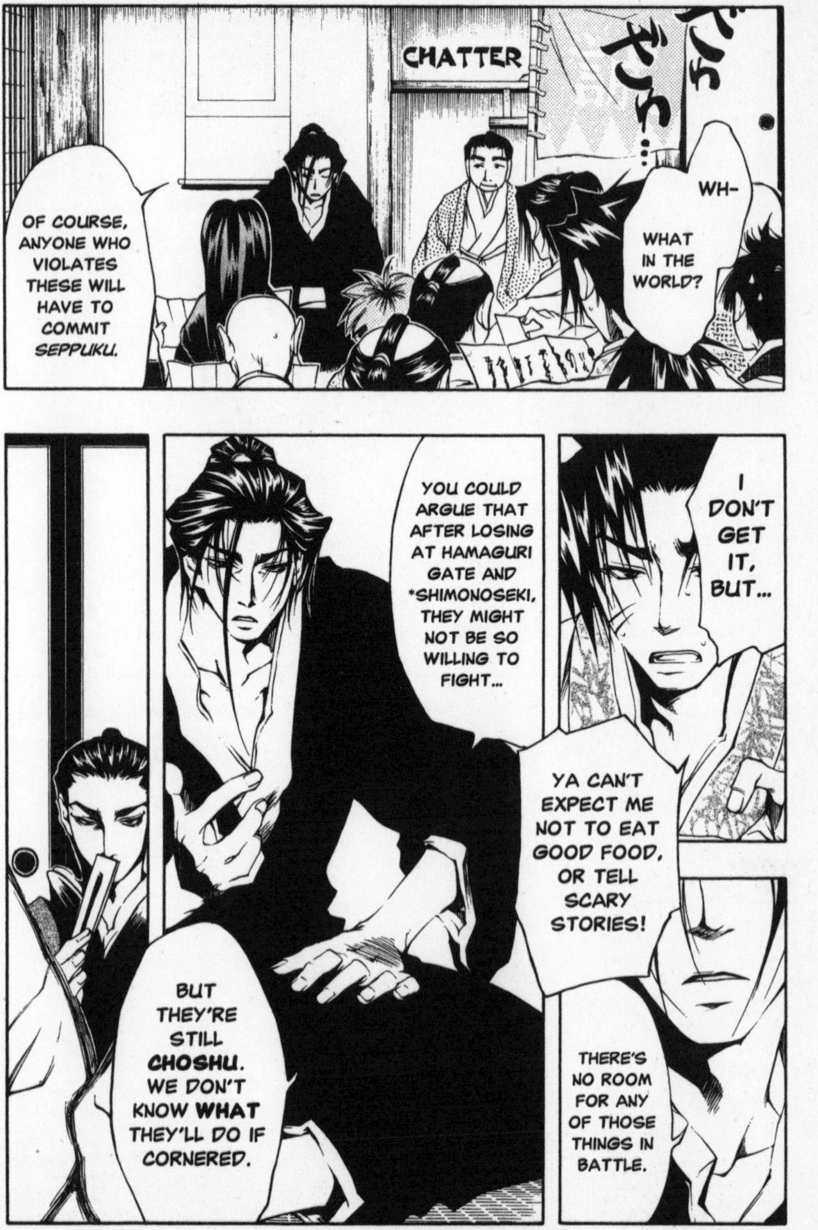
ざわ ざわ…
CHATTER
WH-
WHAT IN THE WORLD?
OF COURSE, ANYONE WHO VIOLATES THESE WILL HAVE TO COMMIT SEPPUKU.
I DON'T GET IT, BUT...
YA CAN'T EXPECT ME NOT TO EAT GOOD FOOD, OR TELL SCARY STORIES!
YOU COULD ARGUE THAT AFTER LOSING AT HAMAGURI GATE AND *SHIMONOSEKI, THEY MIGHT NOT BE SO WILLING TO FIGHT...
THERE'S NO ROOM FOR ANY OF THOSE THINGS IN BATTLE.
BUT THEY'RE STILL **CHOSHU**. WE DON'T KNOW **WHAT** THEY'LL DO IF CORNERED.

* In retaliation for Choshu's attack on foreign ships in the Shimonoseki strait, naval forces from the US, Britain, France, and Holland attacked and destroyed Choshu forts.

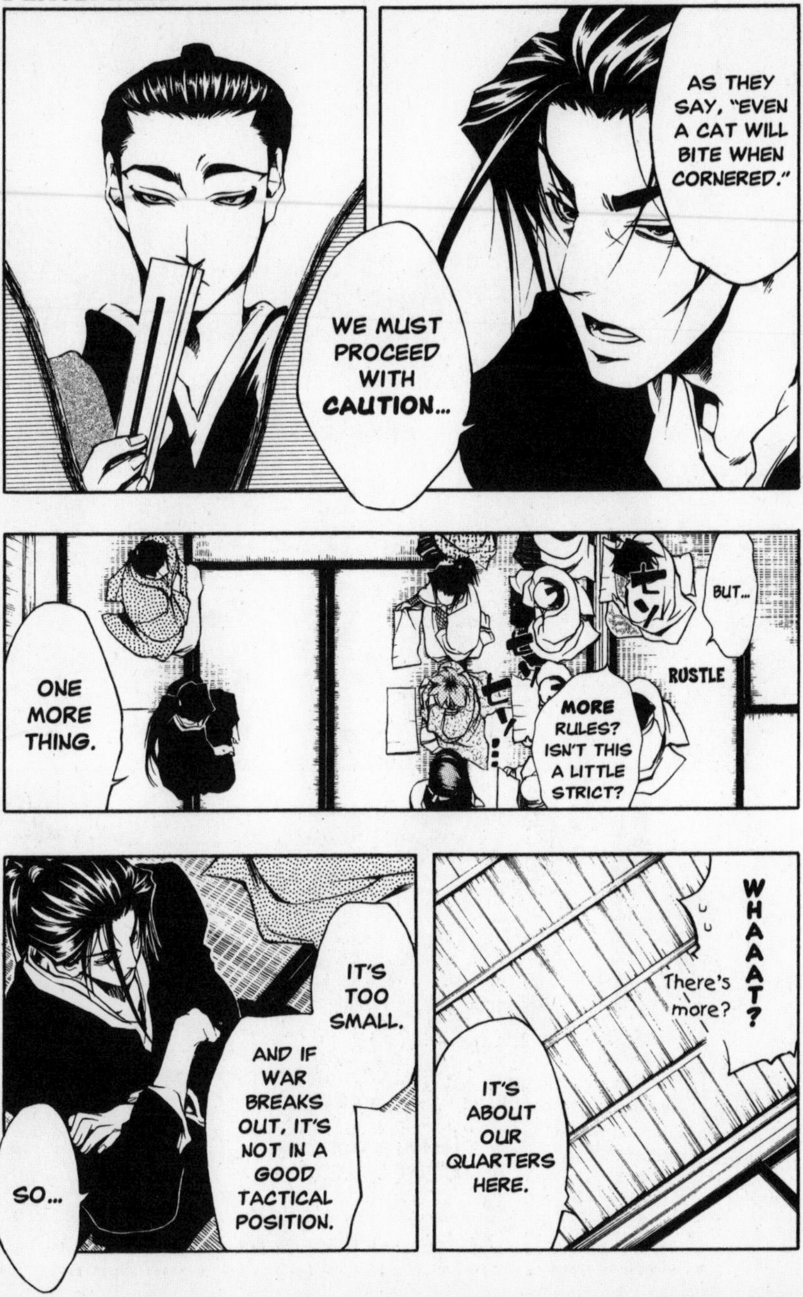
AS THEY SAY, "EVEN A CAT WILL BITE WHEN CORNERED."
WE MUST PROCEED WITH CAUTION...
BUT...
RUSTLE
MORE RULES? ISN'T THIS A LITTLE STRICT?
ONE MORE THING.
WHAAAT?
There's more?
IT'S ABOUT OUR QUARTERS HERE.
IT'S TOO SMALL.
AND IF WAR BREAKS OUT, IT'S NOT IN A GOOD TACTICAL POSITION.
SO...

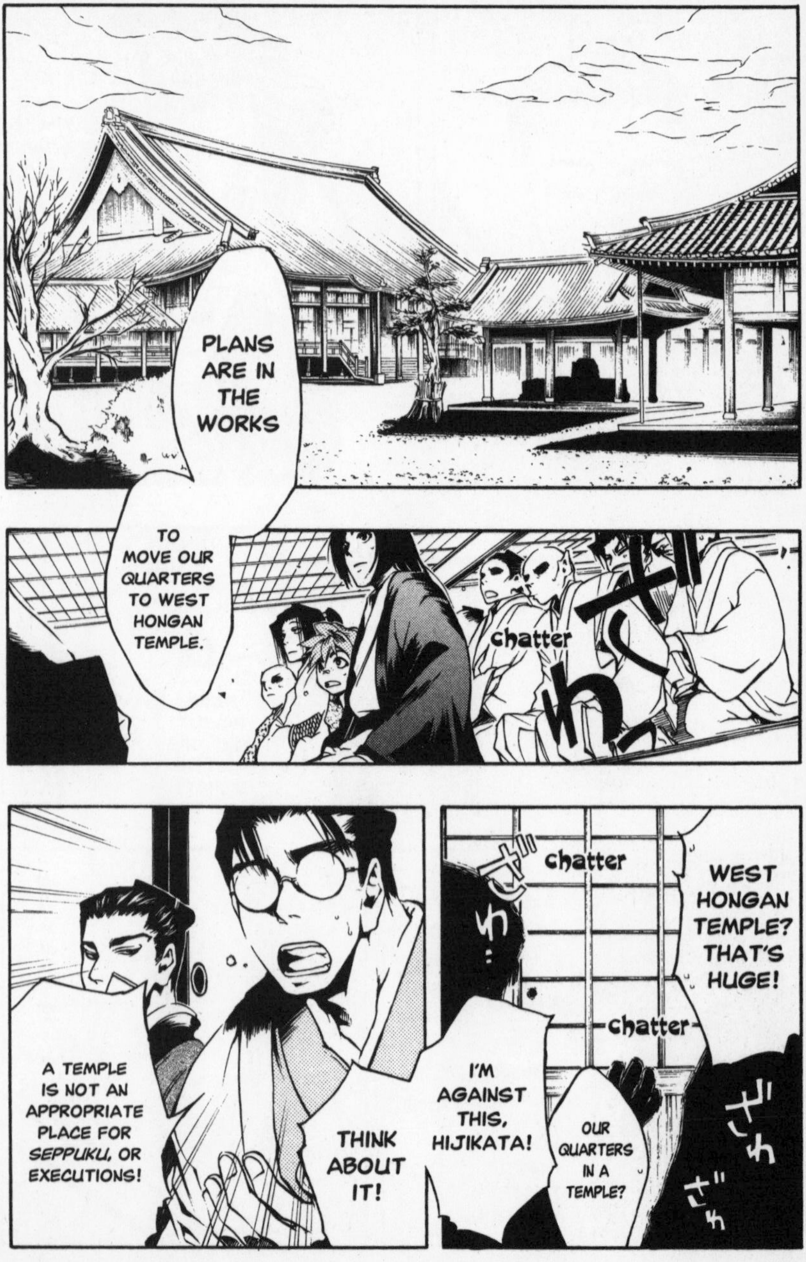
PLANS ARE IN THE WORKS
TO MOVE OUR QUARTERS TO WEST HONGAN TEMPLE.
chatter
chatter
WEST HONGAN TEMPLE? THAT'S HUGE!
chatter
OUR QUARTERS IN A TEMPLE?
I'M AGAINST THIS, HIJIKATA!
THINK ABOUT IT!
A TEMPLE IS NOT AN APPROPRIATE PLACE FOR SEPPUKU, OR EXECUTIONS!

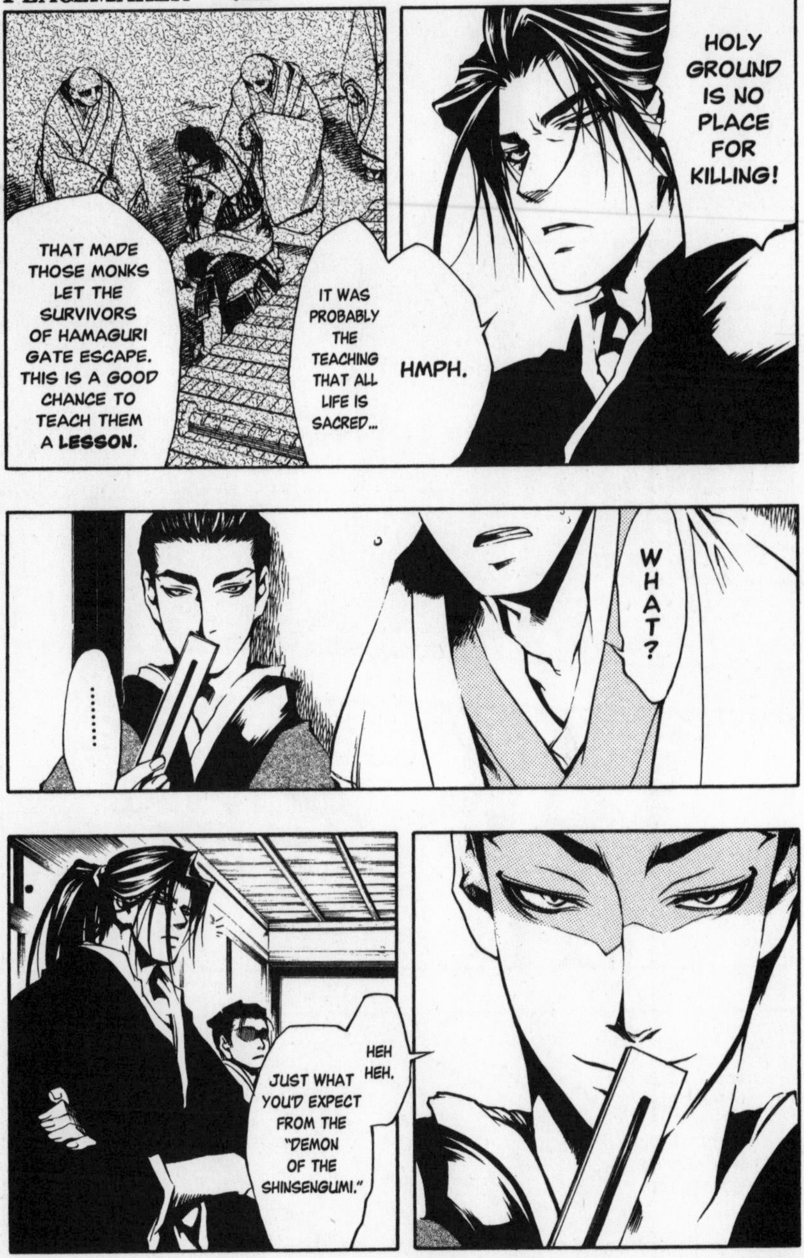
HOLY GROUND IS NO PLACE FOR KILLING!
HMPH.
IT WAS PROBABLY THE TEACHING THAT ALL LIFE IS SACRED...
THAT MADE THOSE MONKS LET THE SURVIVORS OF HAMAGURI GATE ESCAPE. THIS IS A GOOD CHANCE TO TEACH THEM A **LESSON**.
WHAT?
......
HEH HEH.
JUST WHAT YOU'D EXPECT FROM THE "DEMON OF THE SHINSENGUMI."

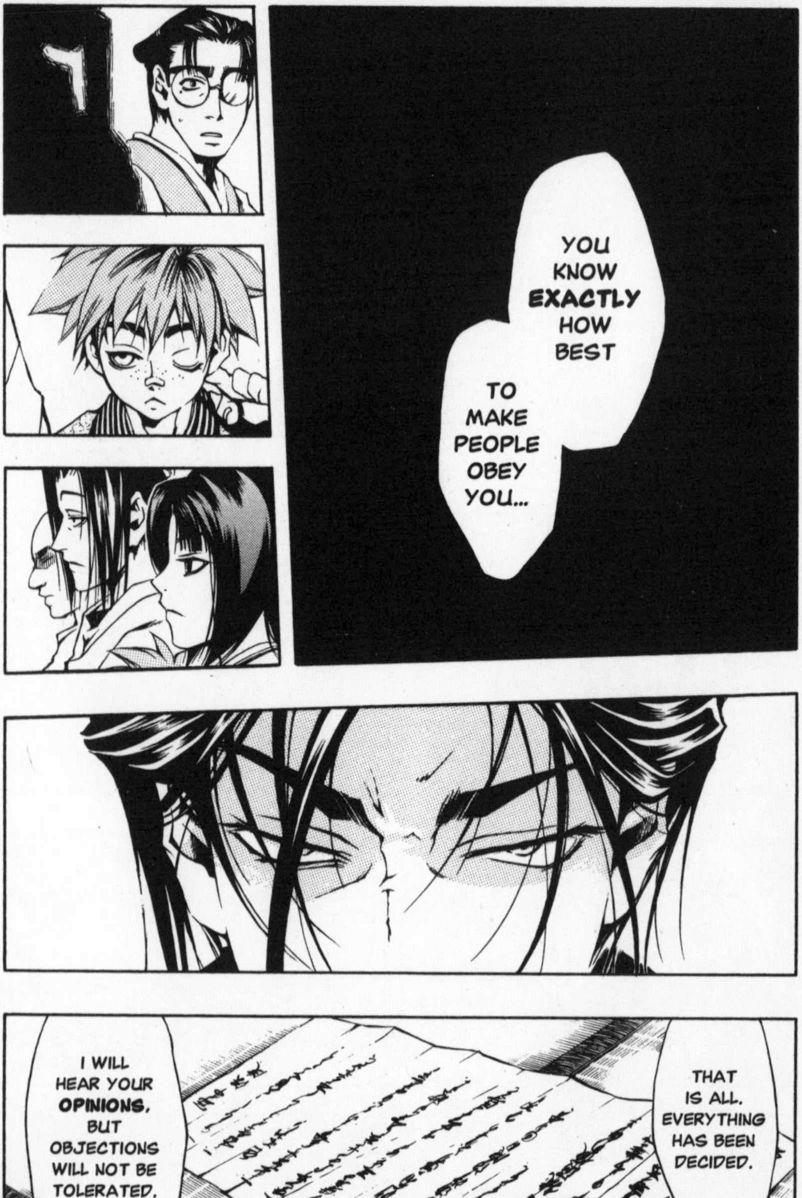
YOU KNOW EXACTLY HOW BEST
TO MAKE PEOPLE OBEY YOU...
THAT IS ALL. EVERYTHING HAS BEEN DECIDED.
I WILL HEAR YOUR OPINIONS, BUT OBJECTIONS WILL NOT BE TOLERATED.

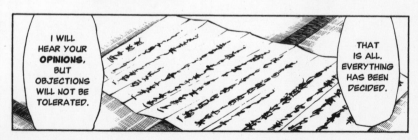

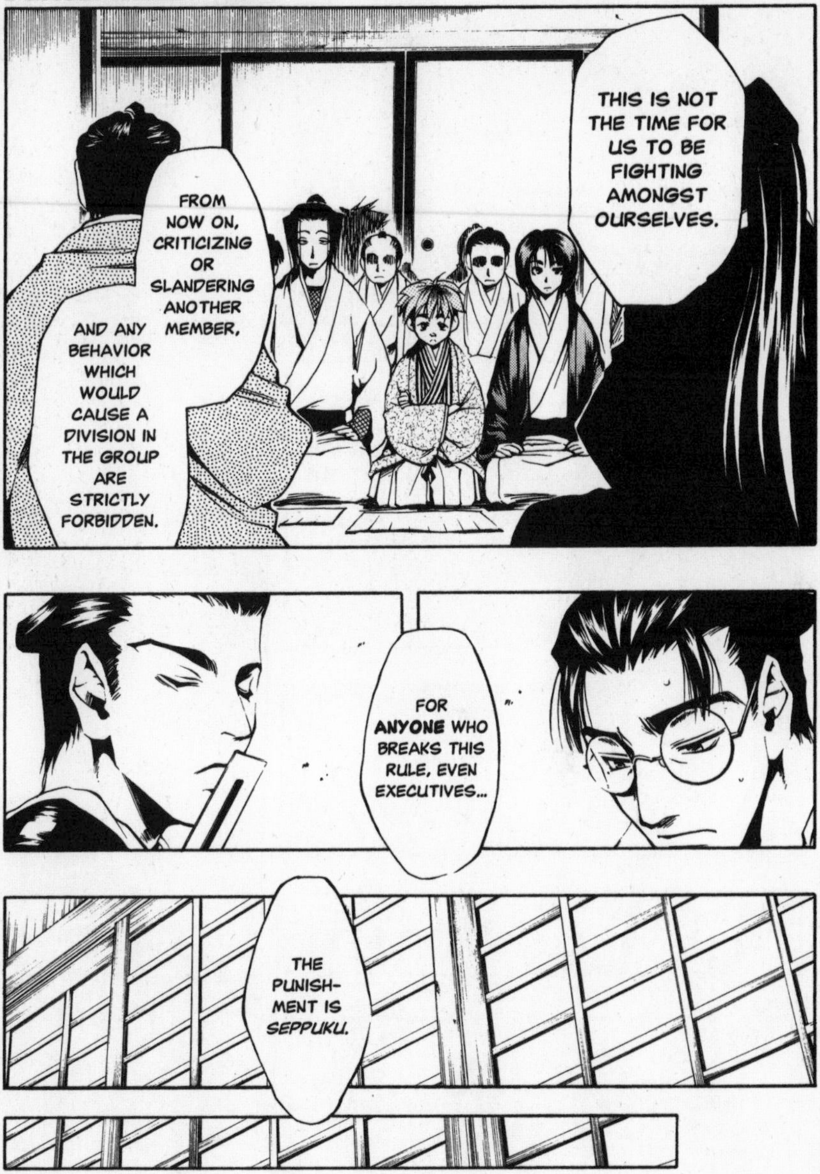
THIS IS NOT THE TIME FOR US TO BE FIGHTING AMONGST OURSELVES.
FROM NOW ON, CRITICIZING OR SLANDERING ANOTHER MEMBER,
AND ANY BEHAVIOR WHICH WOULD CAUSE A DIVISION IN THE GROUP ARE STRICTLY FORBIDDEN.
FOR **ANYONE** WHO BREAKS THIS RULE, EVEN EXECUTIVES...
THE PUNISH-MENT IS SEPPUKU.

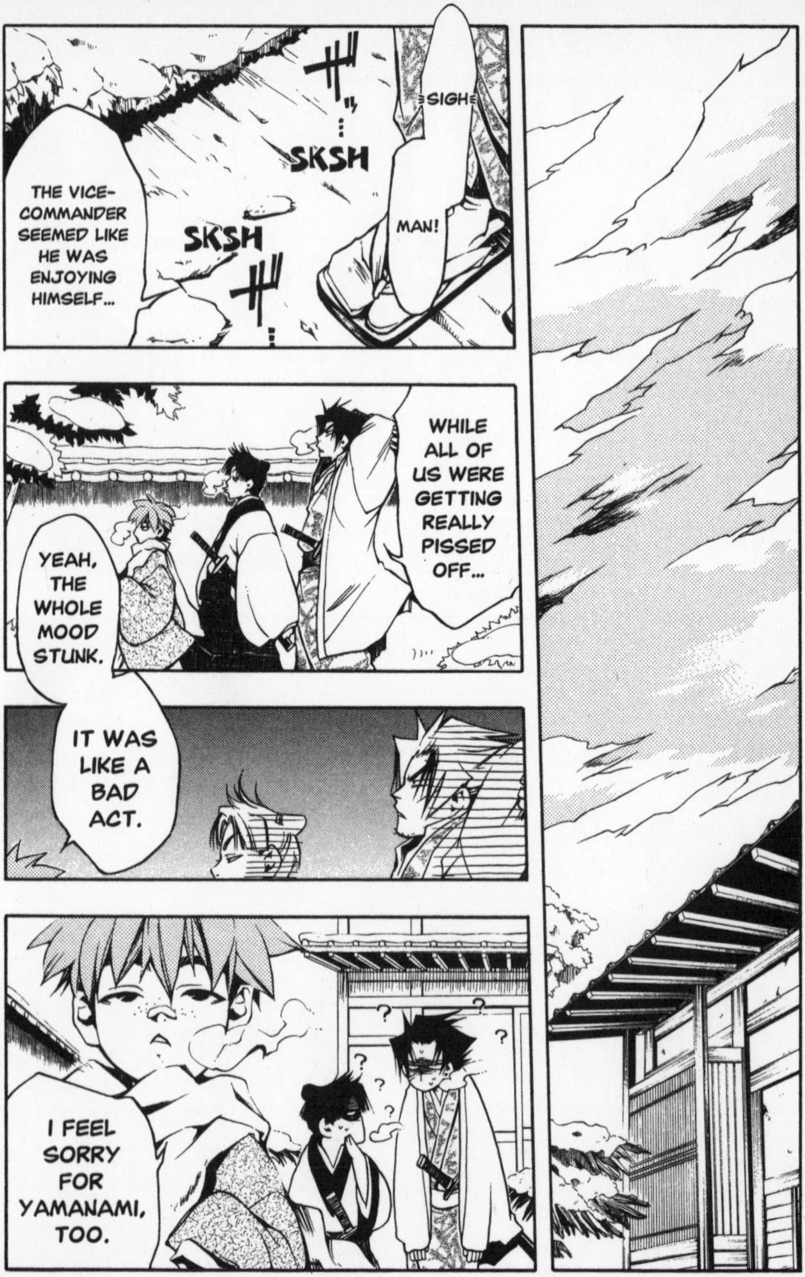
SIGH
MAN!
SKSH
SKSH
THE VICE-COMMANDER SEEMED LIKE HE WAS ENJOYING HIMSELF...
WHILE ALL OF US WERE GETTING REALLY PISSED OFF...
YEAH, THE WHOLE MOOD STUNK.
IT WAS LIKE A BAD ACT.
I FEEL SORRY FOR YAMANAMI, TOO.

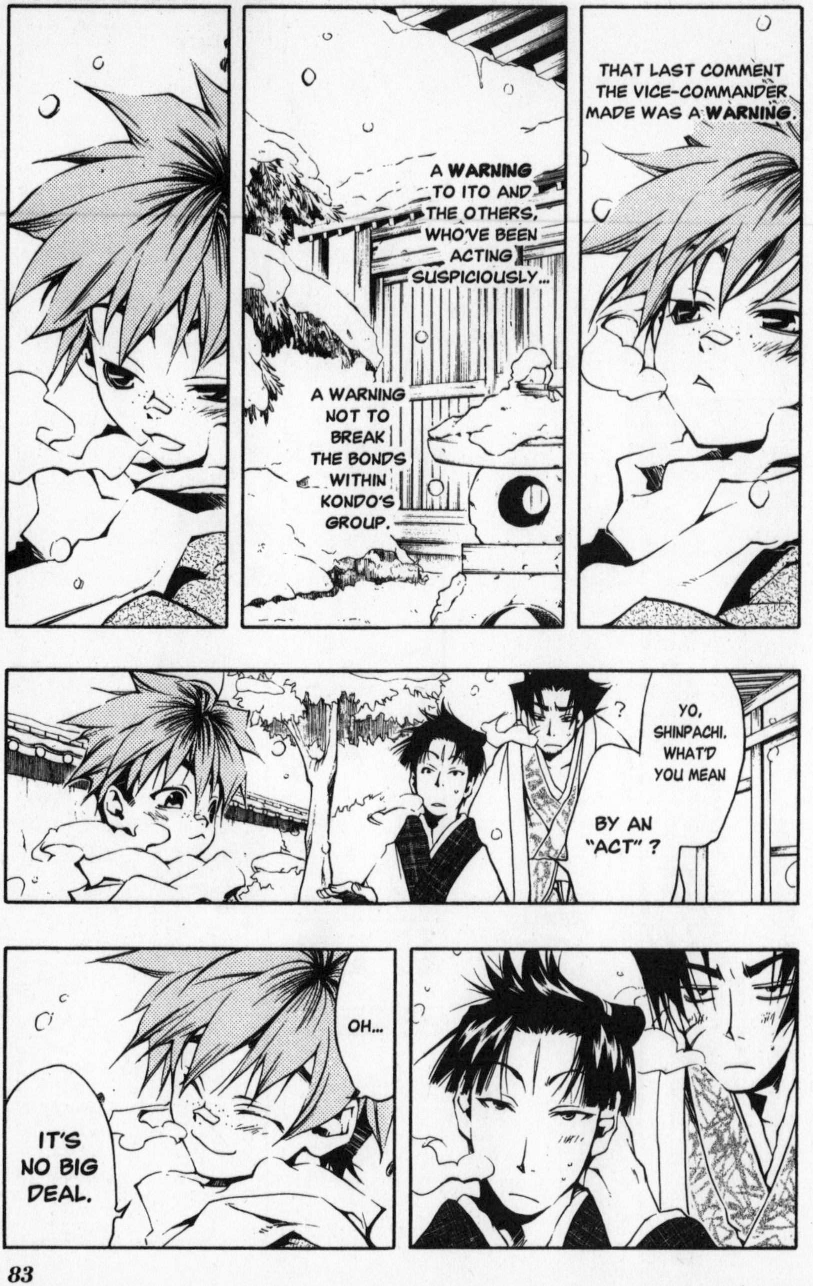
THAT LAST COMMENT THE VICE-COMMANDER MADE WAS A WARNING.
A WARNING TO ITO AND THE OTHERS, WHO'VE BEEN ACTING SUSPICIOUSLY...
A WARNING NOT TO BREAK THE BONDS WITHIN KONDO'S GROUP.
YO, SHINPACHI. WHAT'D YOU MEAN
BY AN "ACT" ?
OH...
IT'S NO BIG DEAL.

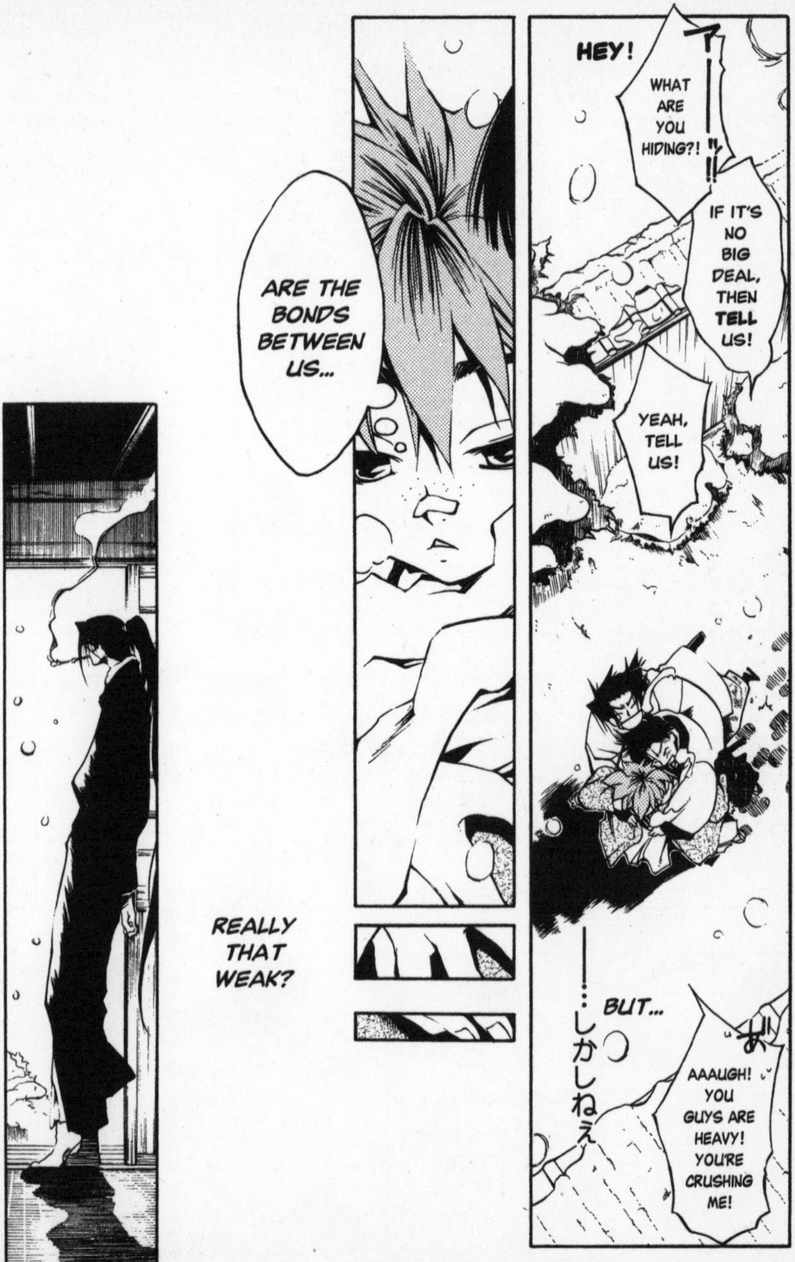
HEY!
WHAT ARE YOU HIDING?!
IF IT'S NO BIG DEAL, THEN TELL US!
YEAH, TELL US!
BUT...
……しかしねぇ
AAAUGH! YOU GUYS ARE HEAVY! YOU'RE CRUSHING ME!
ARE THE BONDS BETWEEN US...
REALLY THAT WEAK?

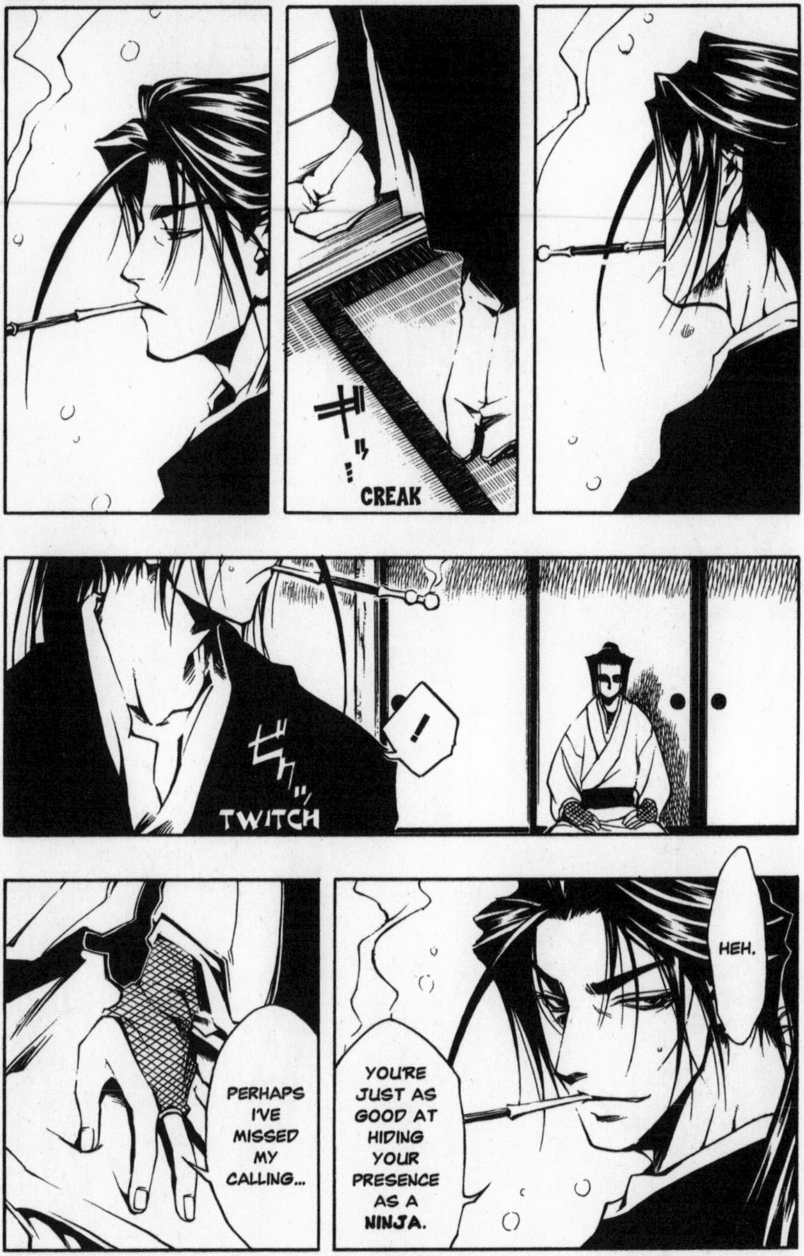
CREAK
!
TWITCH
HEH.
YOU'RE JUST AS GOOD AT HIDING YOUR PRESENCE AS A NINJA.
PERHAPS I'VE MISSED MY CALLING...

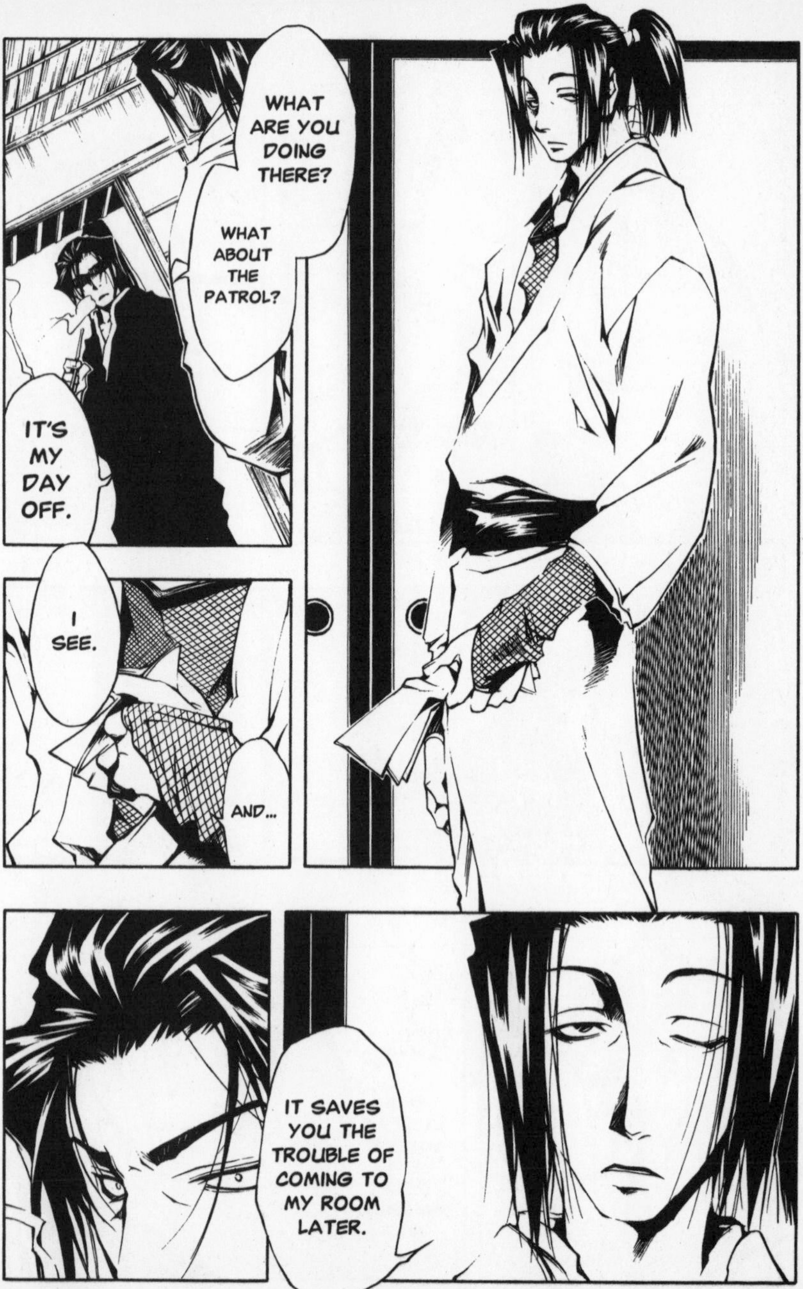
WHAT ARE YOU DOING THERE?
WHAT ABOUT THE PATROL?
IT'S MY DAY OFF.
I SEE.
AND...
IT SAVES YOU THE TROUBLE OF COMING TO MY ROOM LATER.

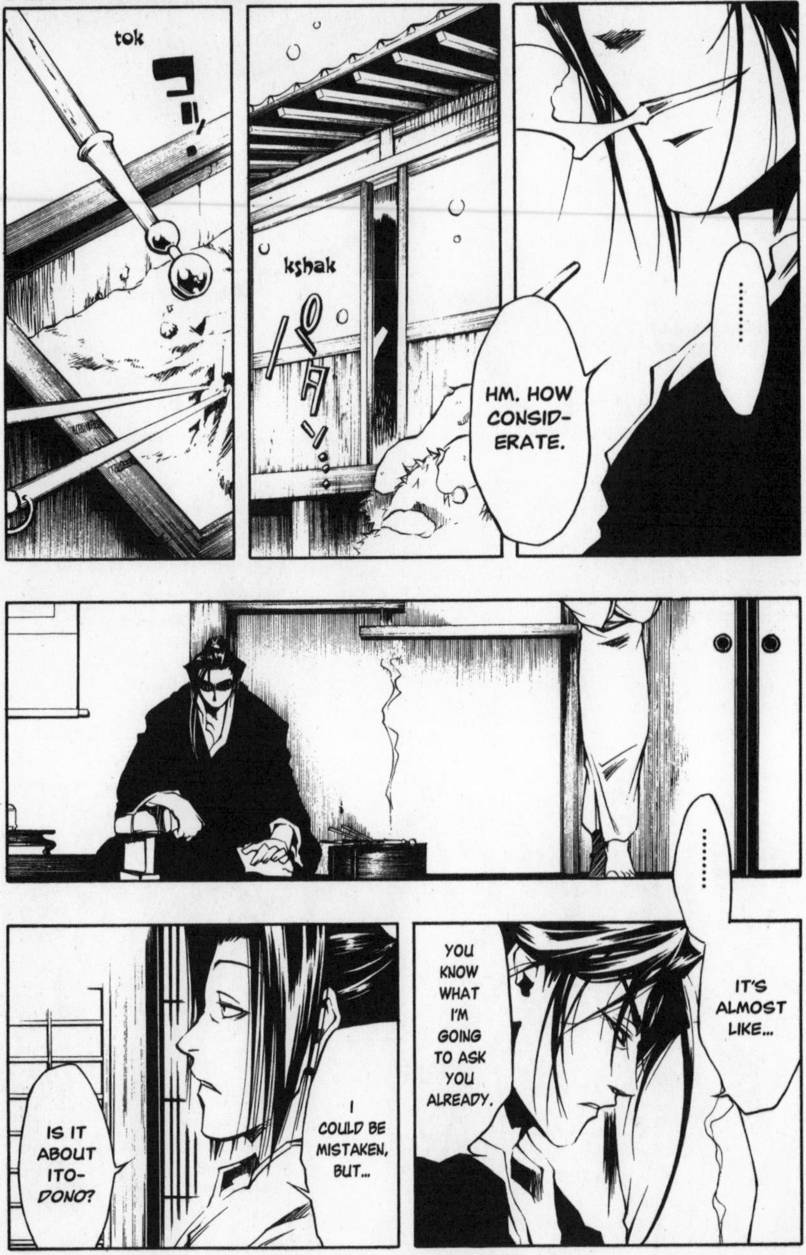
......
HM. HOW CONSID-ERATE.
kshak
tok
......
IT'S ALMOST LIKE...
YOU KNOW WHAT I'M GOING TO ASK YOU ALREADY.
I COULD BE MISTAKEN, BUT...
IS IT ABOUT ITO-DONO?

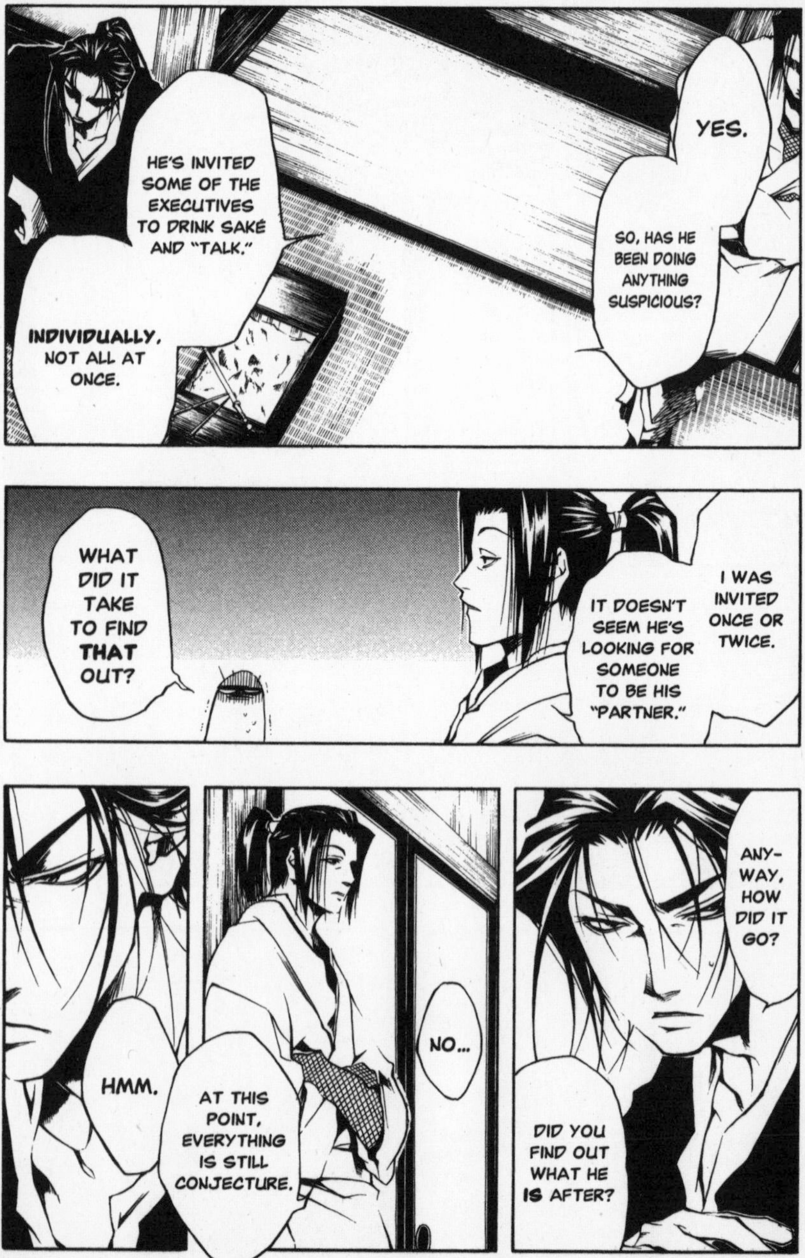
YES.
SO, HAS HE BEEN DOING ANYTHING SUSPICIOUS?
HE'S INVITED SOME OF THE EXECUTIVES TO DRINK SAKÉ AND "TALK."
INDIVIDUALLY, NOT ALL AT ONCE.
I WAS INVITED ONCE OR TWICE.
IT DOESN'T SEEM HE'S LOOKING FOR SOMEONE TO BE HIS "PARTNER."
WHAT DID IT TAKE TO FIND THAT OUT?
ANY-WAY, HOW DID IT GO?
DID YOU FIND OUT WHAT HE IS AFTER?
NO...
AT THIS POINT, EVERYTHING IS STILL CONJECTURE.
HMM.

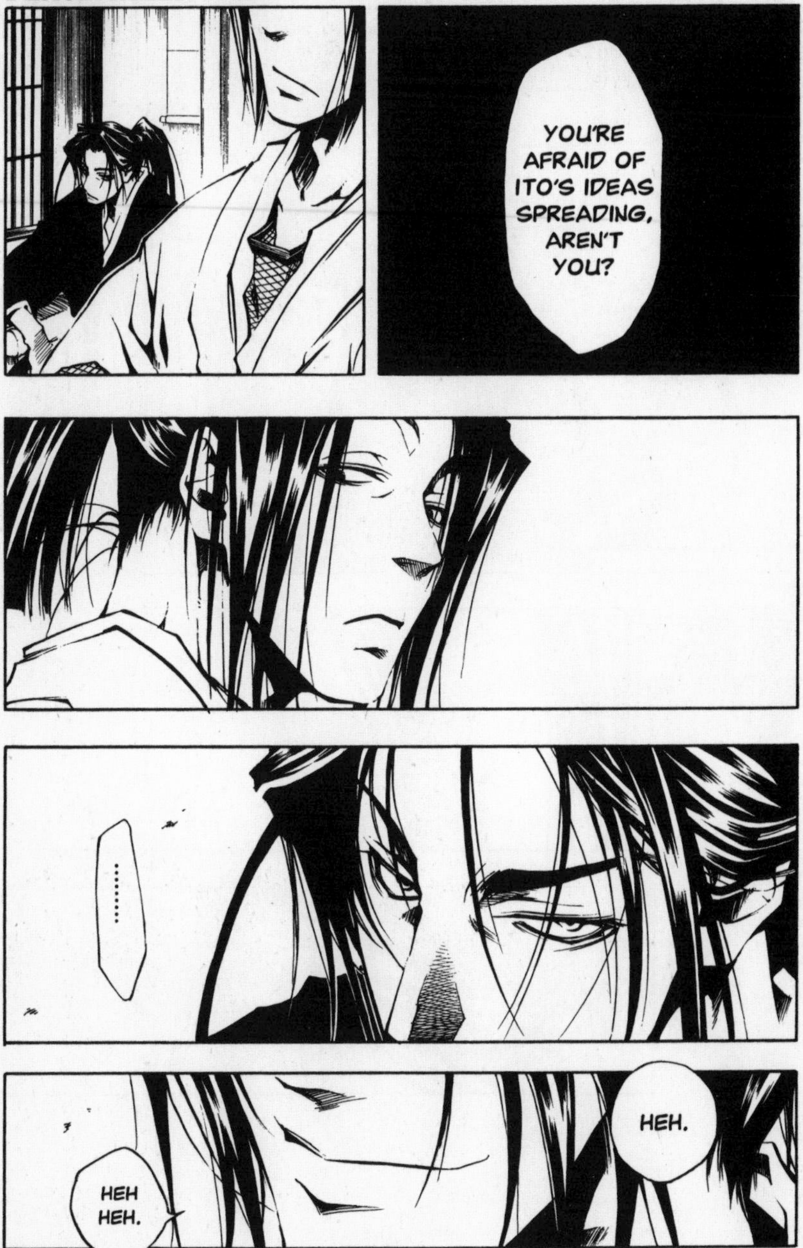
YOU'RE AFRAID OF ITO'S IDEAS SPREADING, AREN'T YOU?
......
HEH.
HEH HEH.

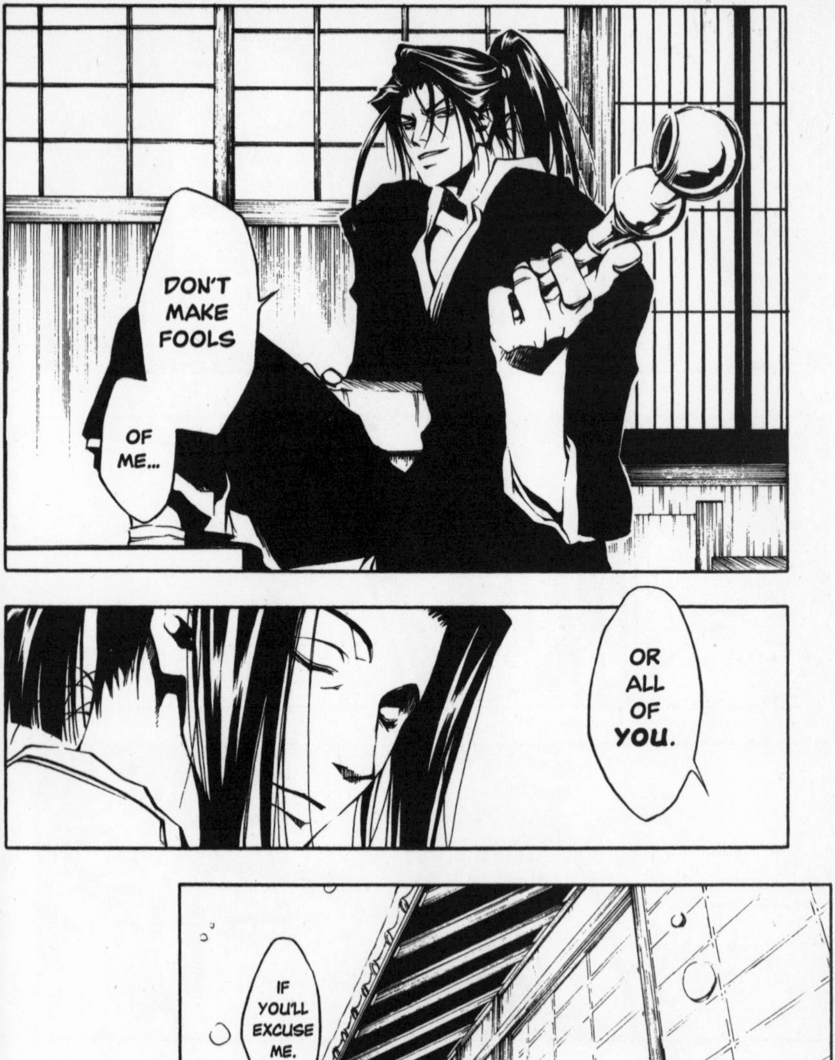
DON'T MAKE FOOLS
OF ME...
OR ALL OF YOU.
IF YOU'LL EXCUSE ME.

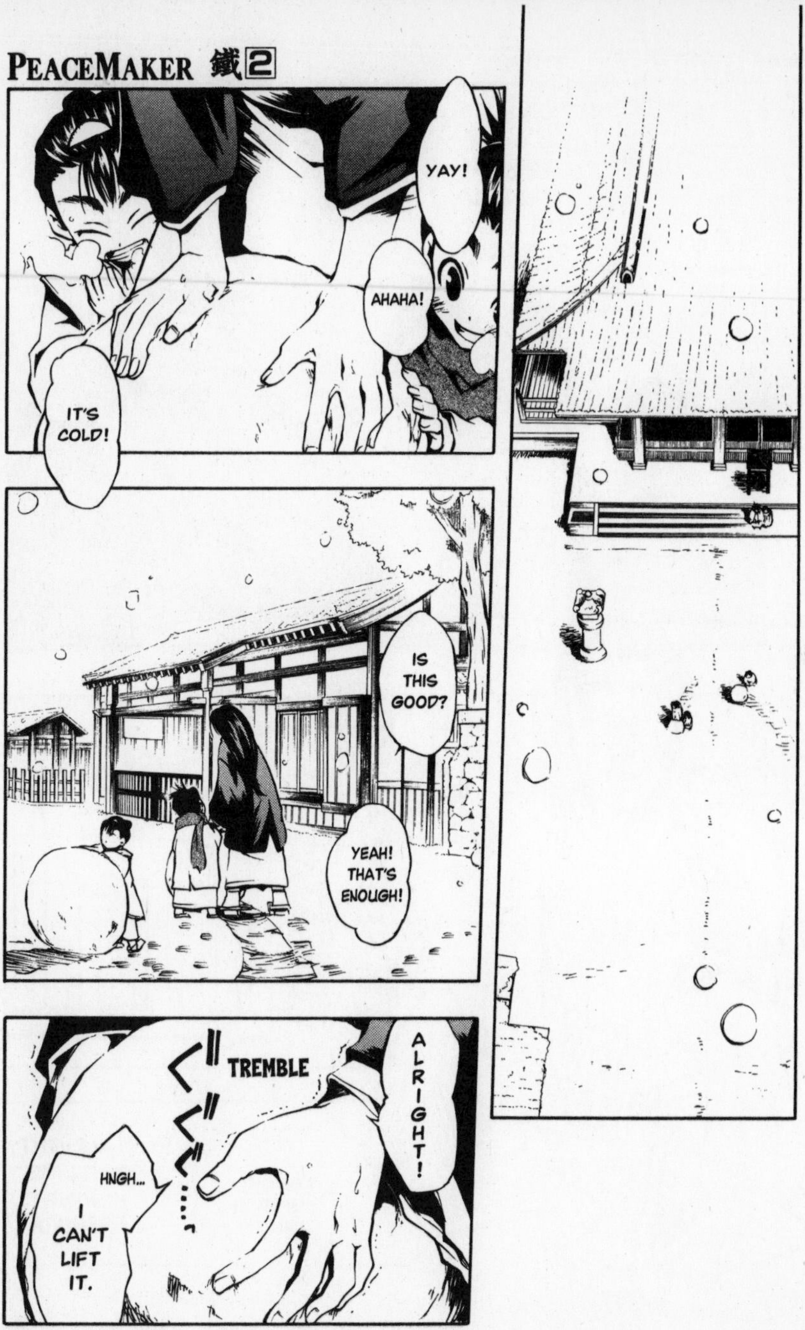
YAY!
AHAHA!
IT'S COLD!
IS THIS GOOD?
YEAH! THAT'S ENOUGH!
ALRIGHT!
TREMBLE
HNGH...
I CAN'T LIFT IT.

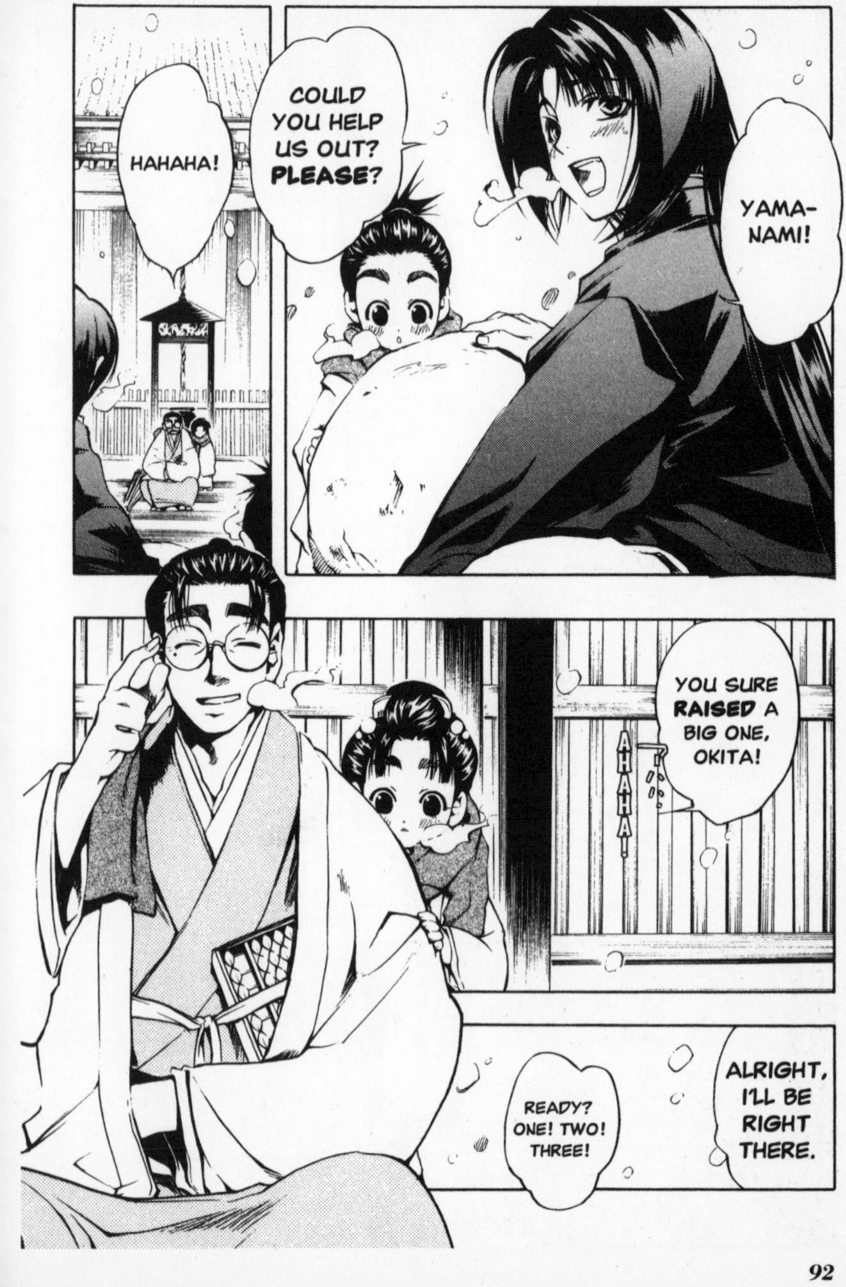
YAMA-NAMI!
COULD YOU HELP US OUT? PLEASE?
HAHAHA!
YOU SURE RAISED A BIG ONE, OKITA!
AHAHAHA!
ALRIGHT, I'LL BE RIGHT THERE.
READY? ONE! TWO! THREE!

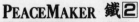

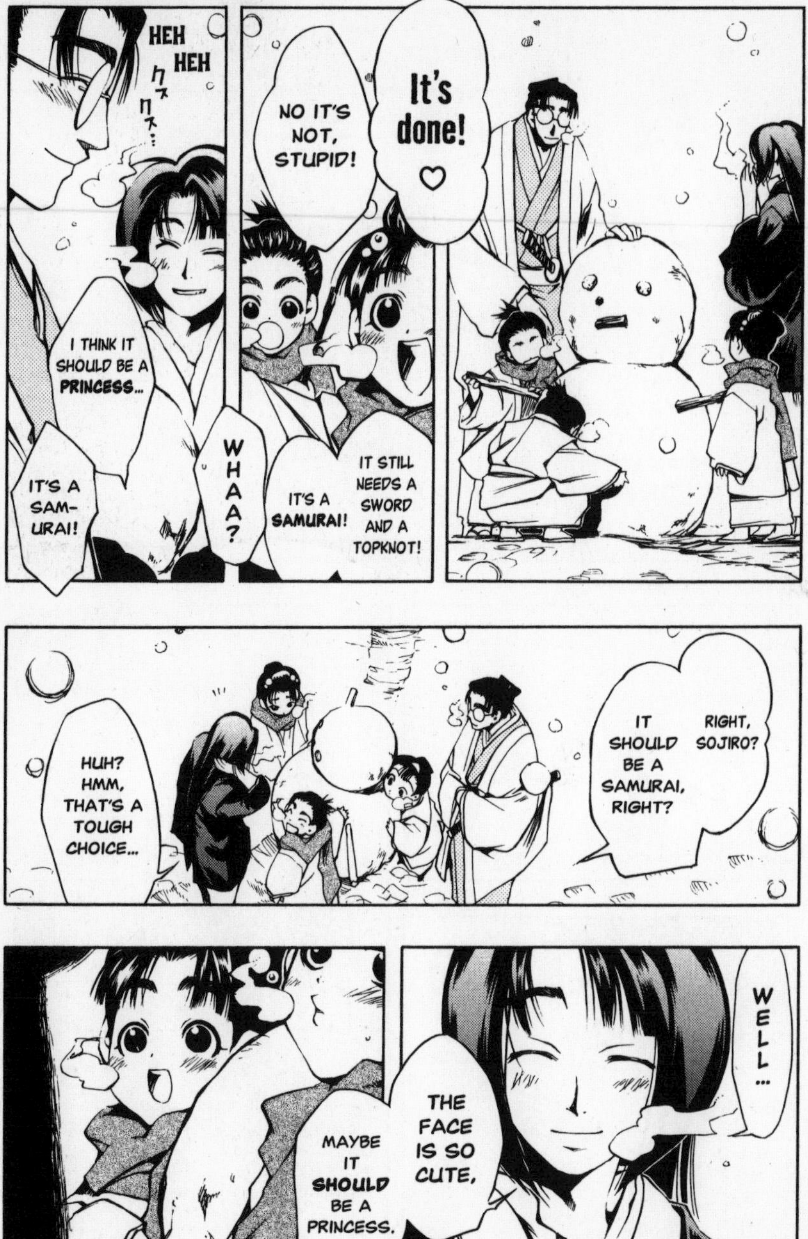
It's done! ♥
NO IT'S NOT, STUPID!
IT STILL NEEDS A SWORD AND A TOPKNOT!
IT'S A **SAMURAI**!
WHAAA?
HEH HEH
クスクス…
I THINK IT SHOULD BE A **PRINCESS**...
IT'S A SAMURAI!
RIGHT, SOJIRO?
IT SHOULD BE A SAMURAI, RIGHT?
HUH? HMM, THAT'S A TOUGH CHOICE...
WELL...
THE FACE IS SO CUTE,
MAYBE IT **SHOULD** BE A PRINCESS.

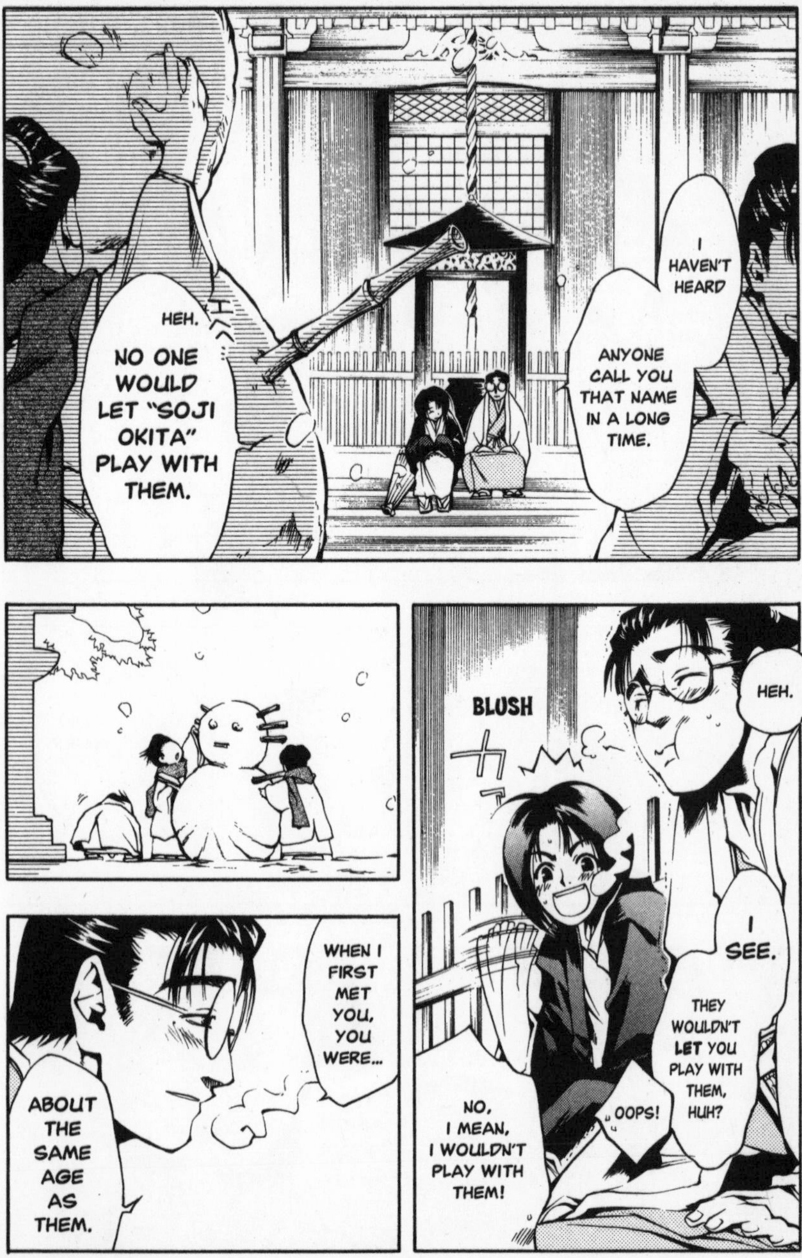
I HAVEN'T HEARD ANYONE CALL YOU THAT NAME IN A LONG TIME.
HEH.
NO ONE WOULD LET "SOJI OKITA" PLAY WITH THEM.
HEH.
BLUSH
I SEE.
THEY WOULDN'T LET YOU PLAY WITH THEM, HUH?
OOPS!
NO, I MEAN, I WOULDN'T PLAY WITH THEM!
WHEN I FIRST MET YOU, YOU WERE...
ABOUT THE SAME AGE AS THEM.

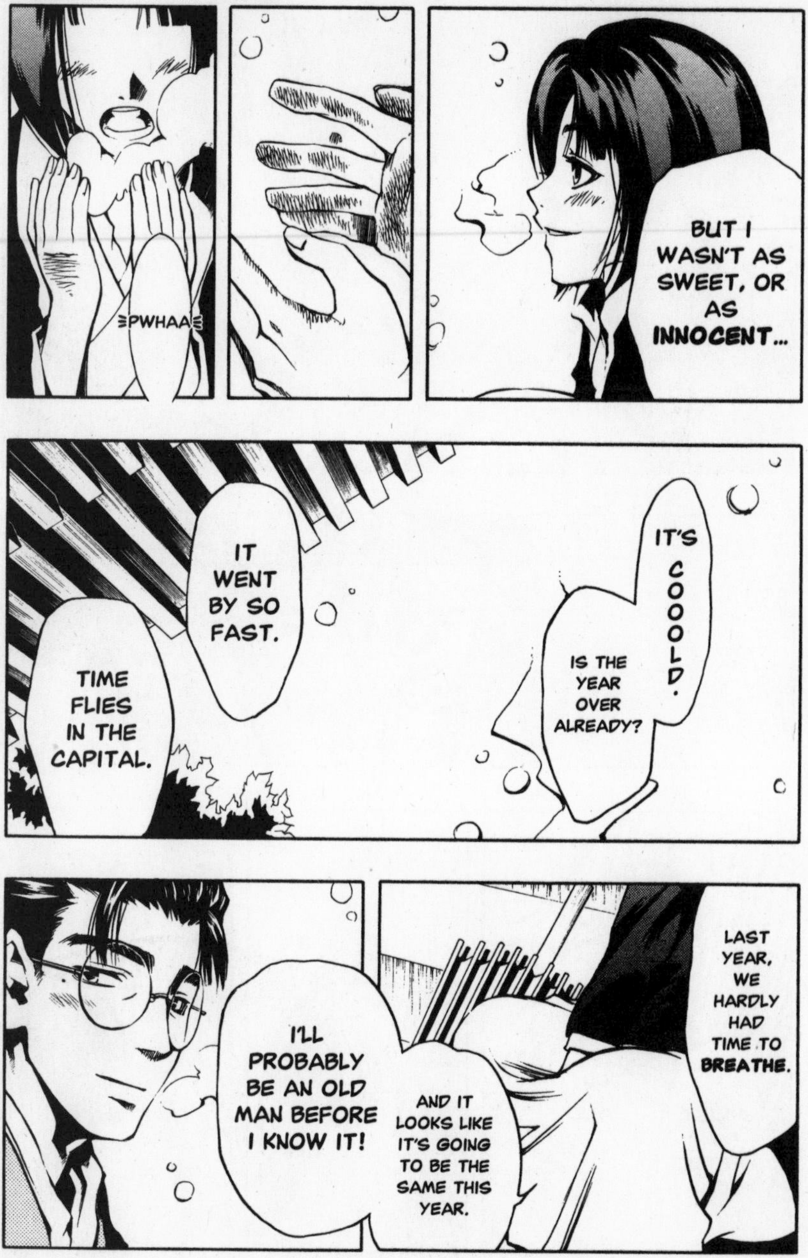
BUT I WASN'T AS SWEET, OR AS INNOCENT...
PWHAA
IT'S COOOOLD.
IS THE YEAR OVER ALREADY?
IT WENT BY SO FAST.
TIME FLIES IN THE CAPITAL.
LAST YEAR, WE HARDLY HAD TIME TO BREATHE.
AND IT LOOKS LIKE IT'S GOING TO BE THE SAME THIS YEAR.
I'LL PROBABLY BE AN OLD MAN BEFORE I KNOW IT!

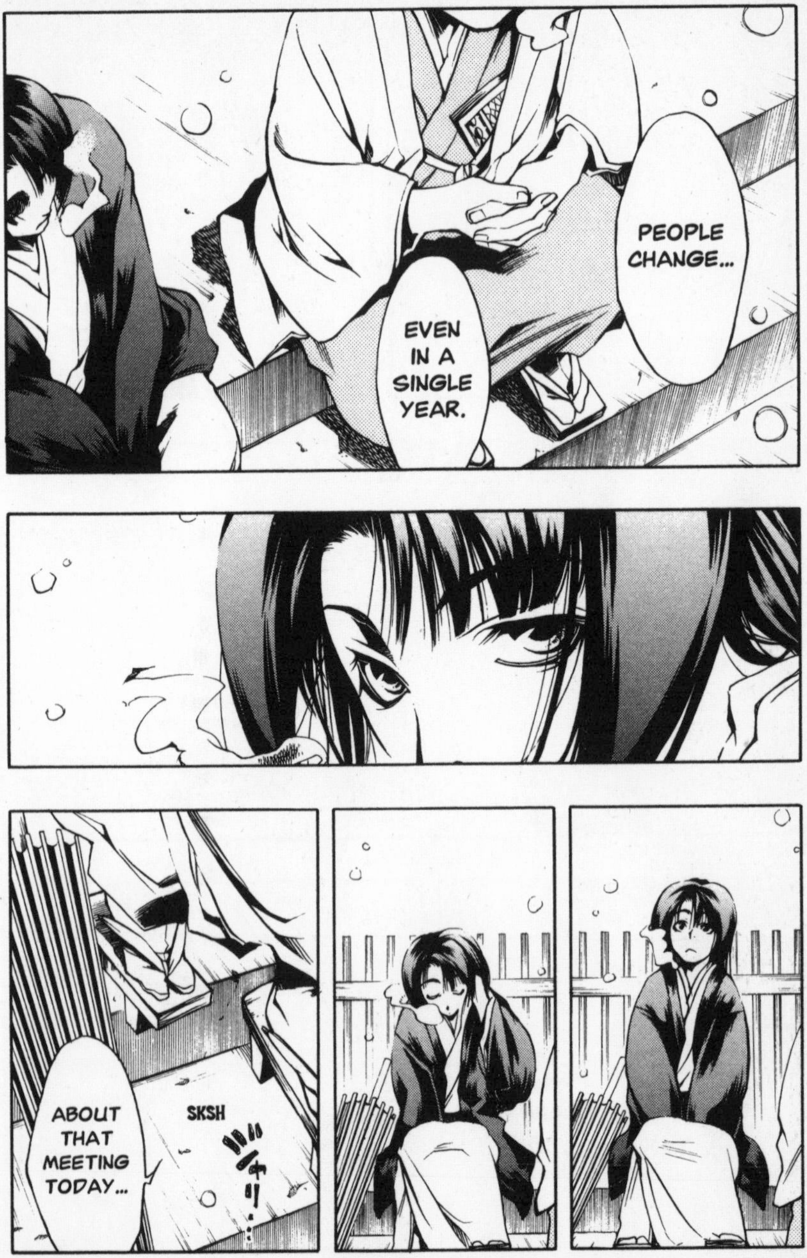
PEOPLE CHANGE...
EVEN IN A SINGLE YEAR.
ABOUT THAT MEETING TODAY...
SKSH

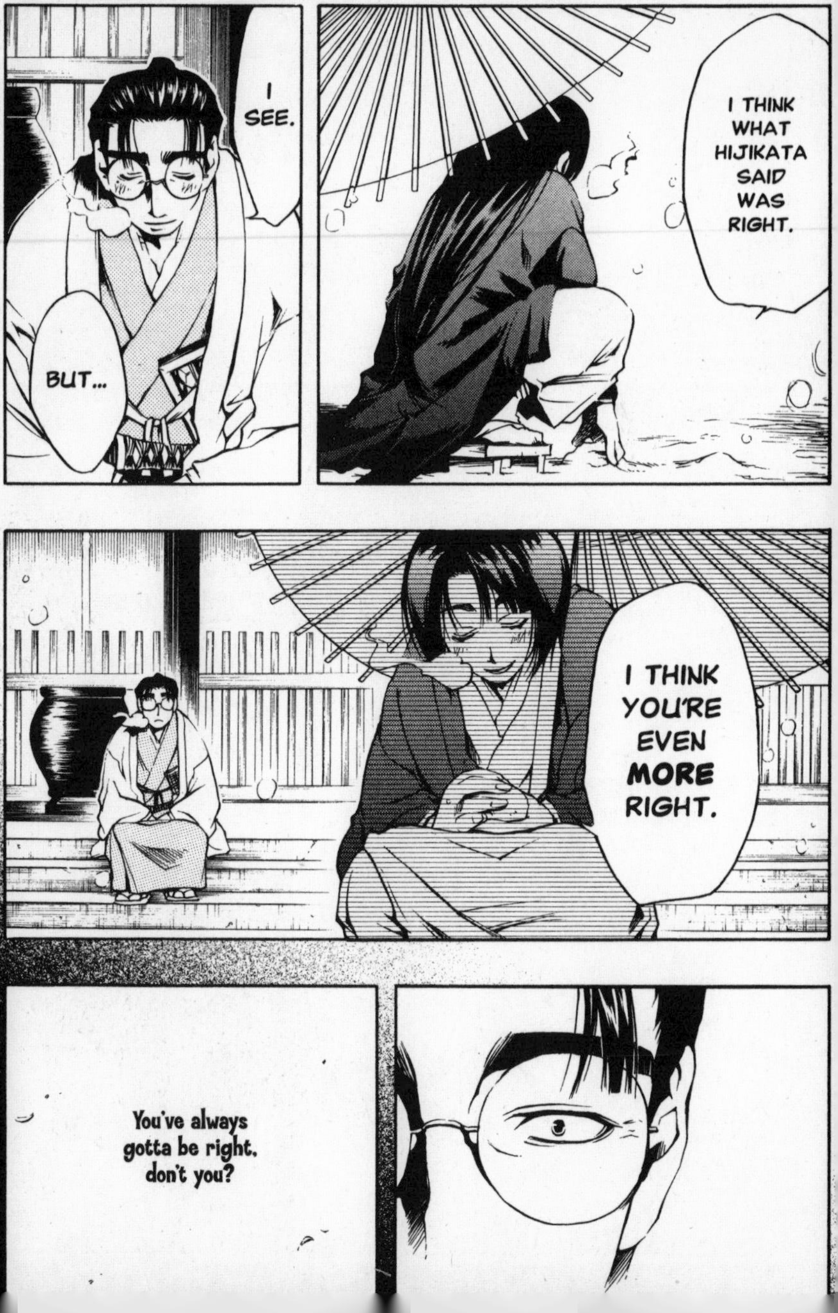
I THINK WHAT HIJIKATA SAID WAS RIGHT.
I SEE.
BUT...
I THINK YOU'RE EVEN **MORE** RIGHT.
You've always gotta be right, don't you?

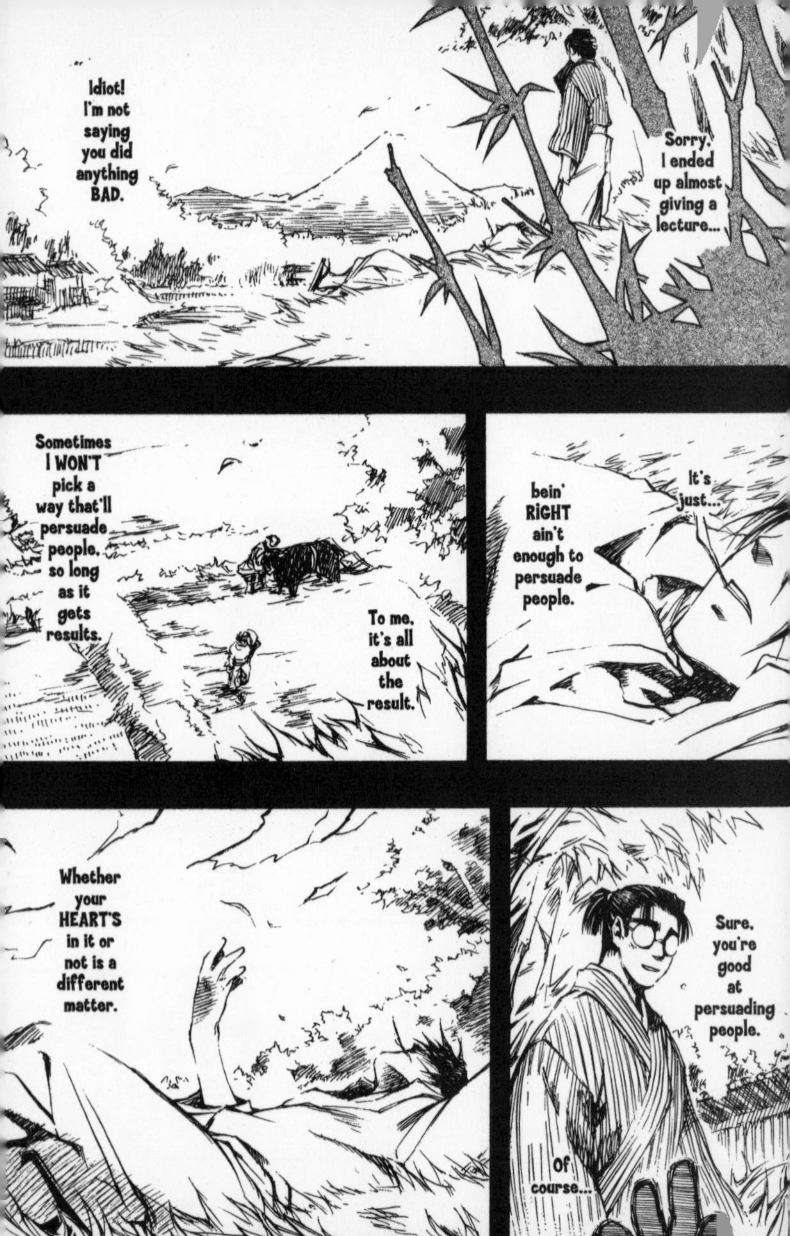
Sorry, I ended up almost giving a lecture...
Idiot! I'm not saying you did anything BAD.
It's just...
bein' RIGHT ain't enough to persuade people.
To me, it's all about the result.
Sometimes I WON'T pick a way that'll persuade people, so long as it gets results.
Sure, you're good at persuading people.
Of course...
Whether your HEART'S in it or not is a different matter.

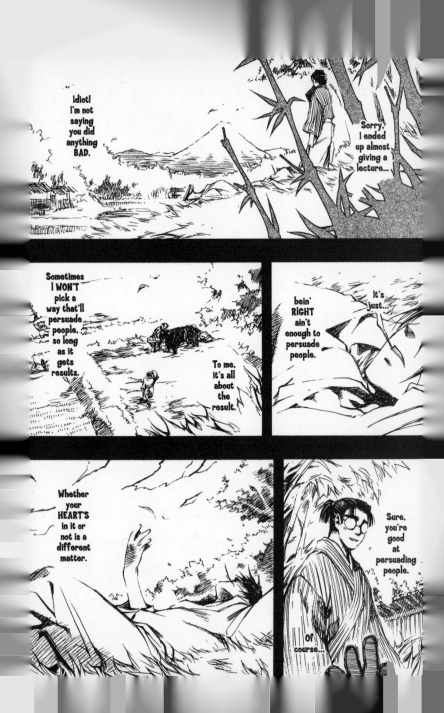

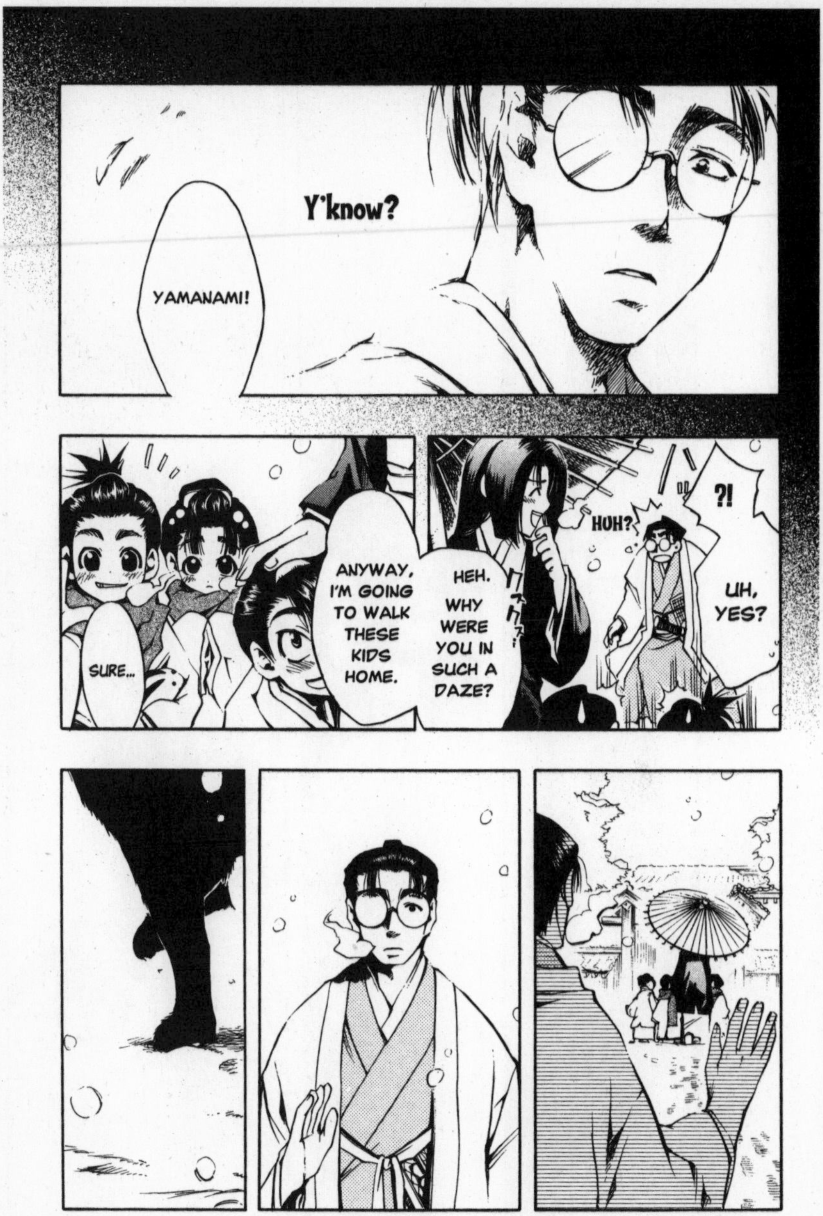
Y'know?
YAMANAMI!
?!
HUH?
UH, YES?
HEH. WHY WERE YOU IN SUCH A DAZE?
ANYWAY, I'M GOING TO WALK THESE KIDS HOME.
SURE...

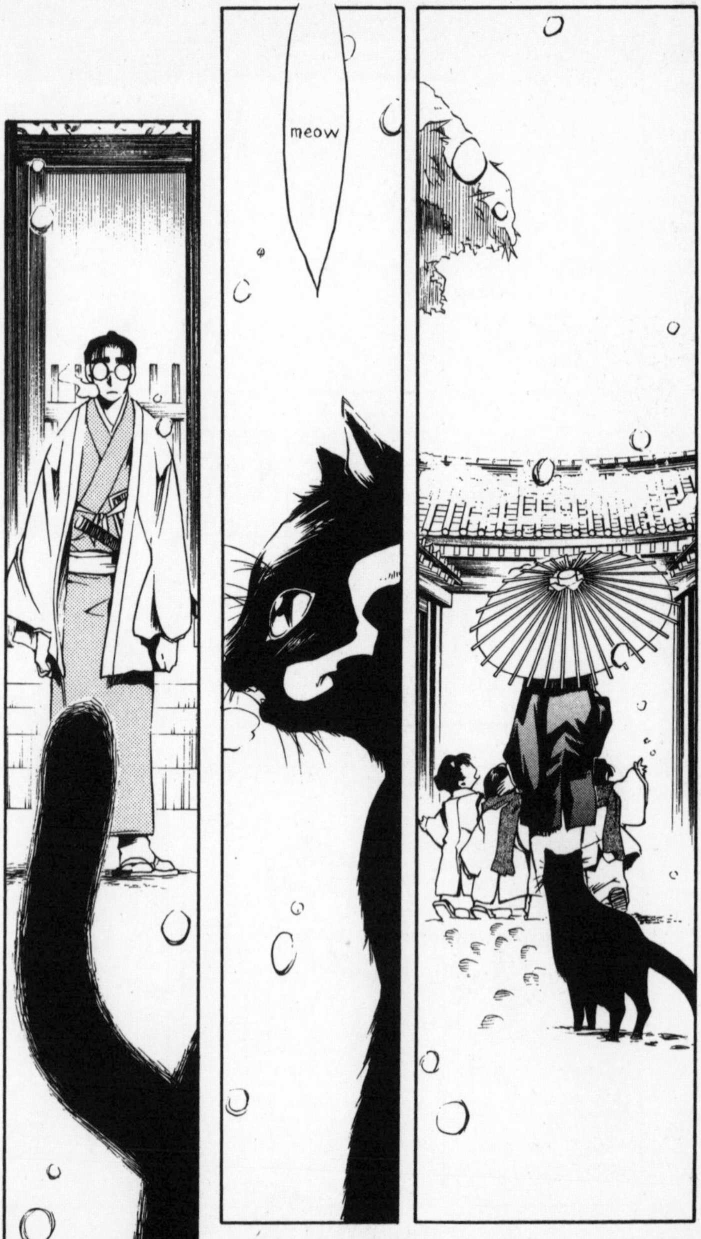
meow

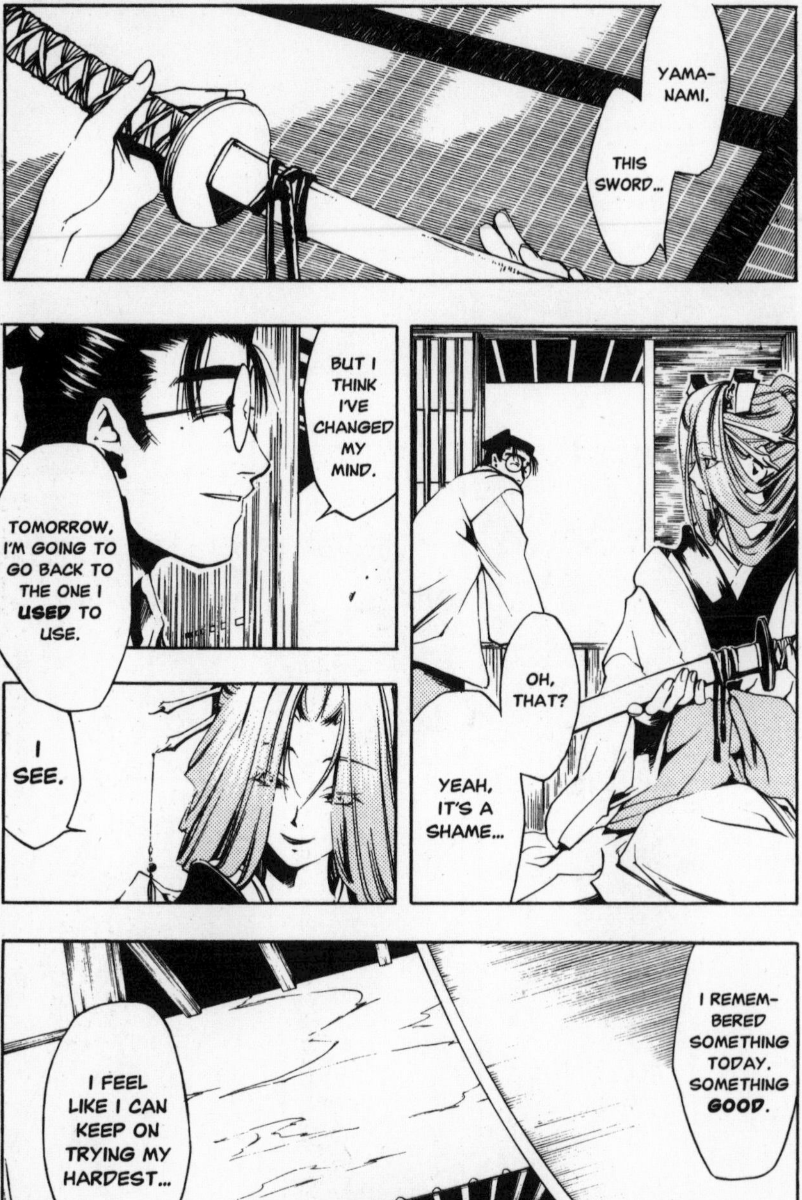
YAMA-NAMI.
THIS SWORD...
OH, THAT?
YEAH, IT'S A SHAME...
BUT I THINK I'VE CHANGED MY MIND.
TOMORROW, I'M GOING TO GO BACK TO THE ONE I **USED** TO USE.
I SEE.
I REMEMBERED SOMETHING TODAY. SOMETHING **GOOD**.
I FEEL LIKE I CAN KEEP ON TRYING MY HARDEST...

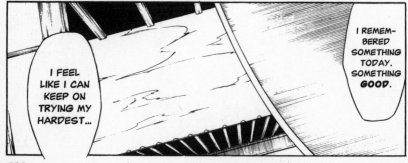

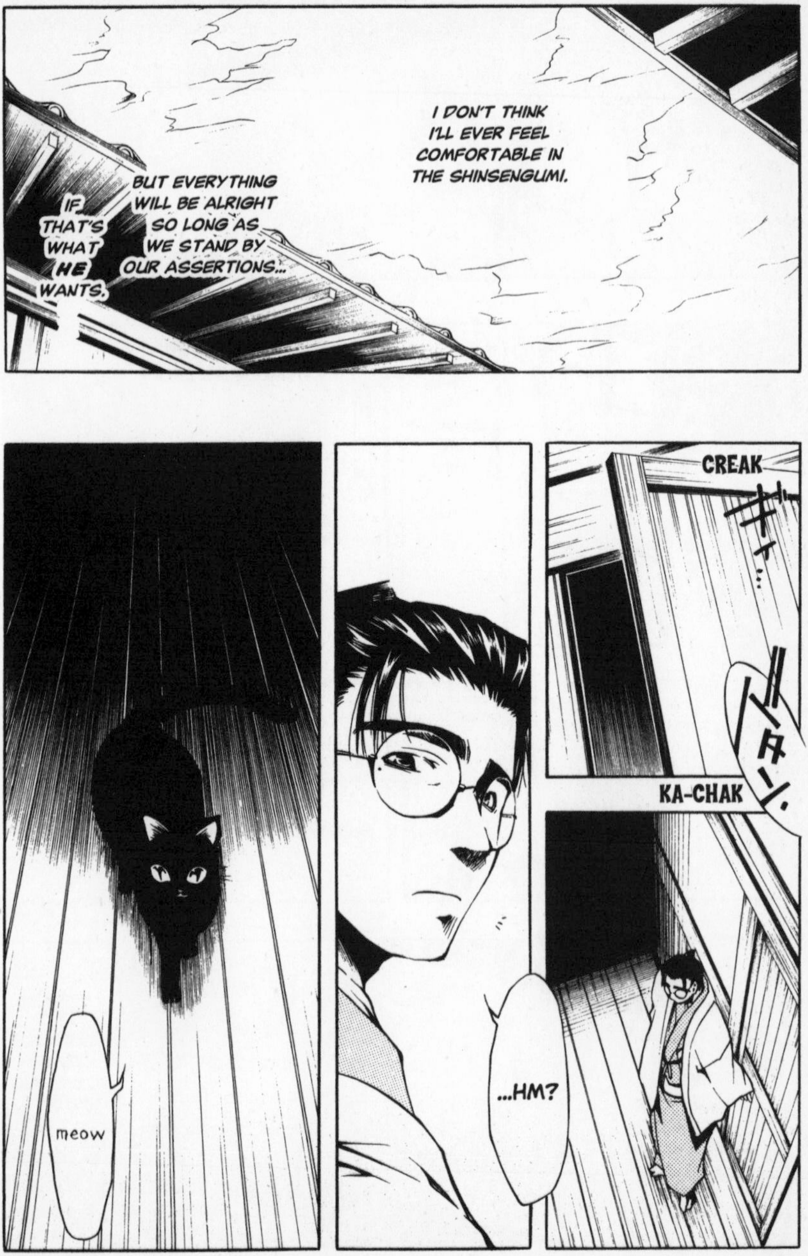
I DON'T THINK I'LL EVER FEEL COMFORTABLE IN THE SHINSENGUMI.
BUT EVERYTHING WILL BE ALRIGHT SO LONG AS WE STAND BY OUR ASSERTIONS...
IF THAT'S WHAT HE WANTS.
CREAK
ギィ…
KA-CHAK
バタン
...HM?
meow

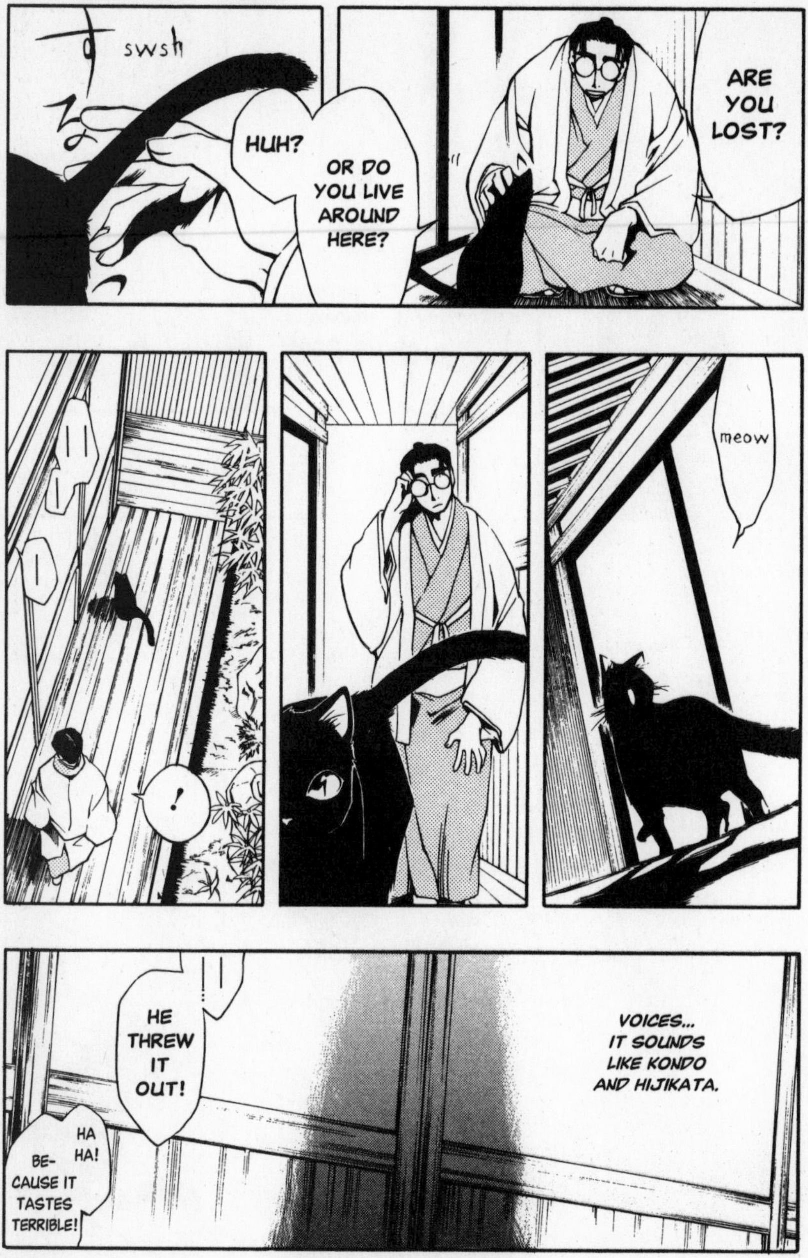
ARE YOU LOST?
HUH?
OR DO YOU LIVE AROUND HERE?
すっ
swsh
meow
!
VOICES... IT SOUNDS LIKE KONDO AND HIJIKATA.
HE THREW IT OUT!
HA HA!
BE-CAUSE IT TASTES TERRIBLE!

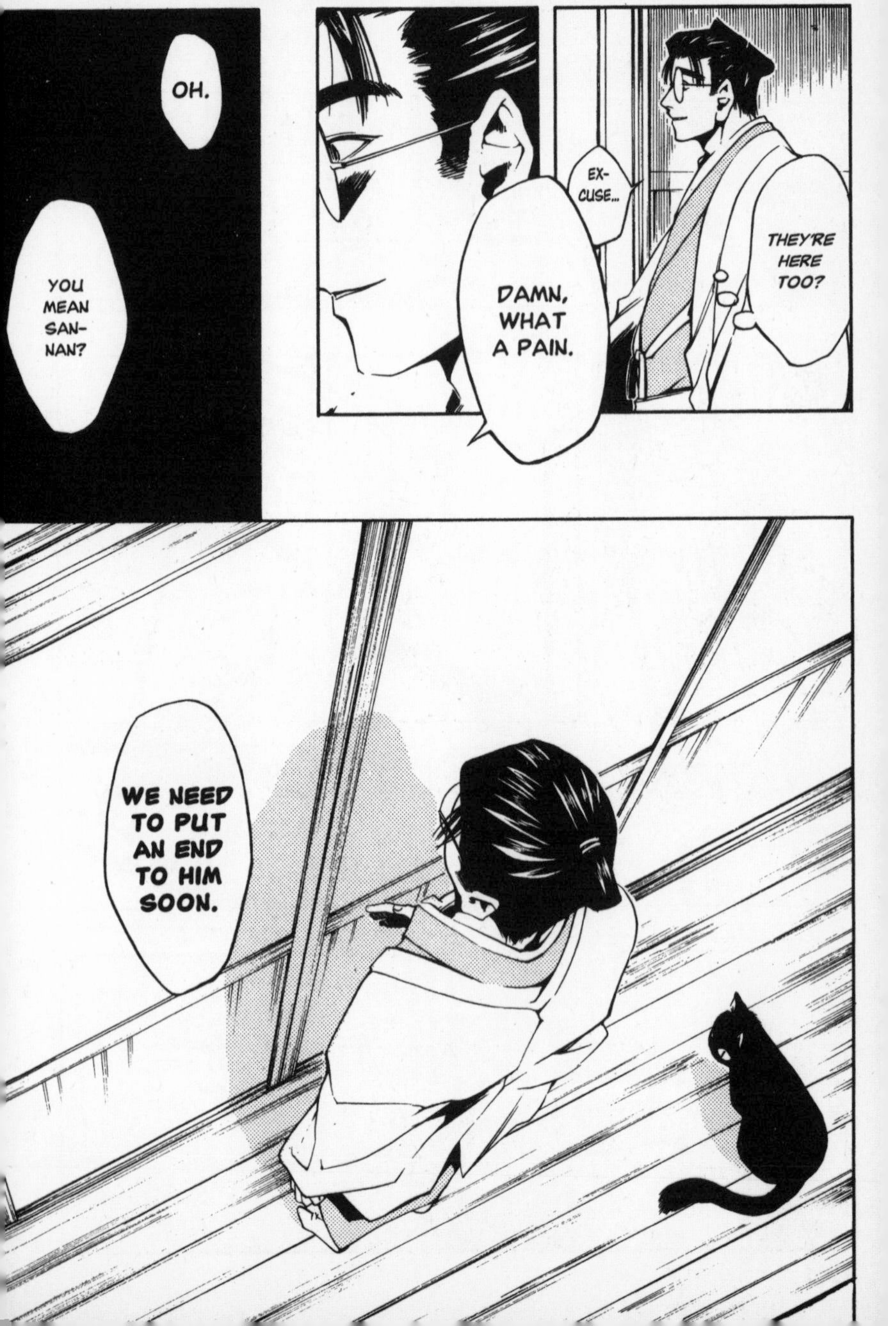
EX-CUSE...
THEY'RE HERE TOO?
DAMN, WHAT A PAIN.
OH.
YOU MEAN SAN-NAN?
WE NEED TO PUT AN END TO HIM SOON.

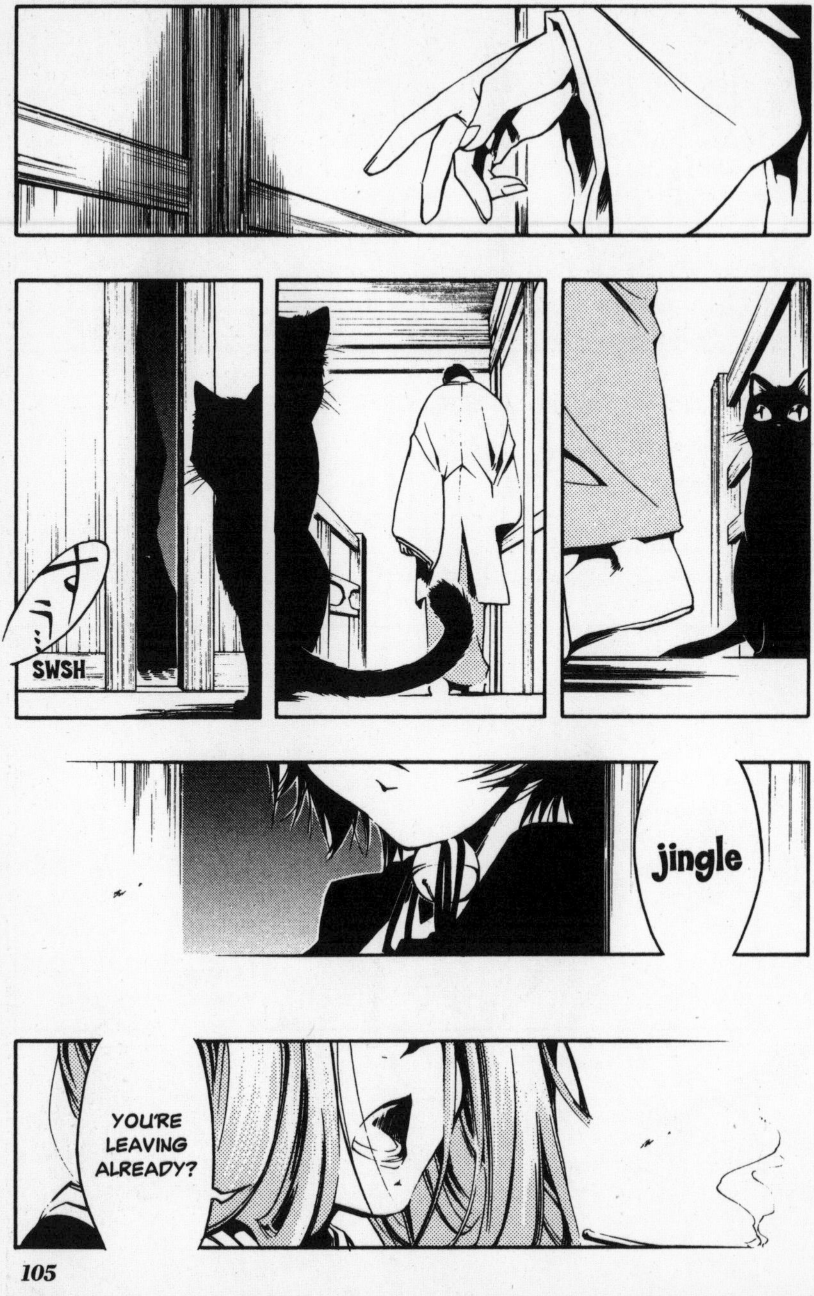
SWSH
jingle
YOU'RE LEAVING ALREADY?

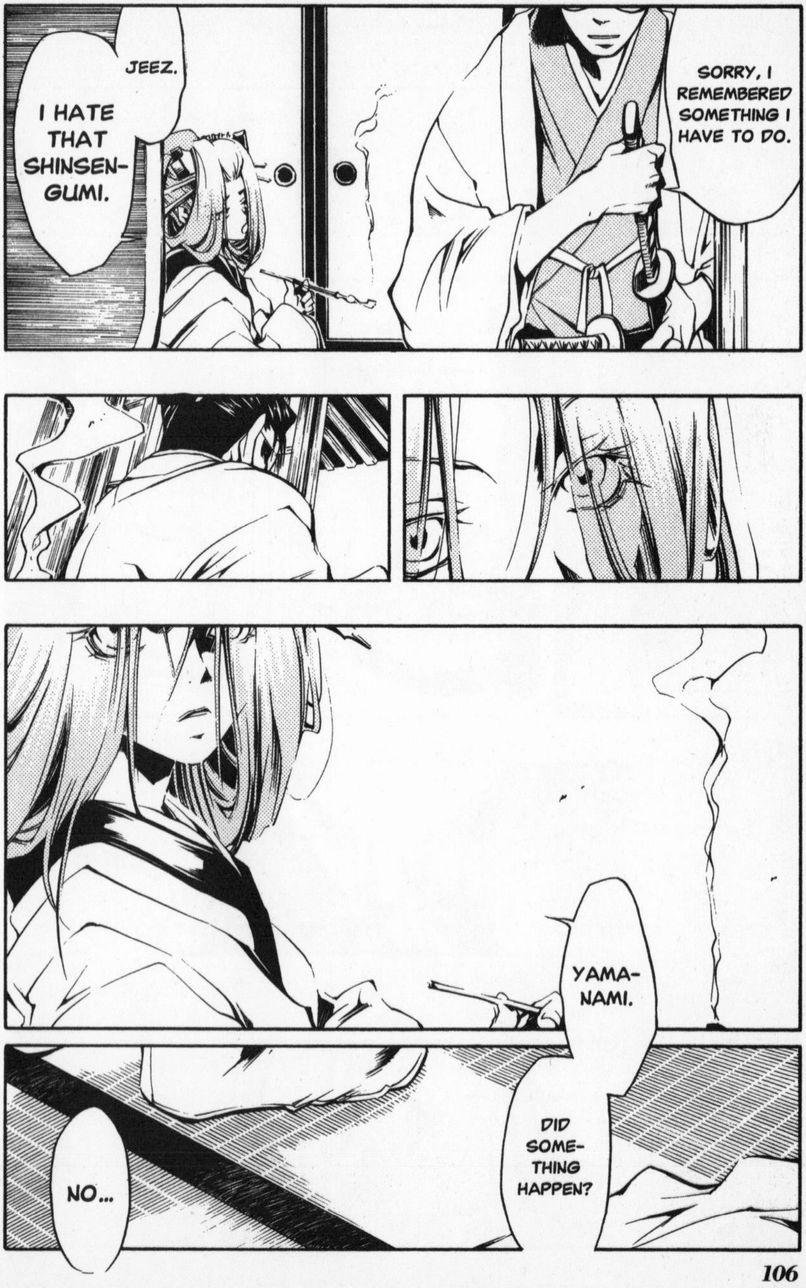
SORRY, I REMEMBERED SOMETHING I HAVE TO DO.
JEEZ.
I HATE THAT SHINSEN-GUMI.
YAMA-NAMI.
DID SOME-THING HAPPEN?
NO...

EVERY-THING'S FINE.
That night...

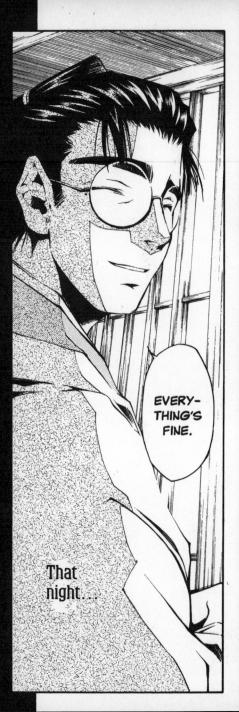

Keisuke Yamanami disappeared.

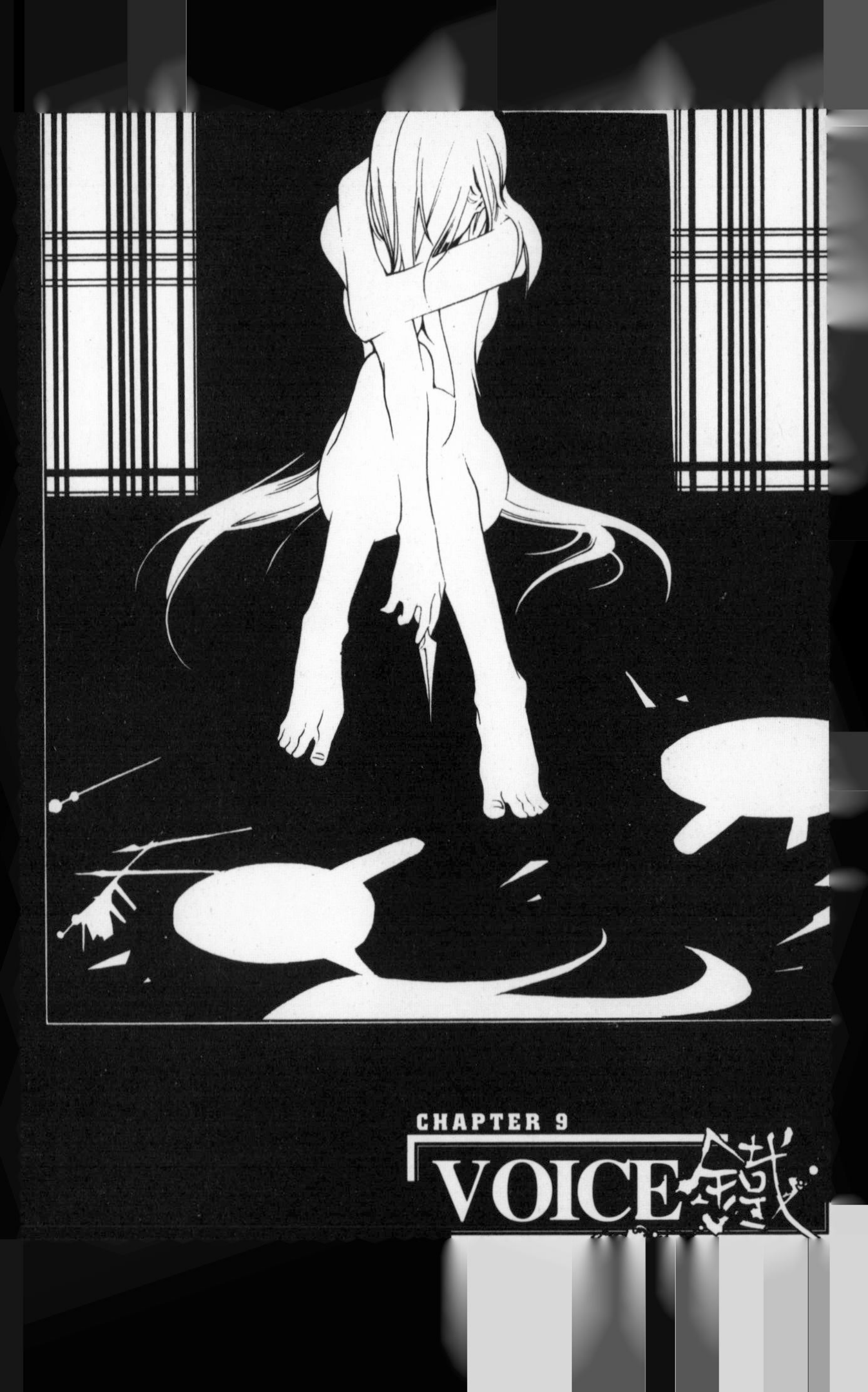

CHAPTER 9

VOICE 鐵

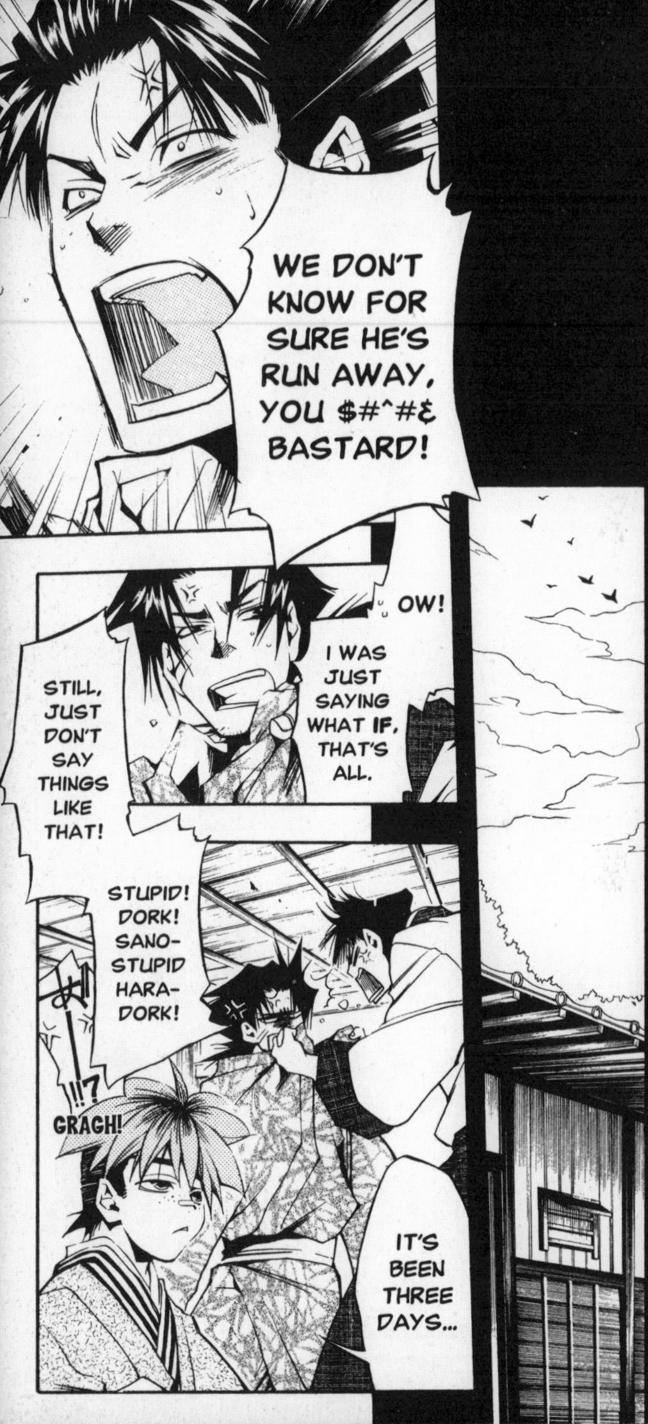
WE DON'T KNOW FOR SURE HE'S RUN AWAY, YOU $#^#& BASTARD!
OW!
I WAS JUST SAYING WHAT IF, THAT'S ALL.
STILL, JUST DON'T SAY THINGS LIKE THAT!
STUPID! DORK! SANO-STUPID HARA-DORK!
!!?
GRAGH!
IT'S BEEN THREE DAYS...

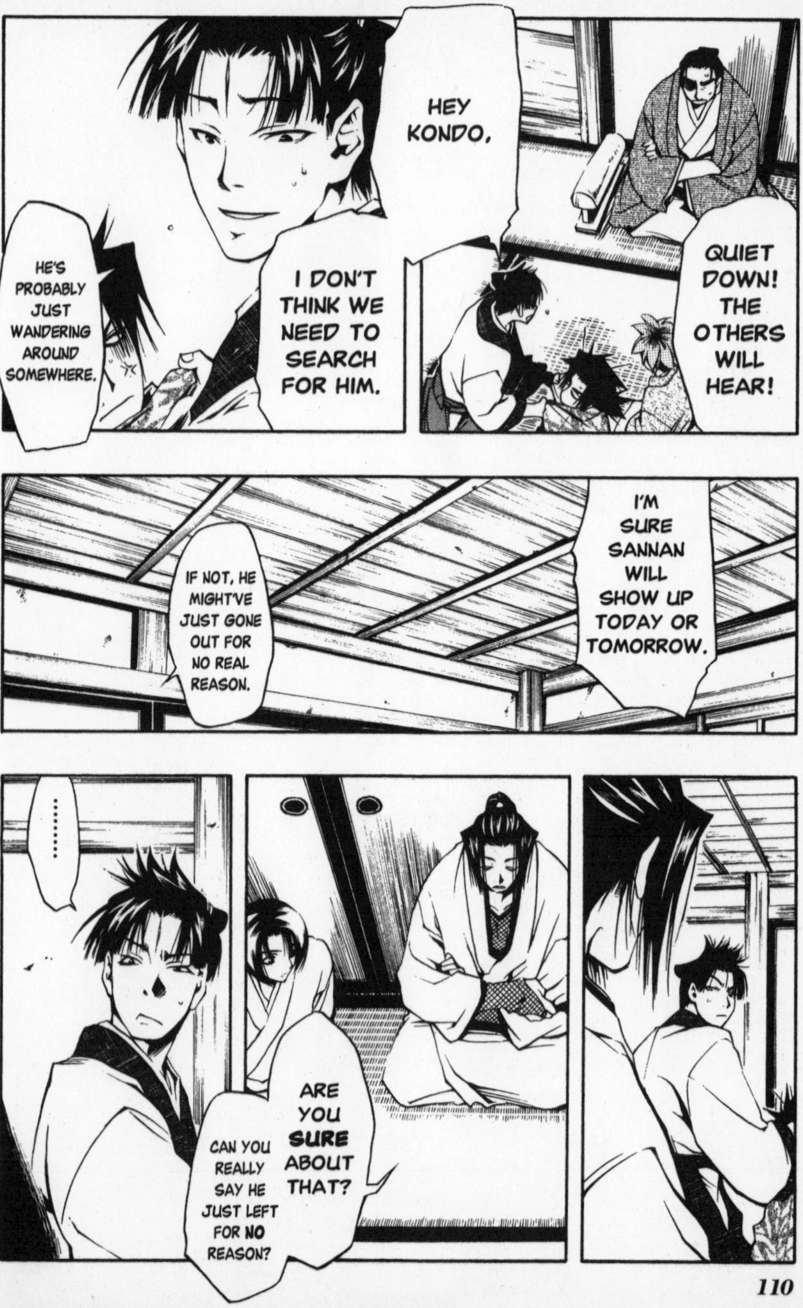
HEY KONDO,
I DON'T THINK WE NEED TO SEARCH FOR HIM.
HE'S PROBABLY JUST WANDERING AROUND SOMEWHERE.
QUIET DOWN! THE OTHERS WILL HEAR!
I'M SURE SANNAN WILL SHOW UP TODAY OR TOMORROW.
IF NOT, HE MIGHT'VE JUST GONE OUT FOR NO REAL REASON.
....
ARE YOU **SURE** ABOUT THAT?
CAN YOU REALLY SAY HE JUST LEFT FOR **NO** REASON?

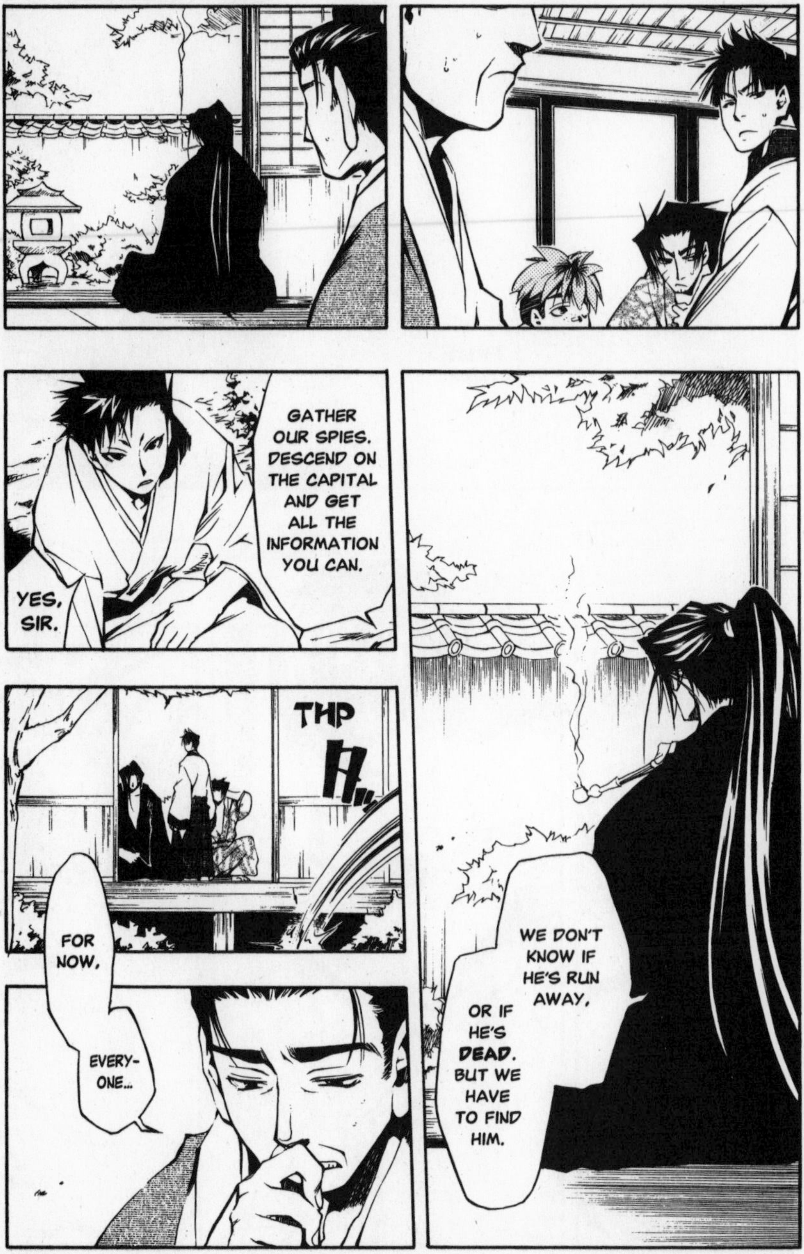

WE DON'T KNOW IF HE'S RUN AWAY,
OR IF HE'S DEAD. BUT WE HAVE TO FIND HIM.
GATHER OUR SPIES. DESCEND ON THE CAPITAL AND GET ALL THE INFORMATION YOU CAN.
YES, SIR.
THP
FOR NOW,
EVERY-ONE...

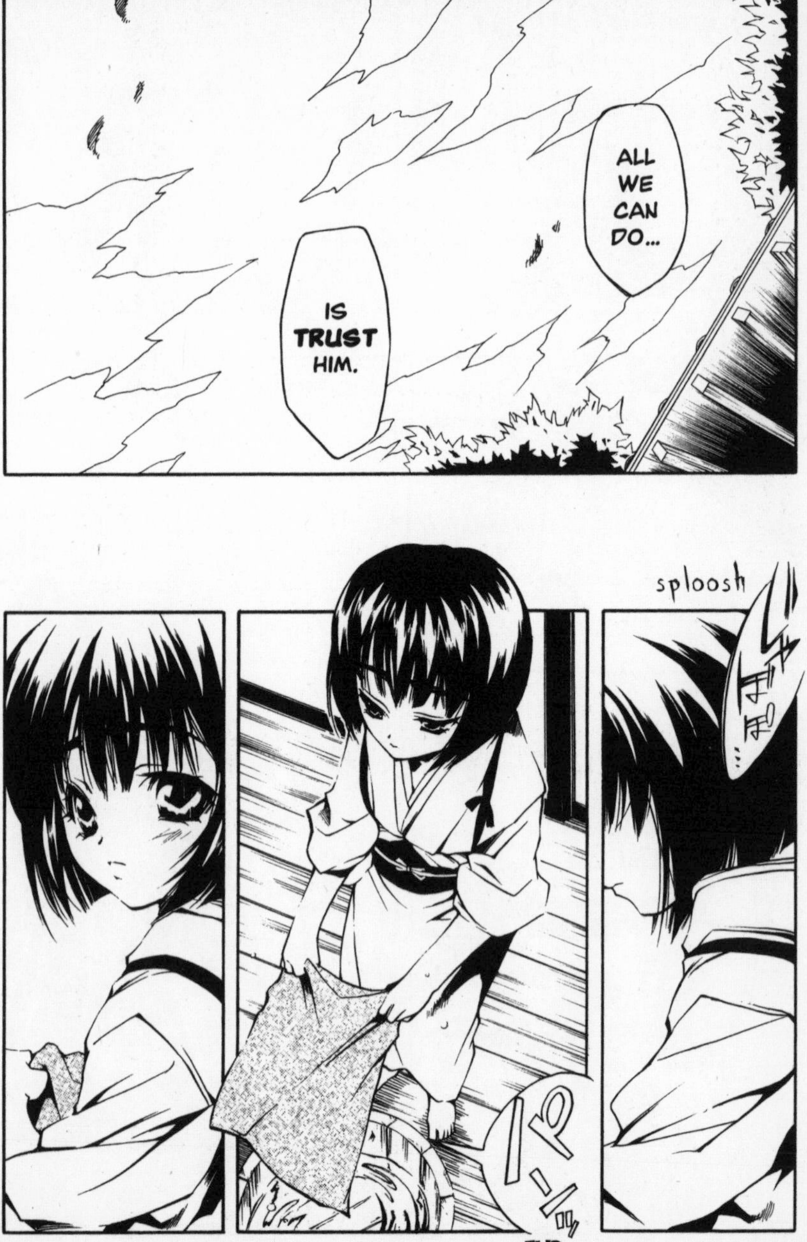
ALL WE CAN DO...
IS TRUST HIM.
sploosh
FWP

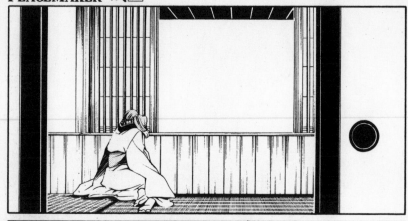

SPLASH

OH, SAYA!

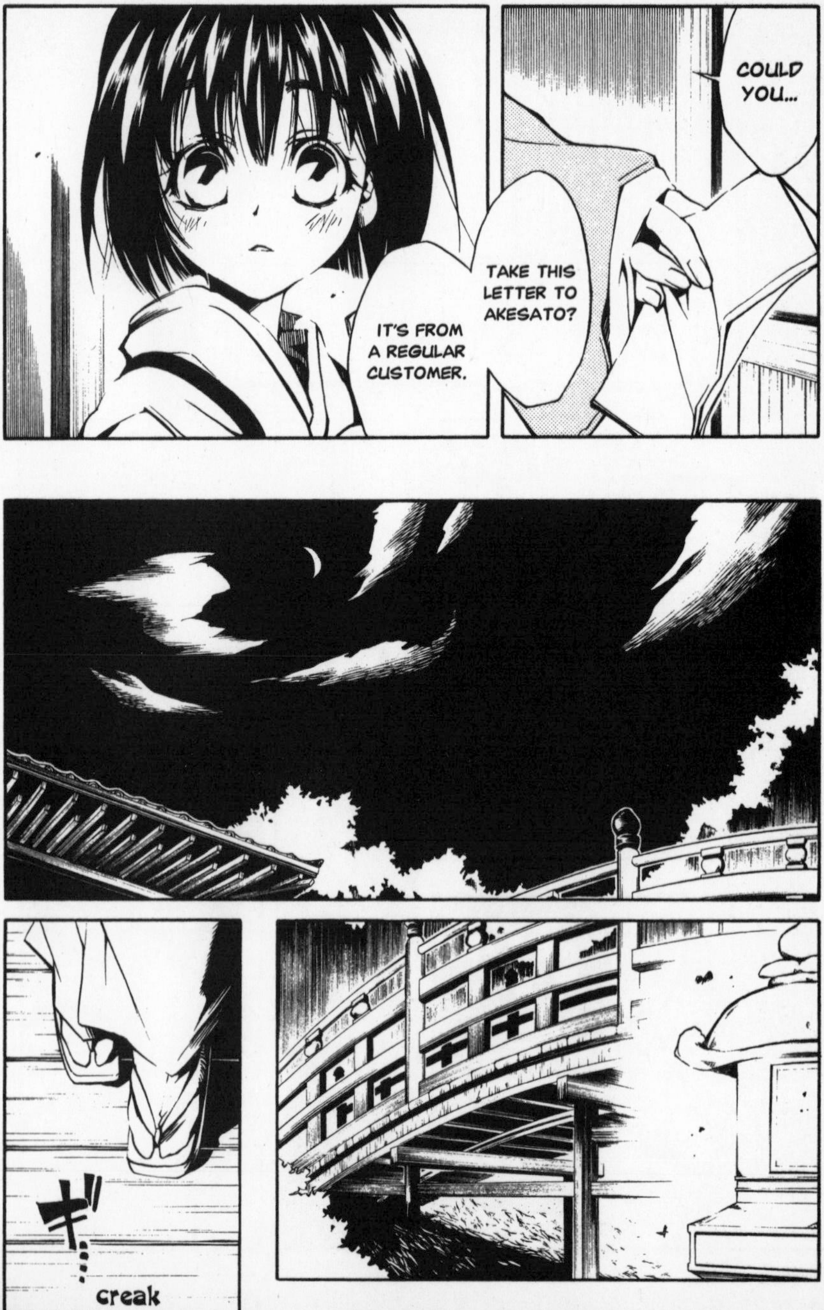
COULD YOU...
TAKE THIS LETTER TO AKESATO?
IT'S FROM A REGULAR CUSTOMER.
ギ...
creak

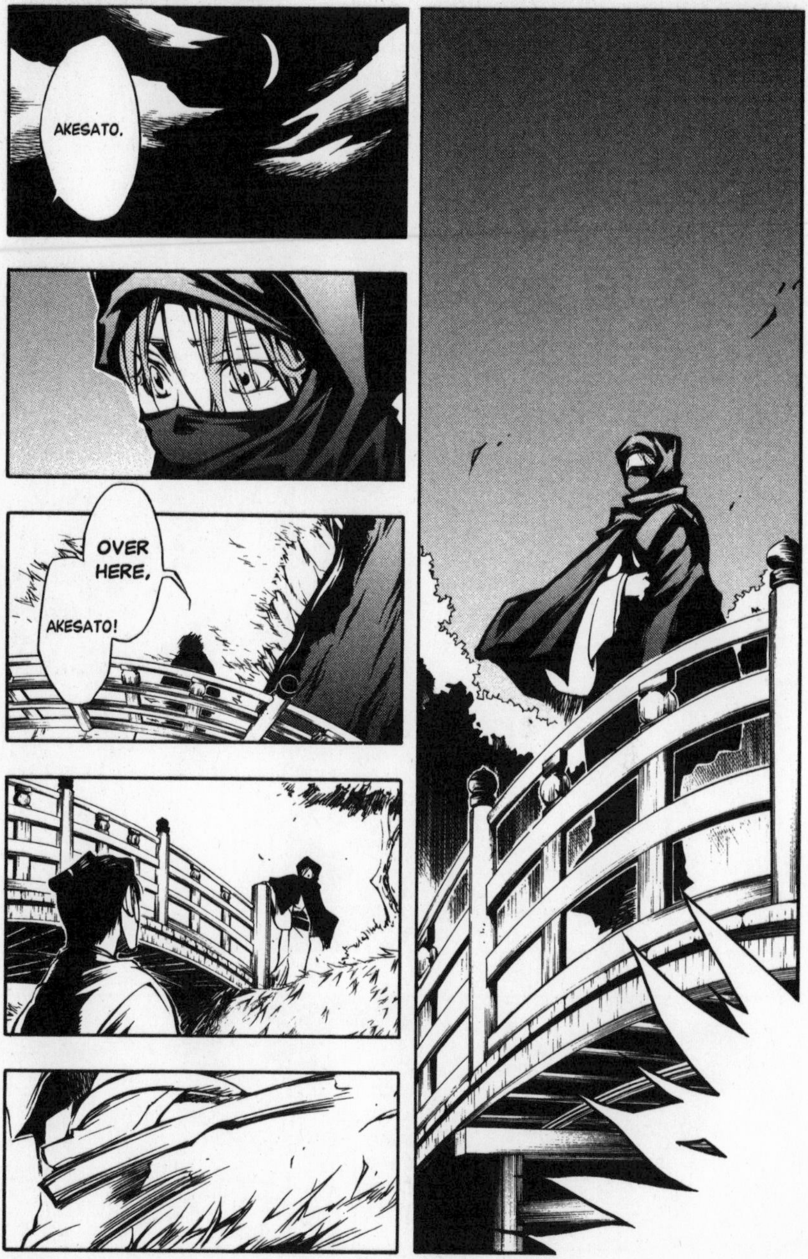
AKESATO.
OVER HERE,
AKESATO!

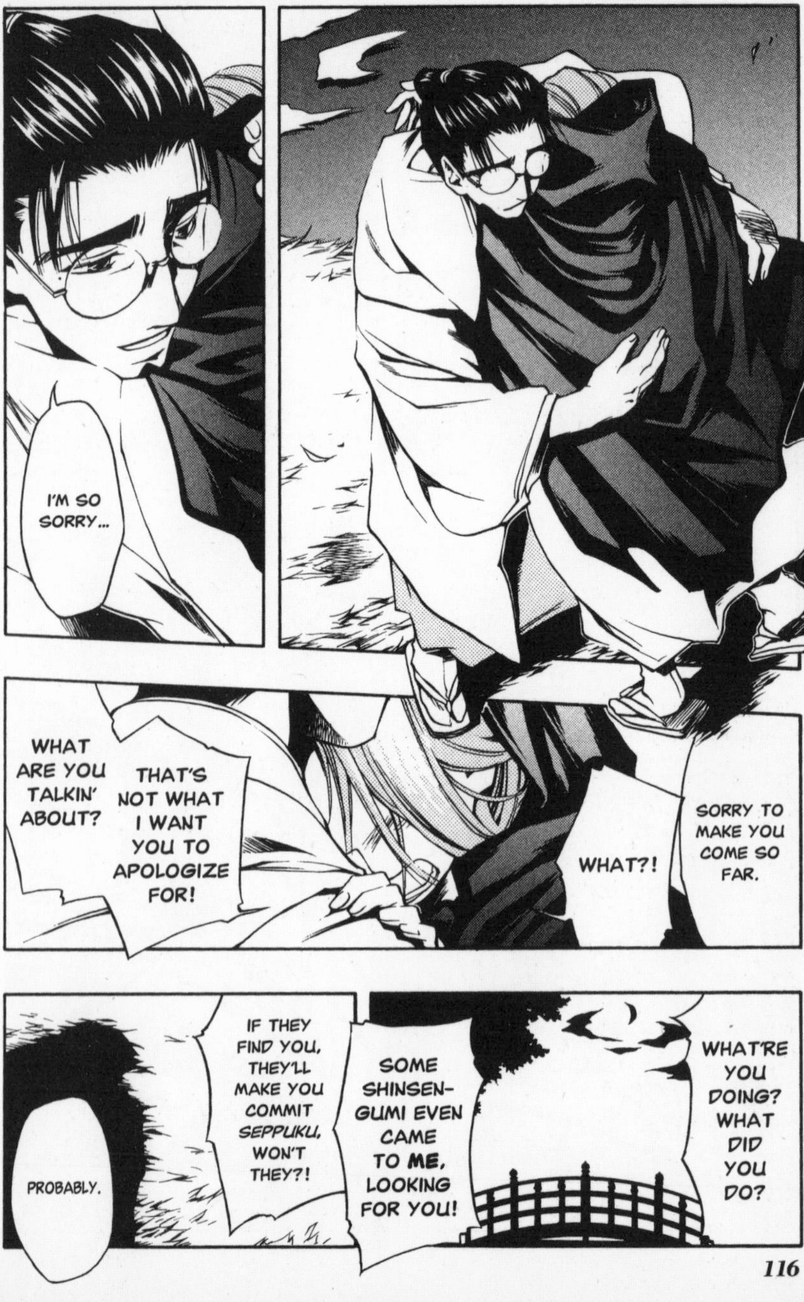
I'M SO SORRY...
SORRY TO MAKE YOU COME SO FAR.
WHAT?!
THAT'S NOT WHAT I WANT YOU TO APOLOGIZE FOR!
WHAT ARE YOU TALKIN' ABOUT?
WHAT'RE YOU DOING? WHAT DID YOU DO?
SOME SHINSEN-GUMI EVEN CAME TO ME, LOOKING FOR YOU!
IF THEY FIND YOU, THEY'LL MAKE YOU COMMIT SEPPUKU, WON'T THEY?!
PROBABLY.

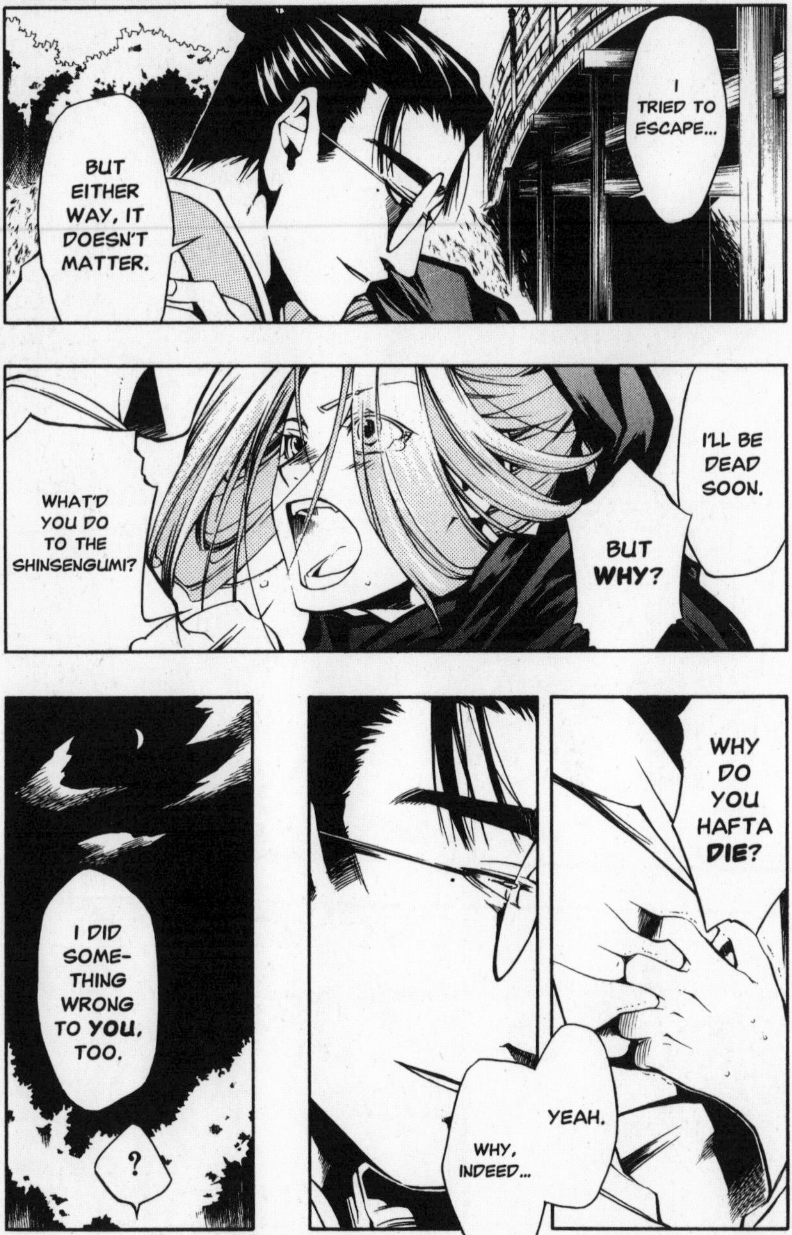
I TRIED TO ESCAPE...
BUT EITHER WAY, IT DOESN'T MATTER.
I'LL BE DEAD SOON.
BUT WHY?
WHAT'D YOU DO TO THE SHINSENGUMI?
WHY DO YOU HAFTA DIE?
YEAH.
WHY, INDEED...
I DID SOMETHING WRONG TO YOU, TOO.
?

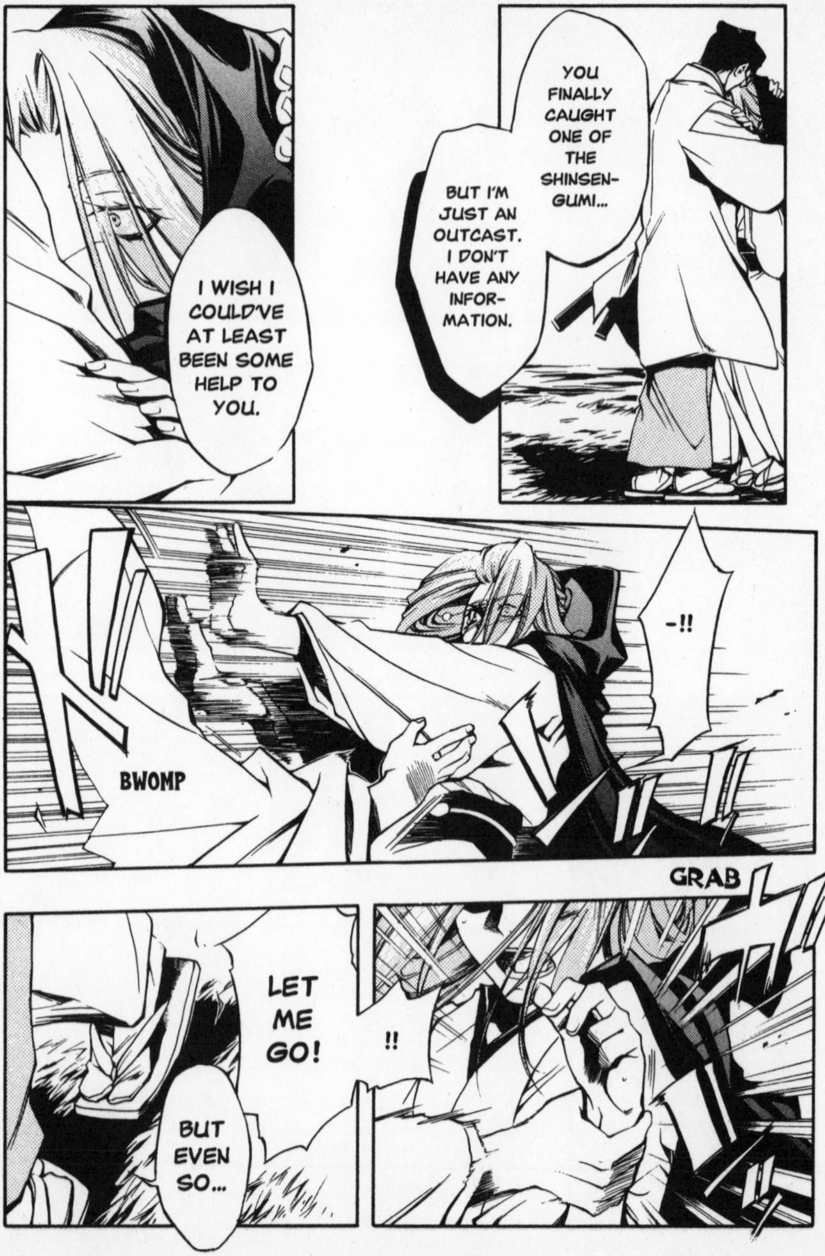
YOU FINALLY CAUGHT ONE OF THE SHINSEN-GUMI...
BUT I'M JUST AN OUTCAST. I DON'T HAVE ANY INFORMATION.
I WISH I COULD'VE AT LEAST BEEN SOME HELP TO YOU.
-!!
BWOMP
GRAB
!!
LET ME GO!
BUT EVEN SO...

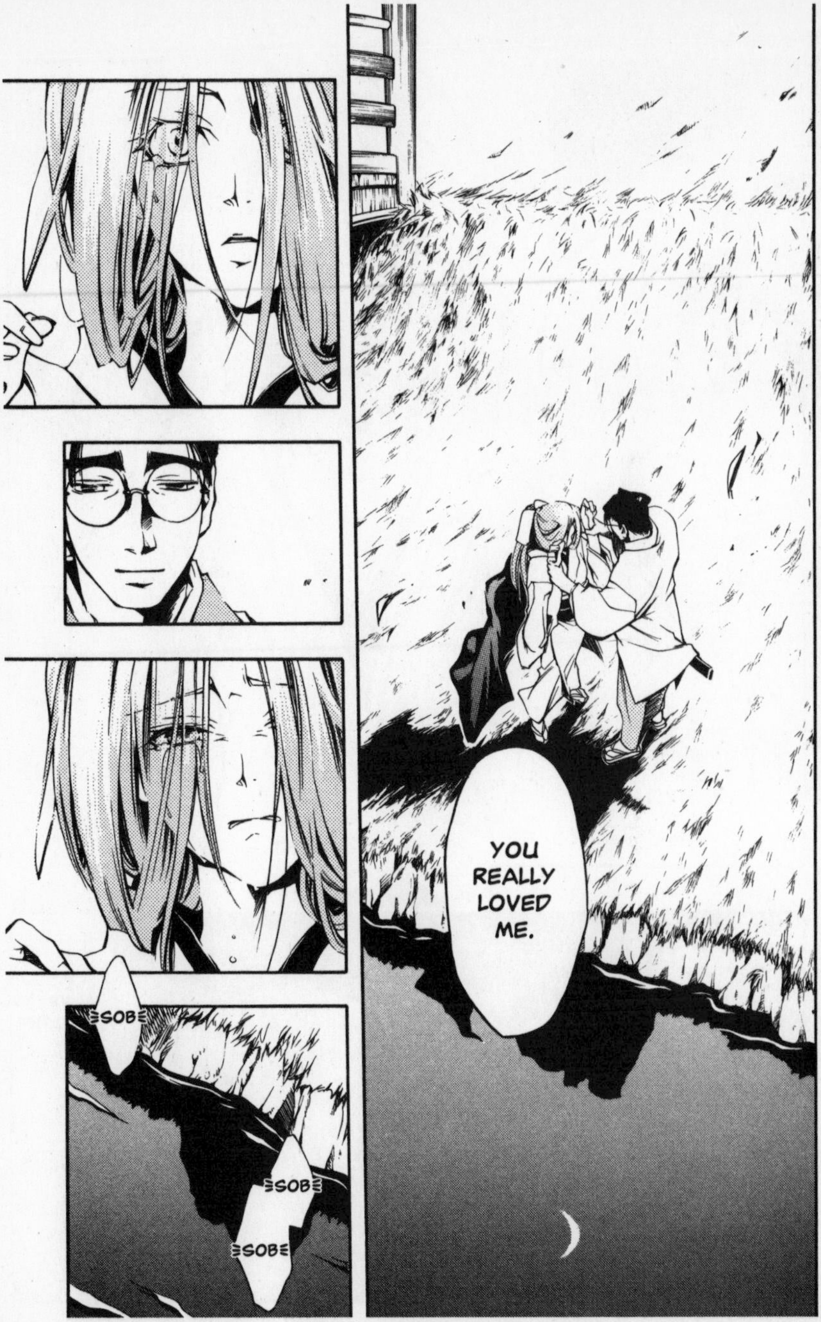
YOU REALLY LOVED ME.
SOB
SOB
SOB

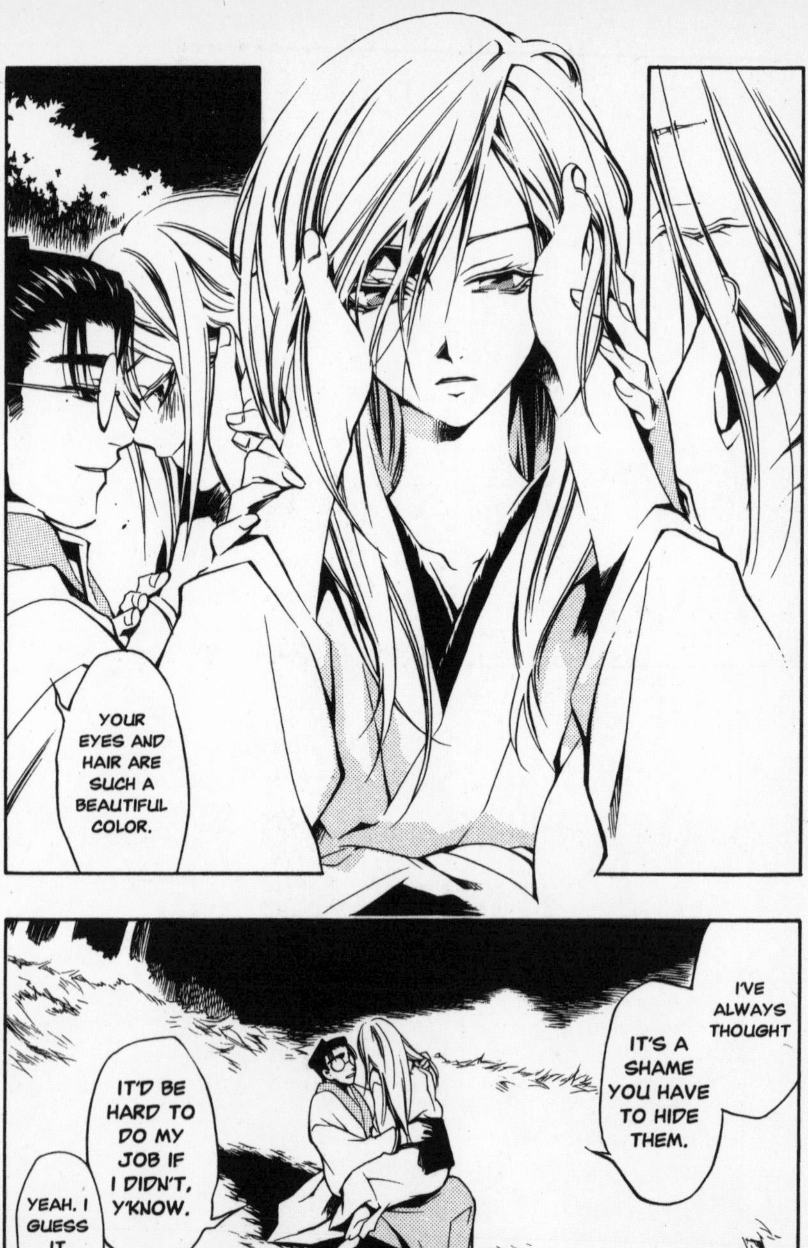

YOUR EYES AND HAIR ARE SUCH A BEAUTIFUL COLOR.
I'VE ALWAYS THOUGHT
IT'S A SHAME YOU HAVE TO HIDE THEM.
IT'D BE HARD TO DO MY JOB IF I DIDN'T, Y'KNOW.
YEAH. I GUESS IT WOULD BE...

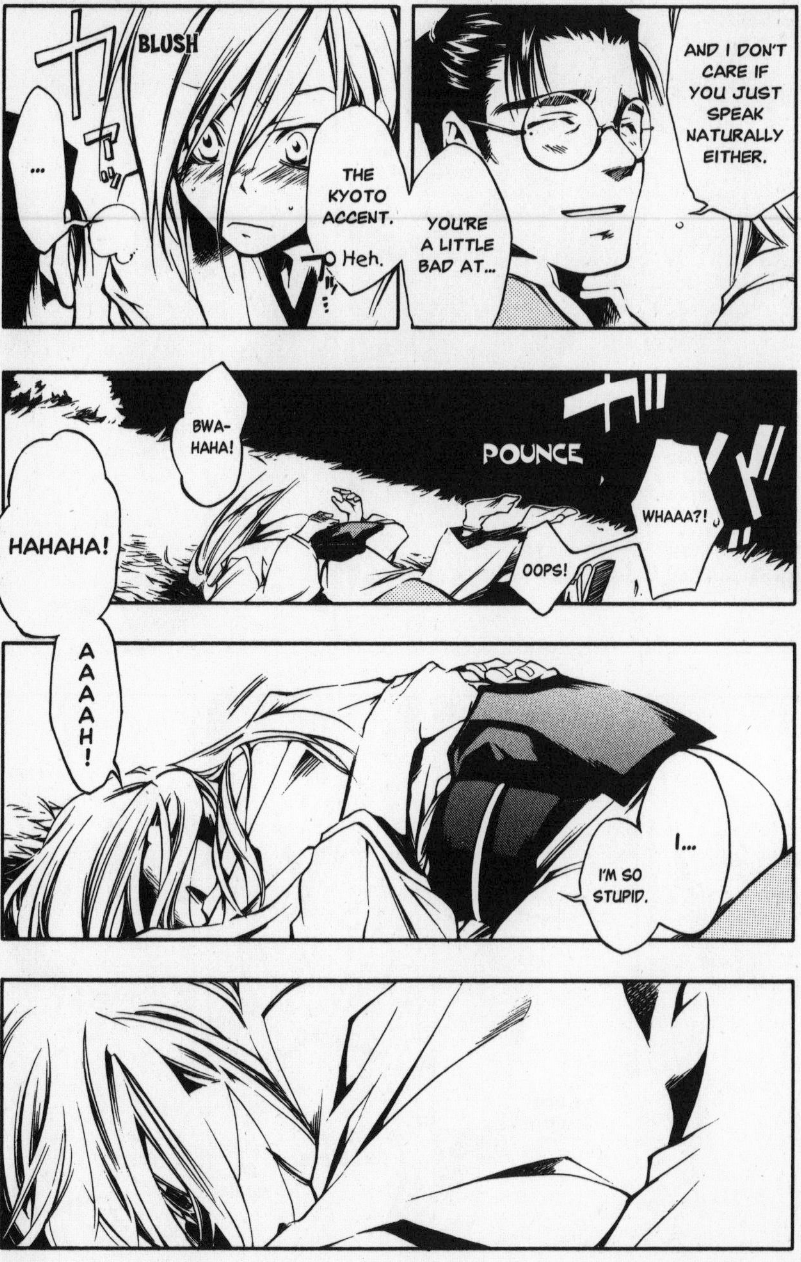
AND I DON'T CARE IF YOU JUST SPEAK NATURALLY EITHER.
YOU'RE A LITTLE BAD AT...
THE KYOTO ACCENT.
Heh.
BLUSH
...
WHAAA?!
OOPS!
POUNCE
BWA-HAHA!
HAHAHA!
I...
I'M SO STUPID.
AAAAAH!

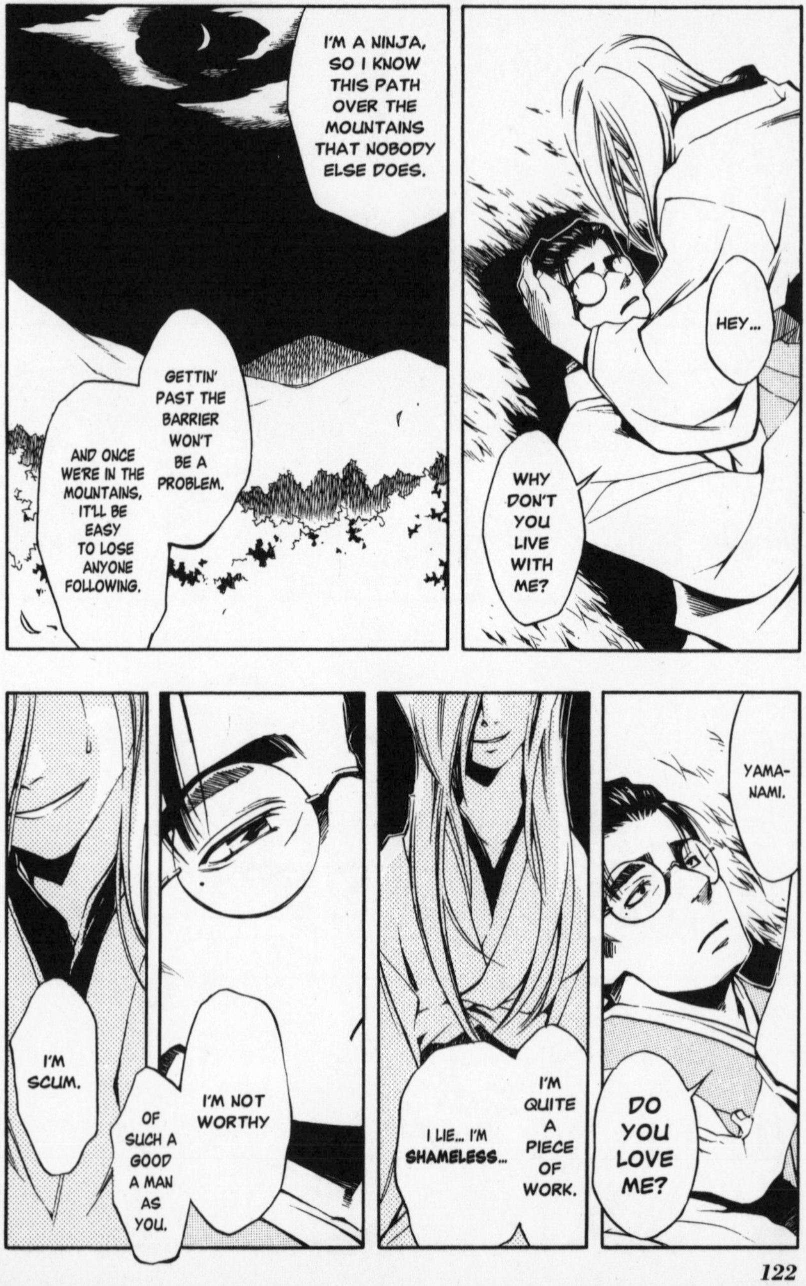
HEY...
WHY DON'T YOU LIVE WITH ME?
I'M A NINJA, SO I KNOW THIS PATH OVER THE MOUNTAINS THAT NOBODY ELSE DOES.
GETTIN' PAST THE BARRIER WON'T BE A PROBLEM.
AND ONCE WE'RE IN THE MOUNTAINS, IT'LL BE EASY TO LOSE ANYONE FOLLOWING.
YAMA-NAMI.
DO YOU LOVE ME?
I'M QUITE A PIECE OF WORK.
I LIE... I'M SHAMELESS...
I'M NOT WORTHY
OF SUCH A GOOD A MAN AS YOU.
I'M SCUM.

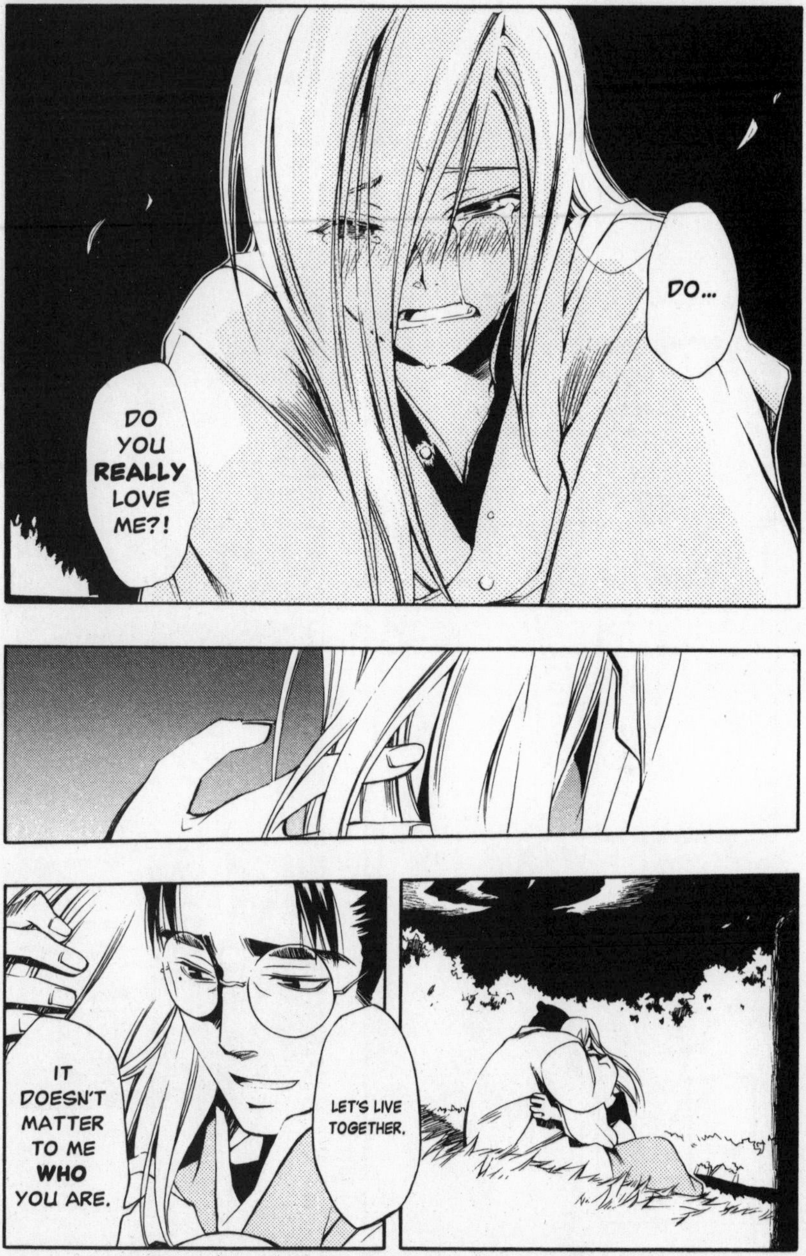
DO...
DO YOU **REALLY** LOVE ME?!
LET'S LIVE TOGETHER.
IT DOESN'T MATTER TO ME **WHO** YOU ARE.

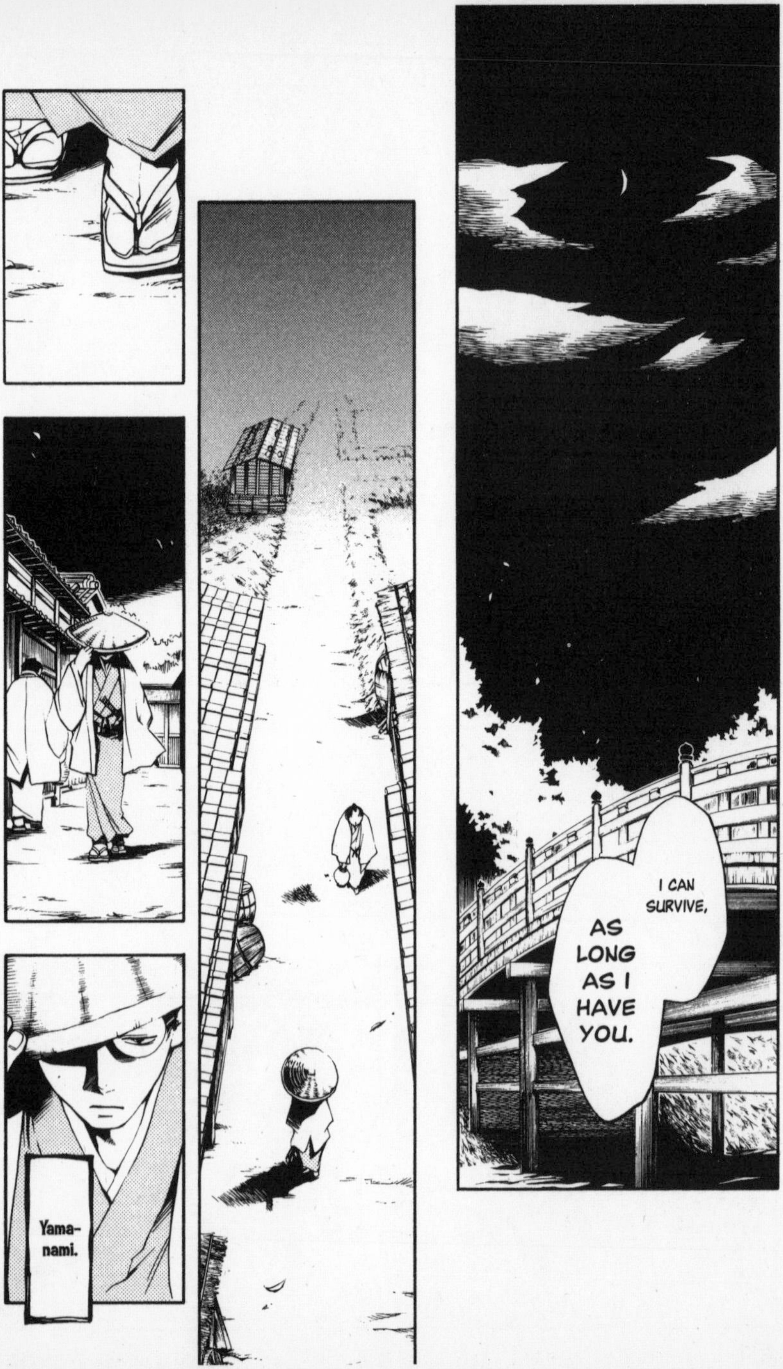
I CAN SURVIVE,
AS LONG AS I HAVE YOU.
Yama-nami.

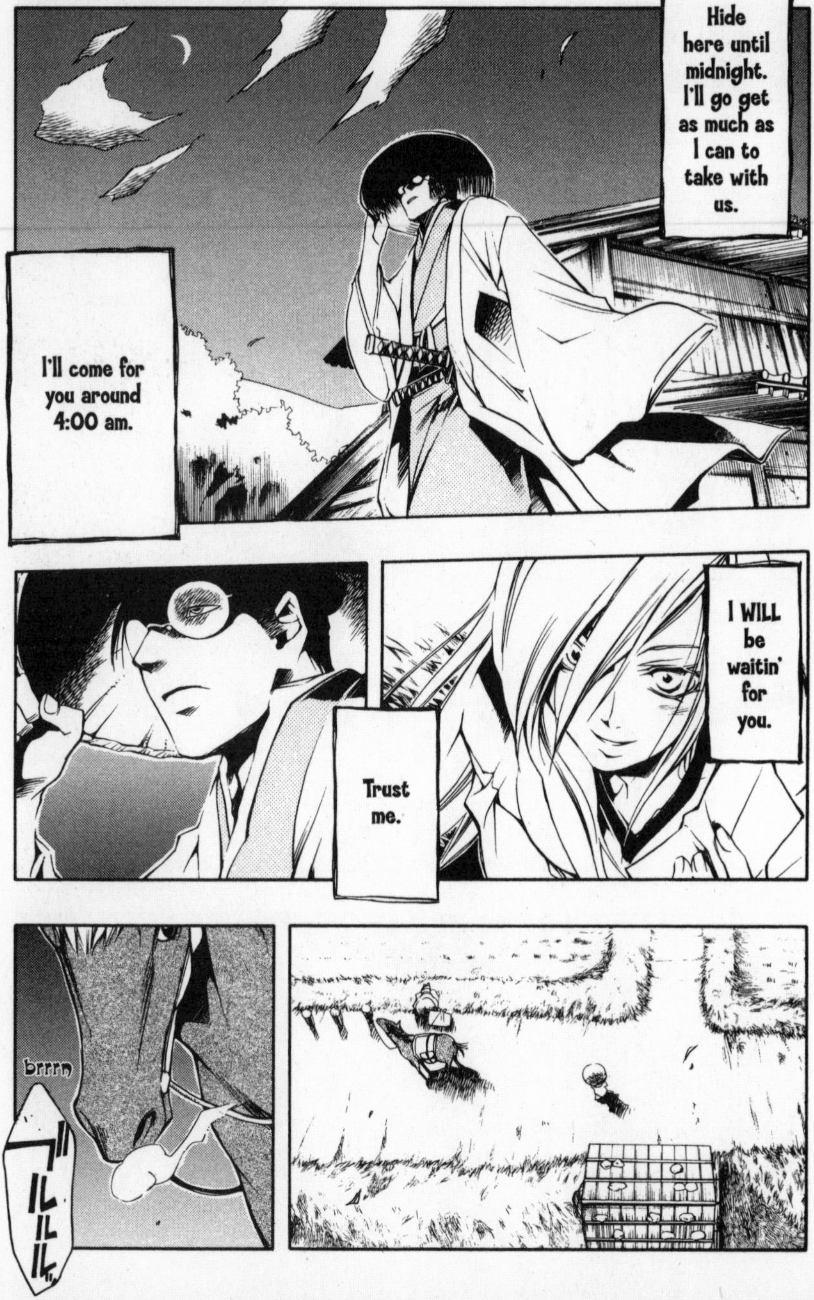
Hide here until midnight. I'll go get as much as I can to take with us.
I'll come for you around 4:00 am.
I WILL be waitin' for you.
Trust me.
brrrn

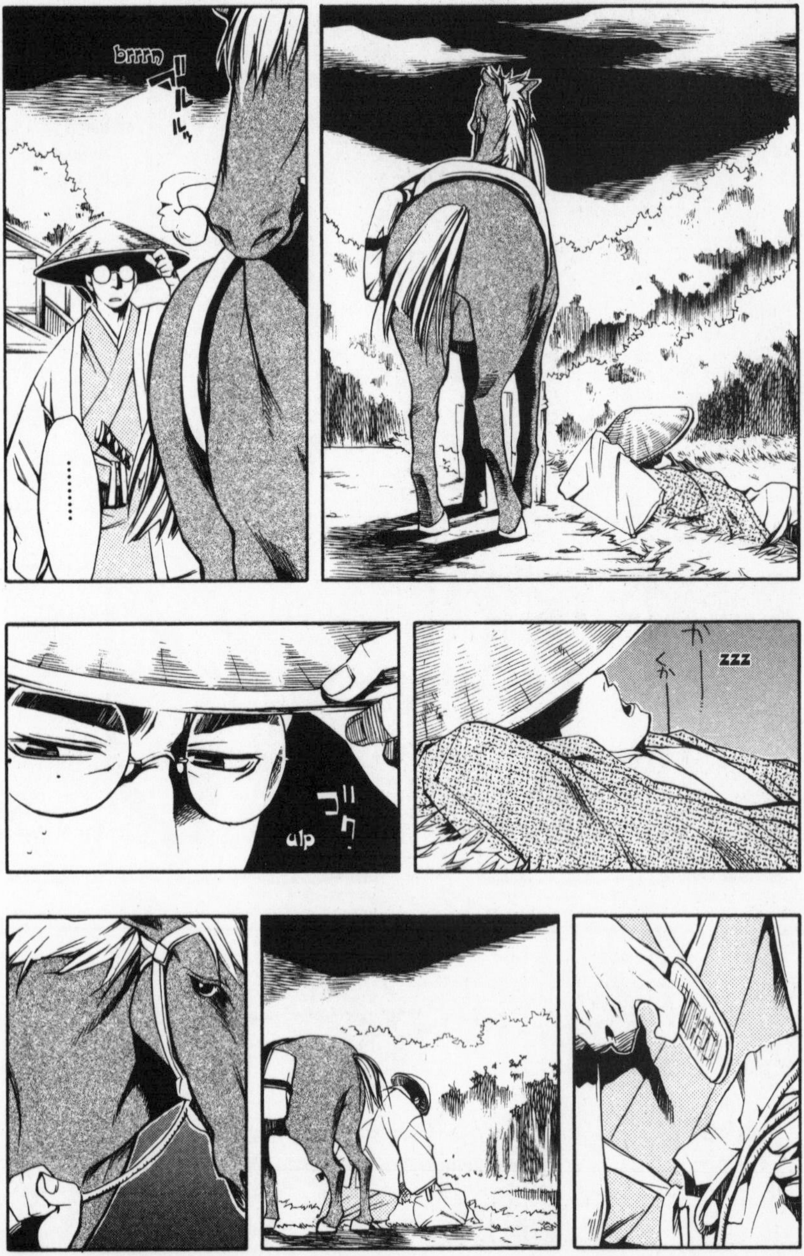
brrrn
ブルルルッ
......
ゴクッ
ulp
かーくかー
zzz

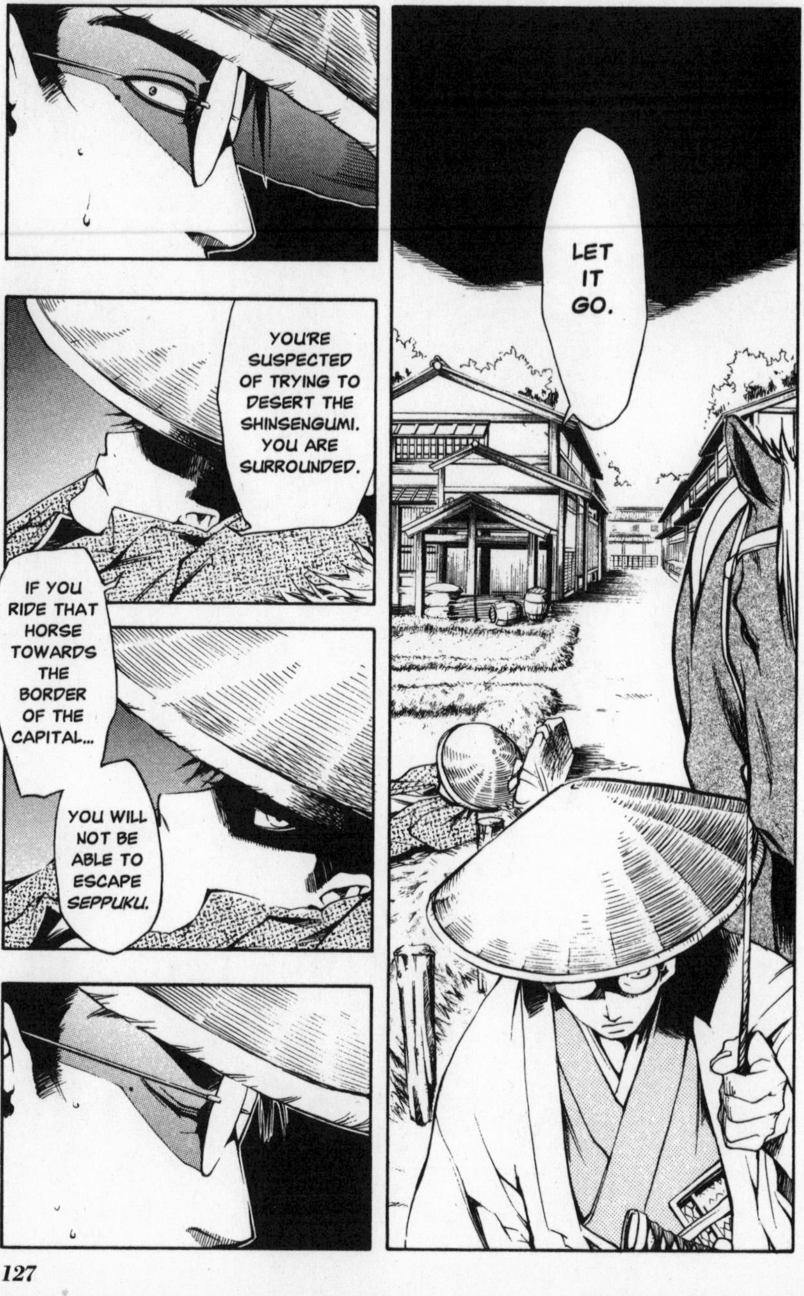
LET IT GO.
YOU'RE SUSPECTED OF TRYING TO DESERT THE SHINSENGUMI. YOU ARE SURROUNDED.
IF YOU RIDE THAT HORSE TOWARDS THE BORDER OF THE CAPITAL...
YOU WILL NOT BE ABLE TO ESCAPE SEPPUKU.

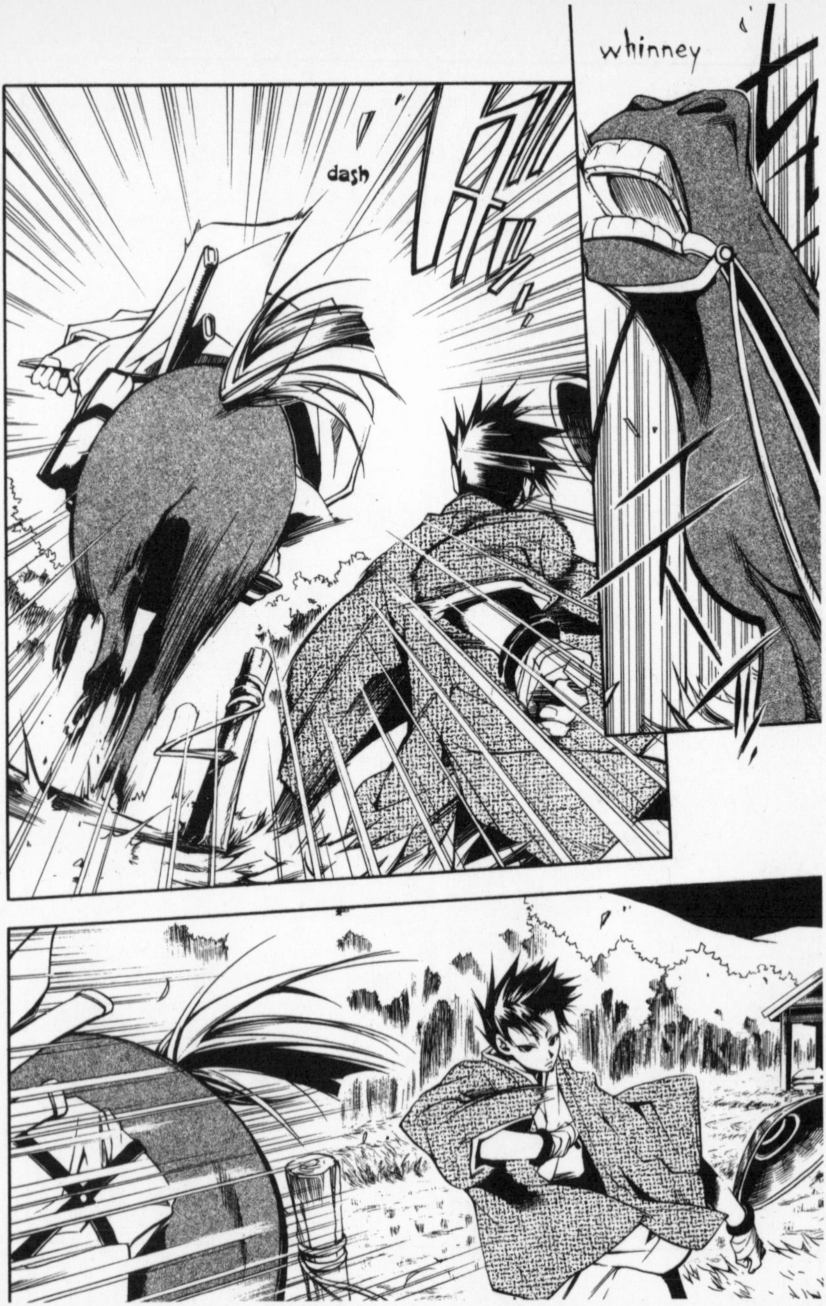
whinney
dash

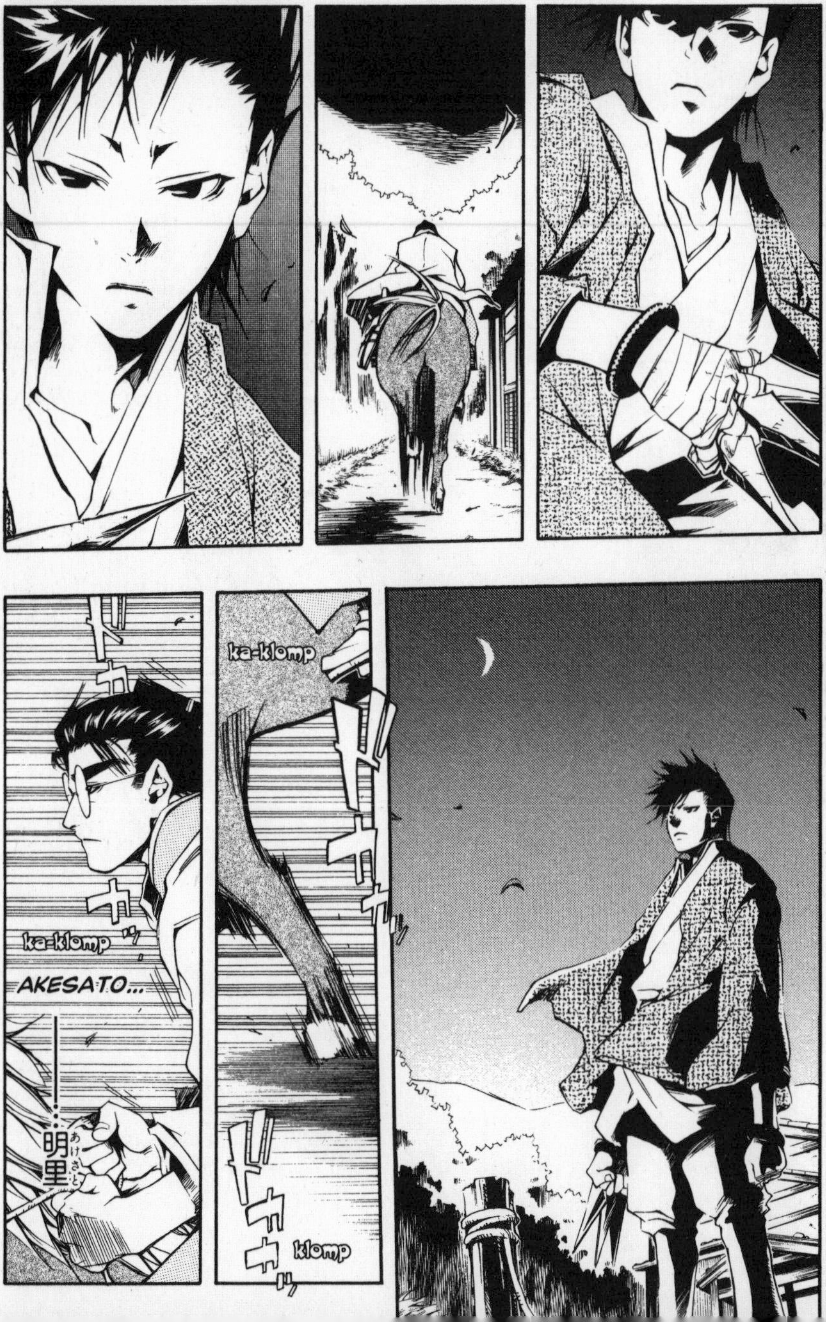
ka-klomp
klomp
ka-klomp
AKESATO...
明里

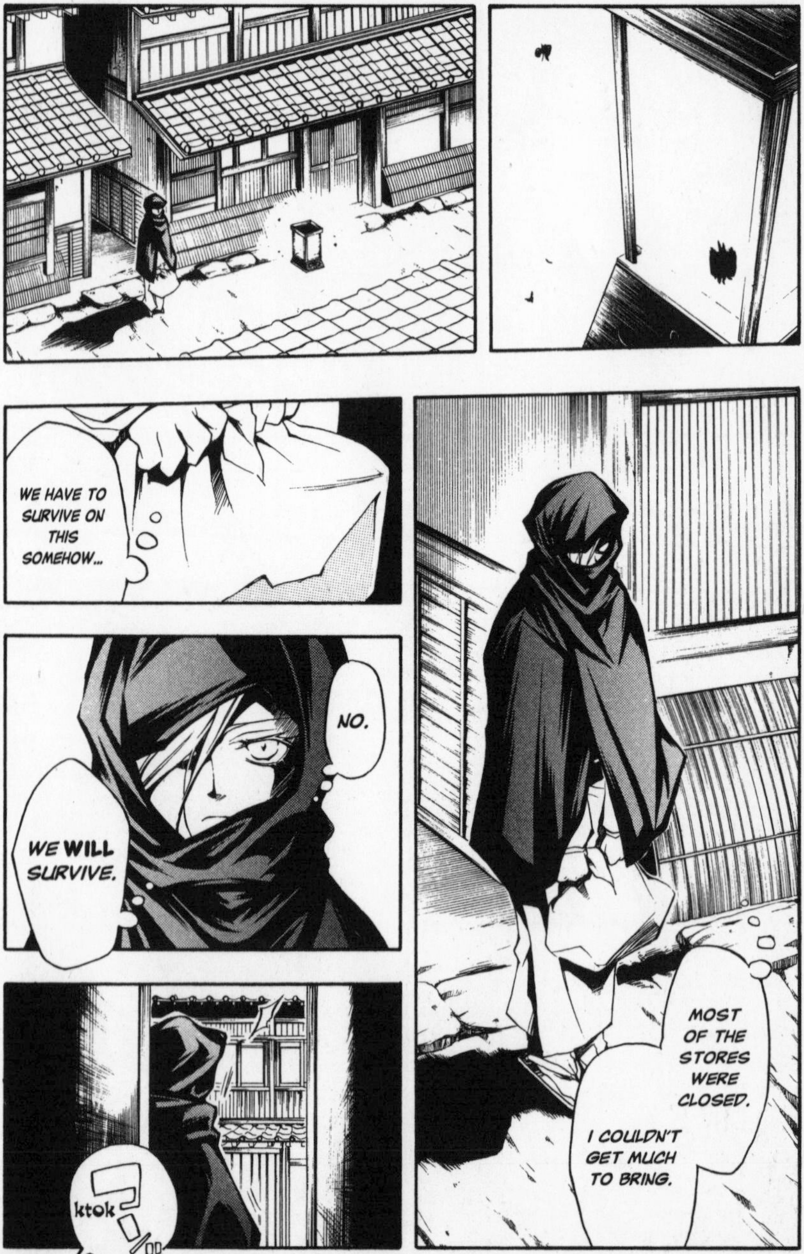
MOST OF THE STORES WERE CLOSED.
I COULDN'T GET MUCH TO BRING.
WE HAVE TO SURVIVE ON THIS SOMEHOW...
NO.
WE **WILL** SURVIVE.
ktok

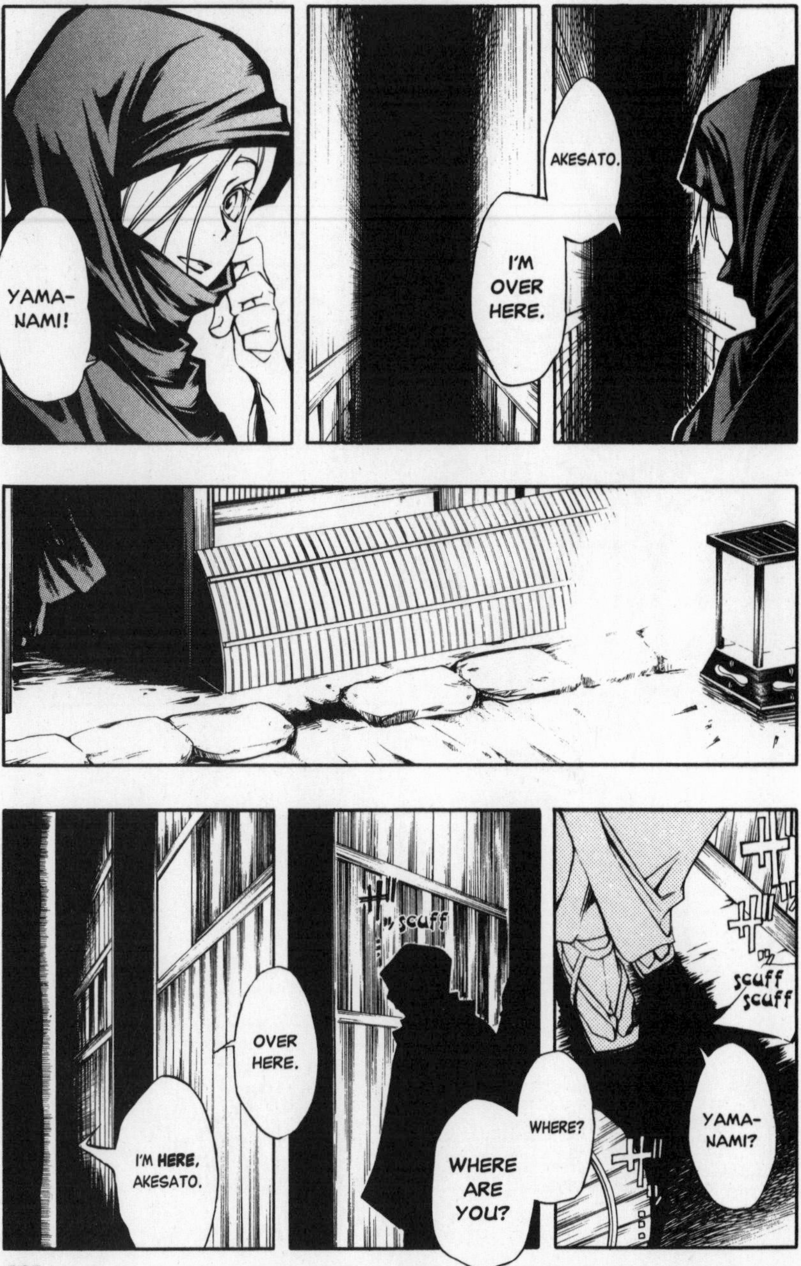
YAMA-NAMI!
AKESATO.
I'M OVER HERE.
OVER HERE.
I'M HERE, AKESATO.
scuff
scuff scuff
YAMA-NAMI?
WHERE?
WHERE ARE YOU?

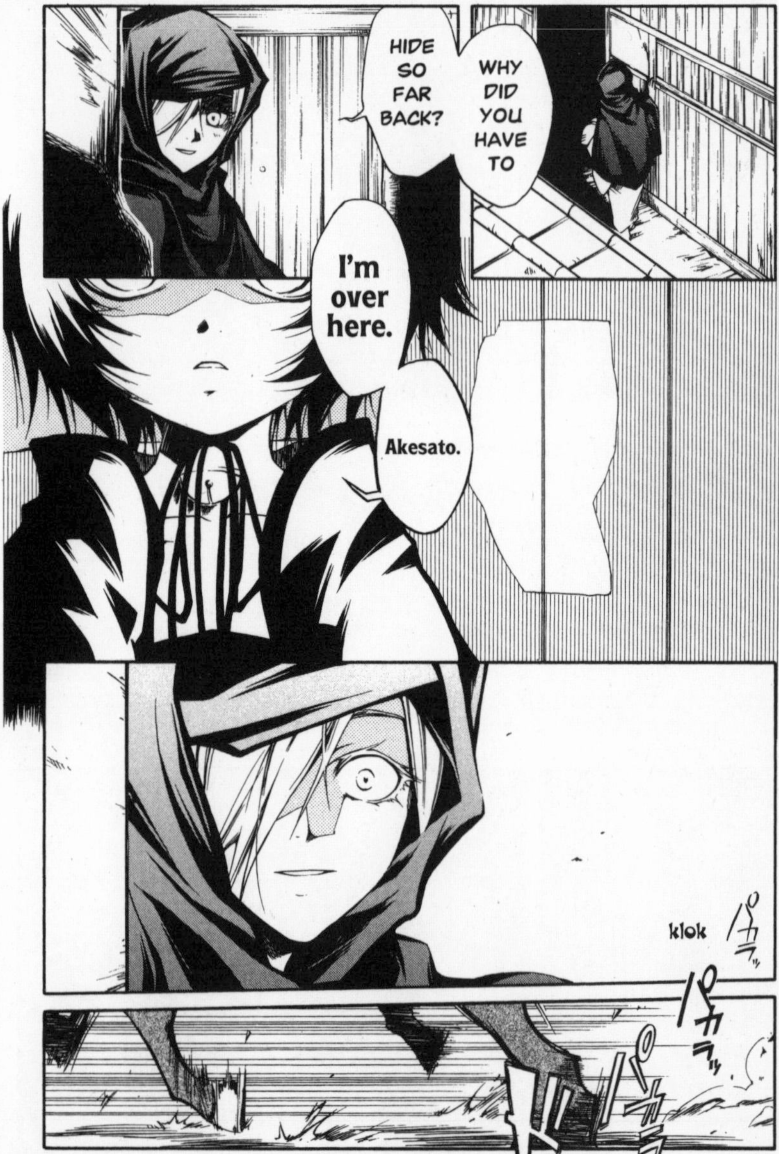

WHY DID YOU HAVE TO
HIDE SO FAR BACK?
I'm over here.
Akesato.
klok
klok KA-KLOK

ka-klok

klok

klok

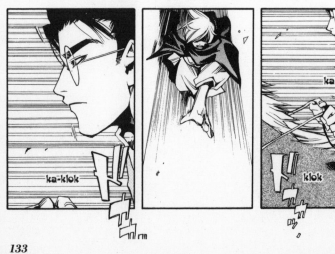

ka-klok

ka-klok

klok

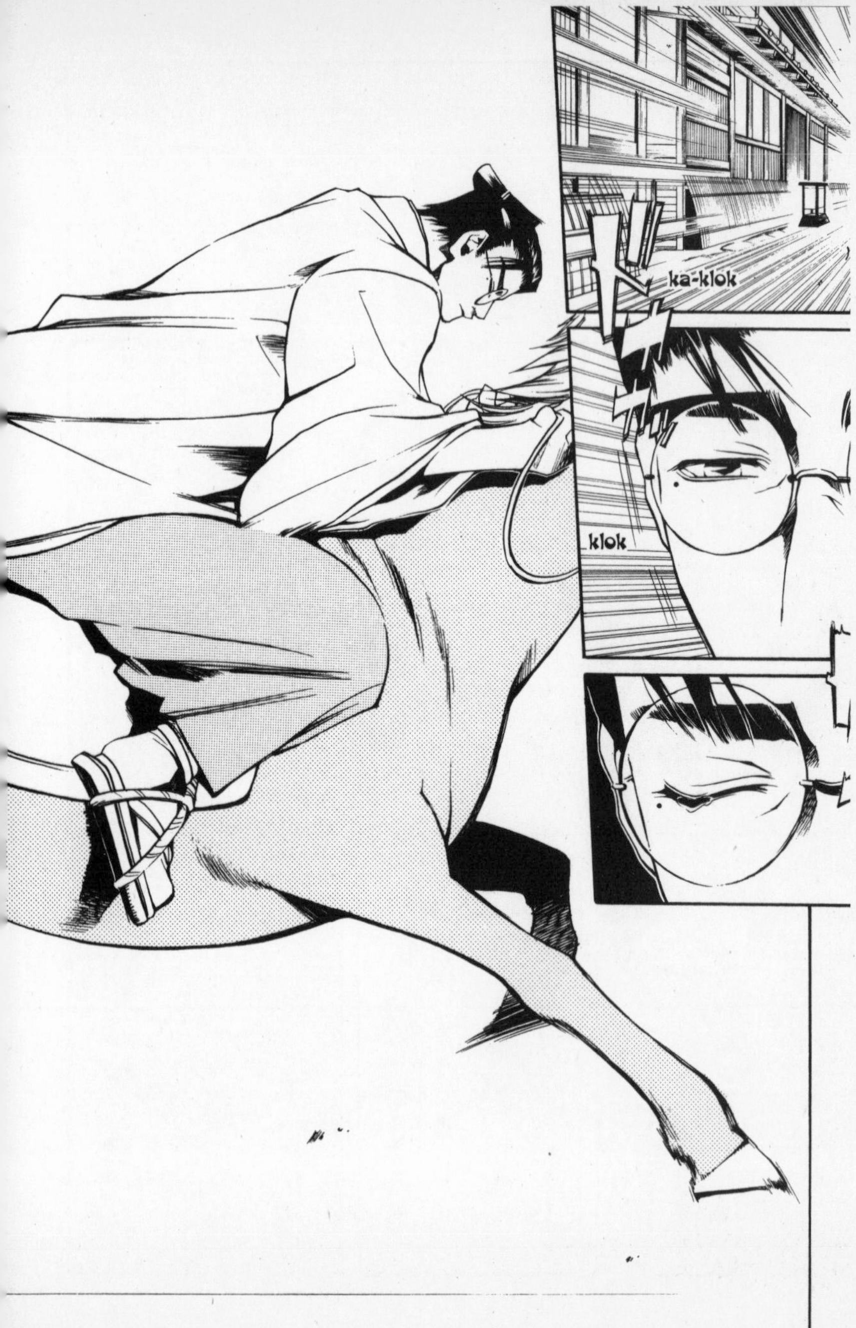
ka-klok
klok

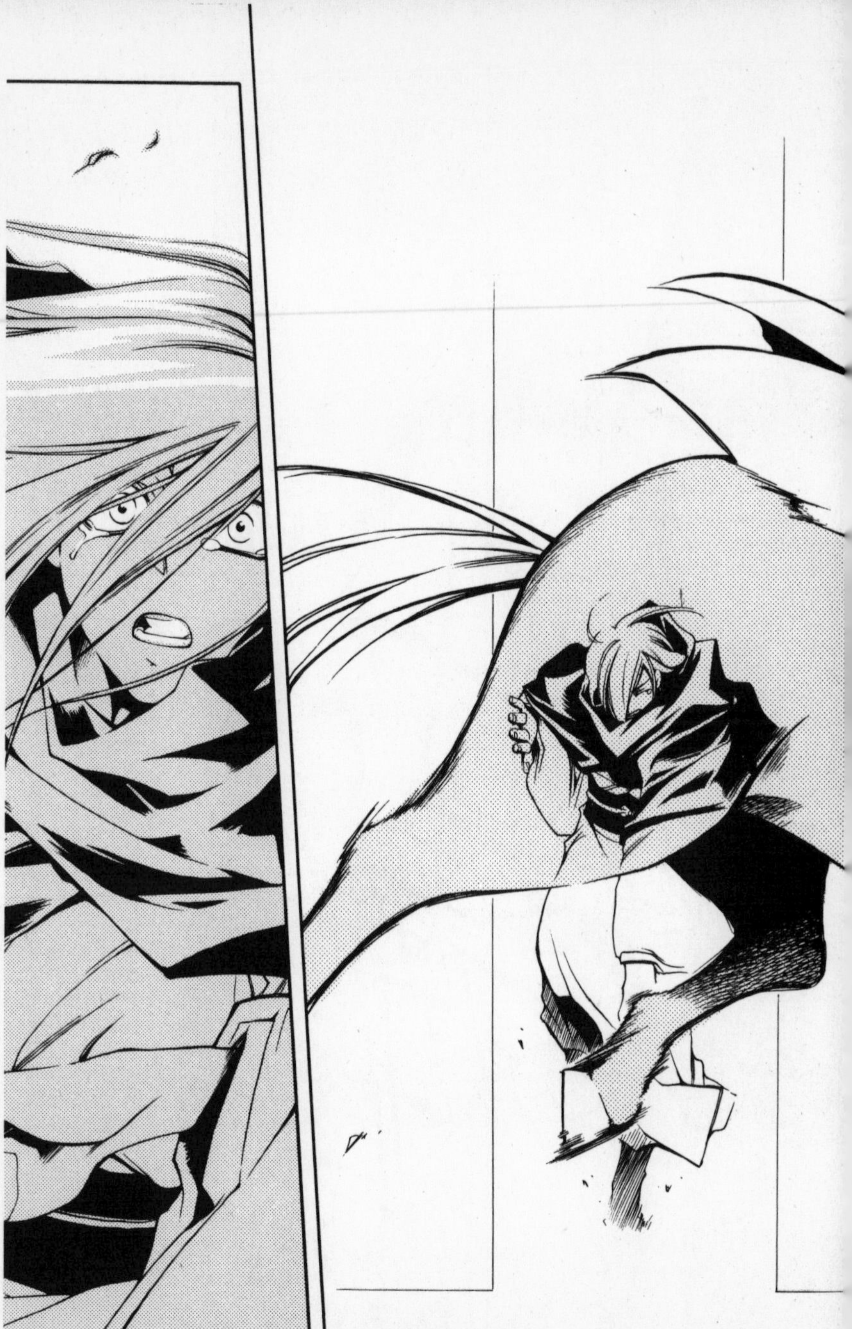

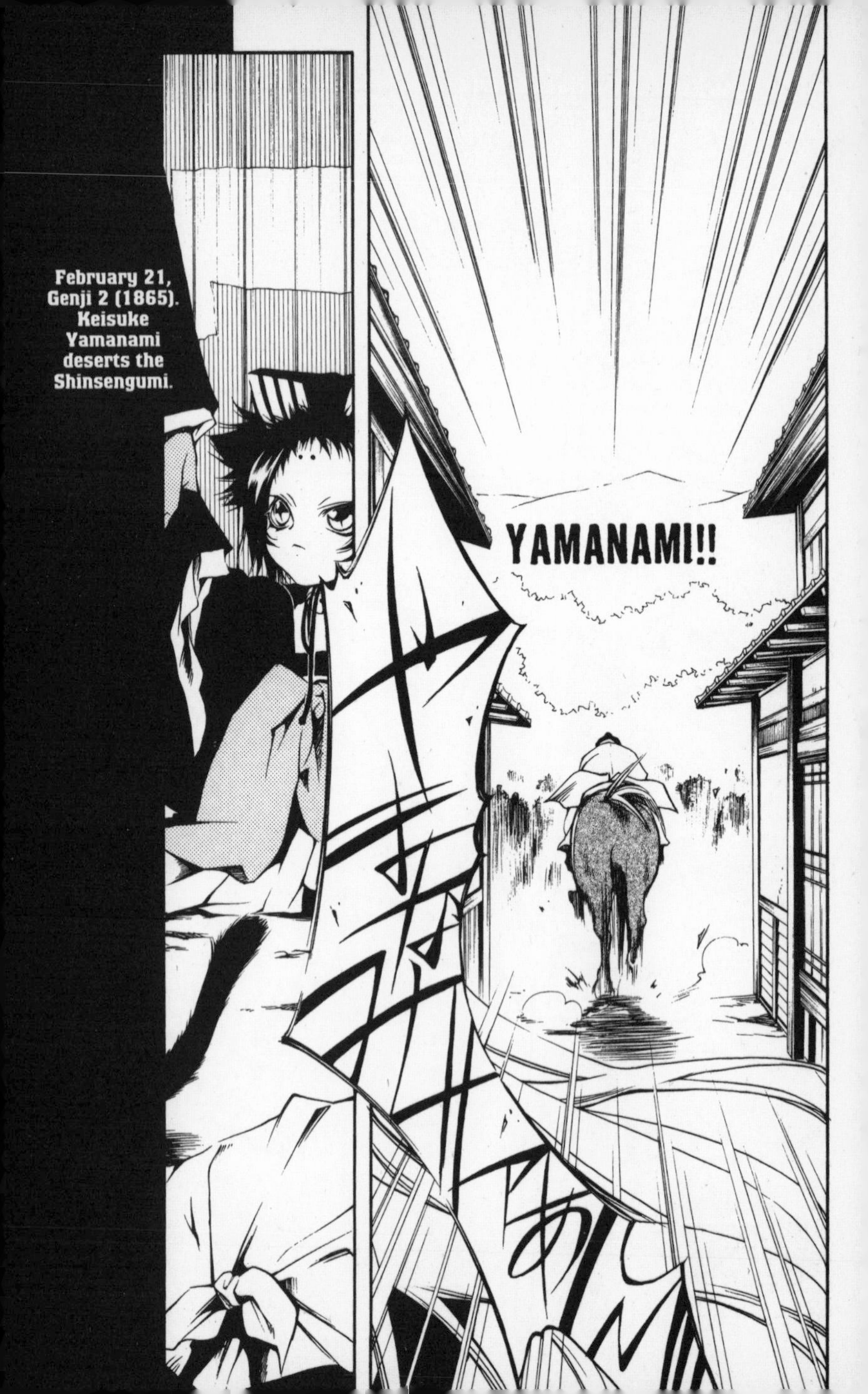
February 21, Genji 2 (1865). Keisuke Yamanami deserts the Shinsengumi.
YAMANAMI!!

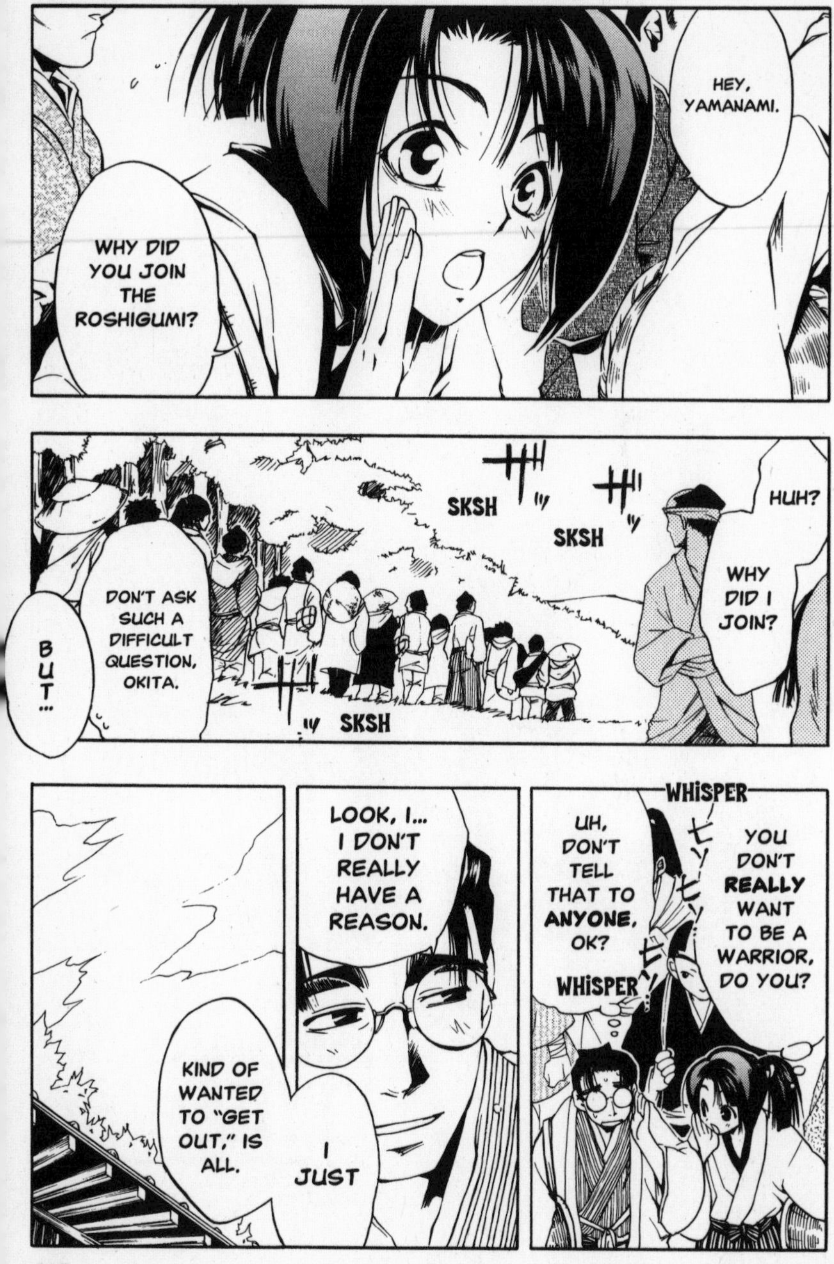
HEY, YAMANAMI.
WHY DID YOU JOIN THE ROSHIGUMI?
HUH?
WHY DID I JOIN?
SKSH
SKSH
SKSH
DON'T ASK SUCH A DIFFICULT QUESTION, OKITA.
BUT...
WHISPER
YOU DON'T REALLY WANT TO BE A WARRIOR, DO YOU?
UH, DON'T TELL THAT TO ANYONE, OK?
WHISPER
LOOK, I... I DON'T REALLY HAVE A REASON.
I JUST
KIND OF WANTED TO "GET OUT," IS ALL.

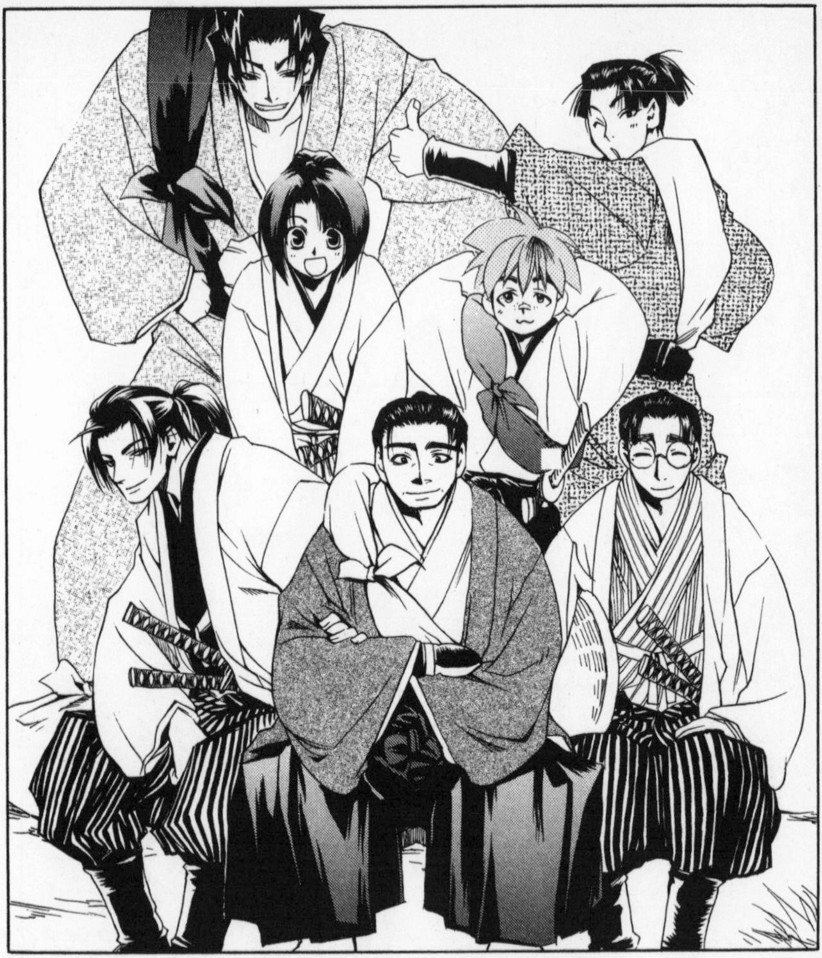

CHAPTER 10
TIES 鐵

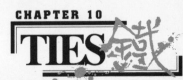

ka-tonk

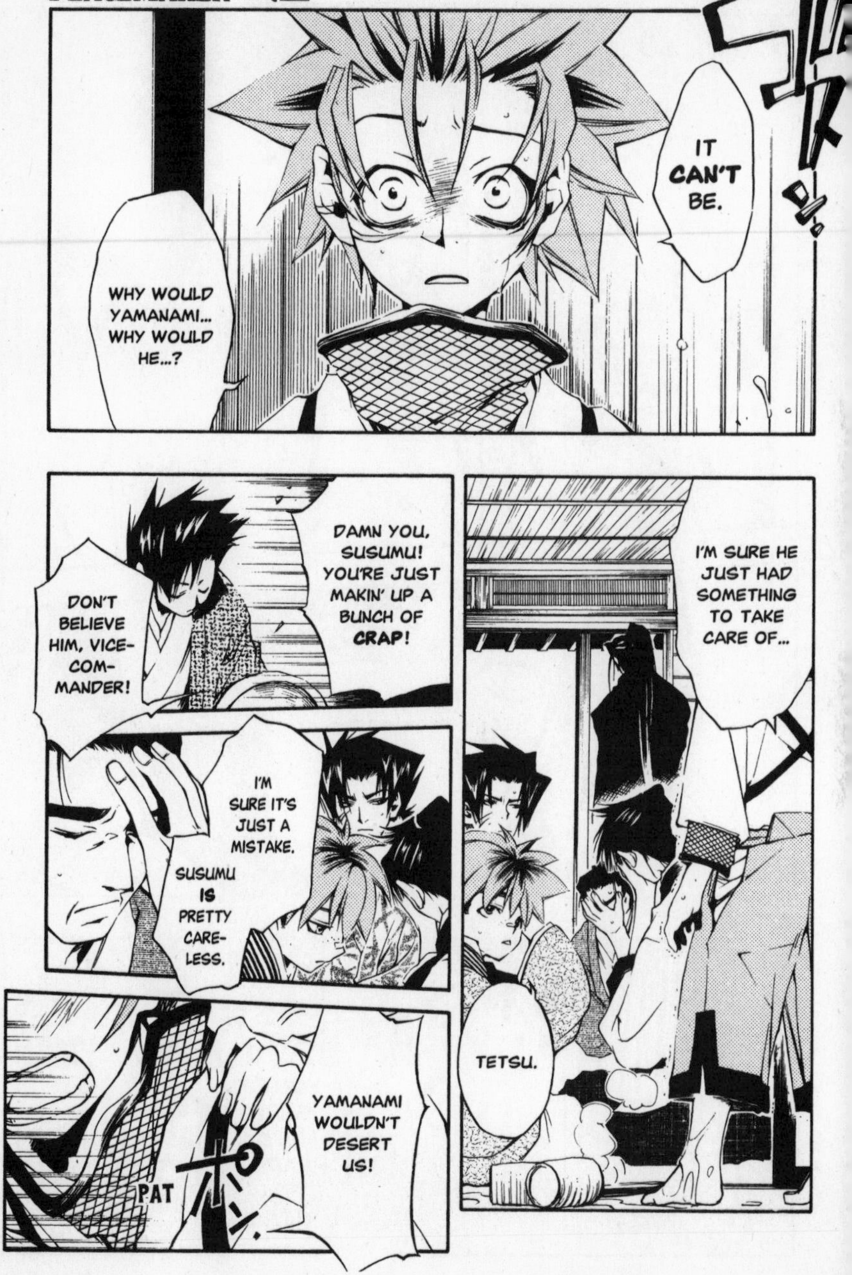
IT CAN'T BE.
WHY WOULD YAMANAMI... WHY WOULD HE...?
I'M SURE HE JUST HAD SOMETHING TO TAKE CARE OF...
DAMN YOU, SUSUMU! YOU'RE JUST MAKIN' UP A BUNCH OF CRAP!
DON'T BELIEVE HIM, VICE-COMMANDER!
I'M SURE IT'S JUST A MISTAKE.
SUSUMU IS PRETTY CARELESS.
TETSU.
YAMANAMI WOULDN'T DESERT US!
PAT

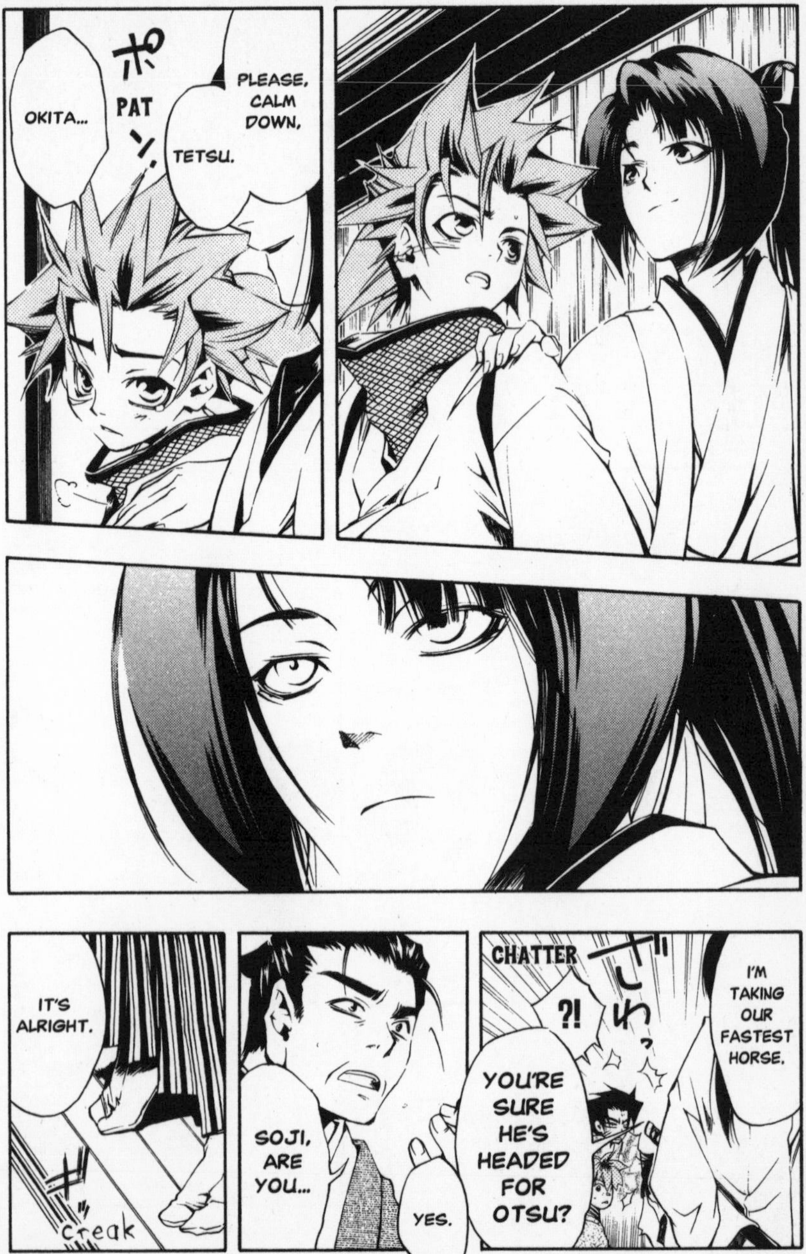
PLEASE, CALM DOWN,
TETSU.
ポン
PAT
OKITA...
I'M TAKING OUR FASTEST HORSE.
CHATTER
?!
YOU'RE SURE HE'S HEADED FOR OTSU?
YES.
SOJI, ARE YOU...
IT'S ALRIGHT.
creak

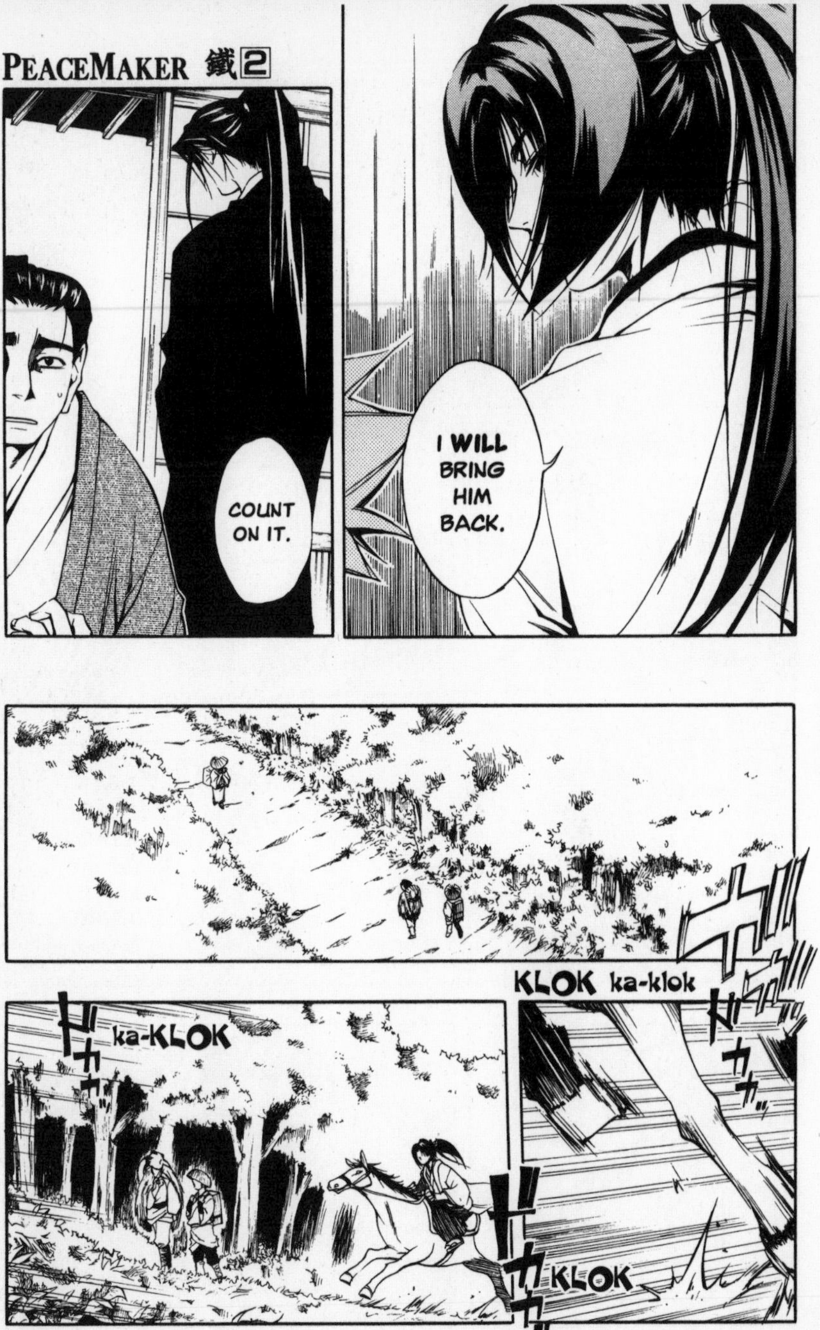
I WILL BRING HIM BACK.
COUNT ON IT.
KLOK ka-klok
ka-KLOK
KLOK

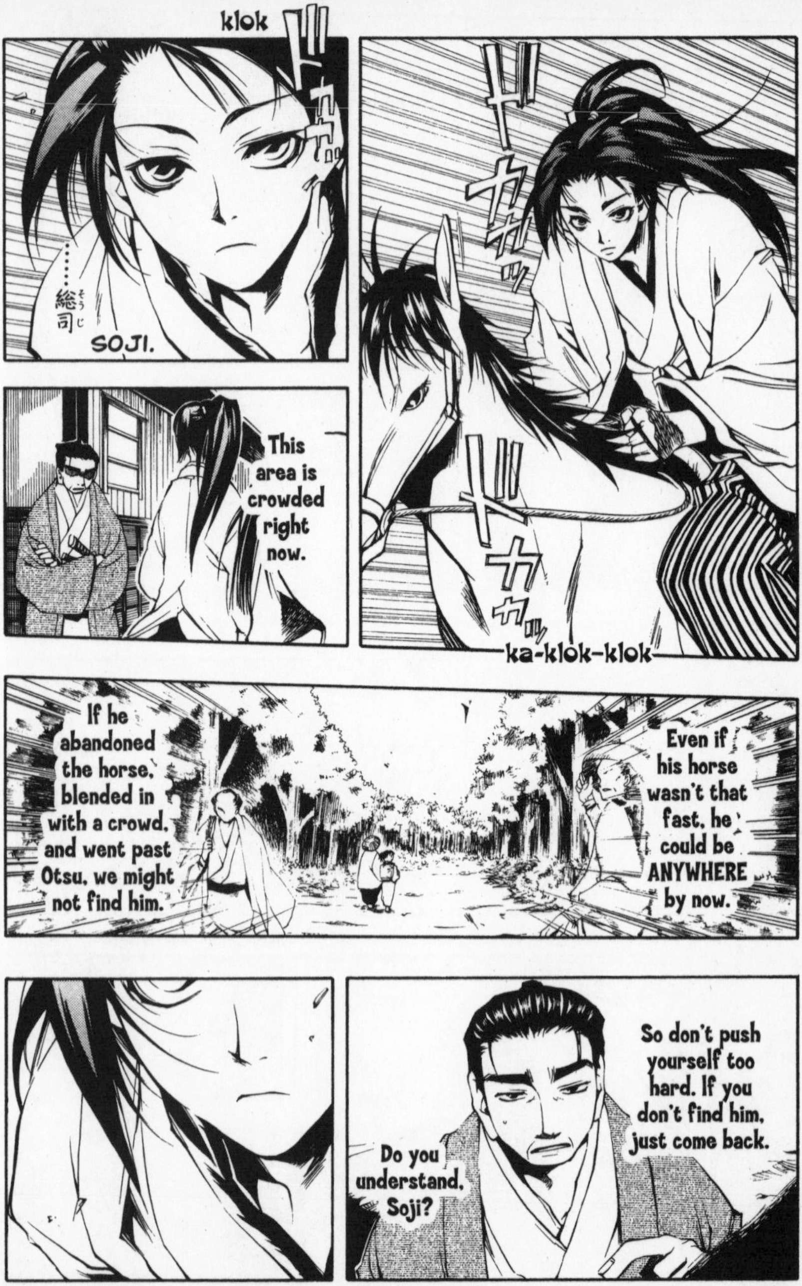
ka-klok-klok
klok
……総司
SOJI.
This area is crowded right now.
Even if his horse wasn't that fast, he could be ANYWHERE by now.
If he abandoned the horse, blended in with a crowd, and went past Otsu, we might not find him.
So don't push yourself too hard. If you don't find him, just come back.
Do you understand, Soji?

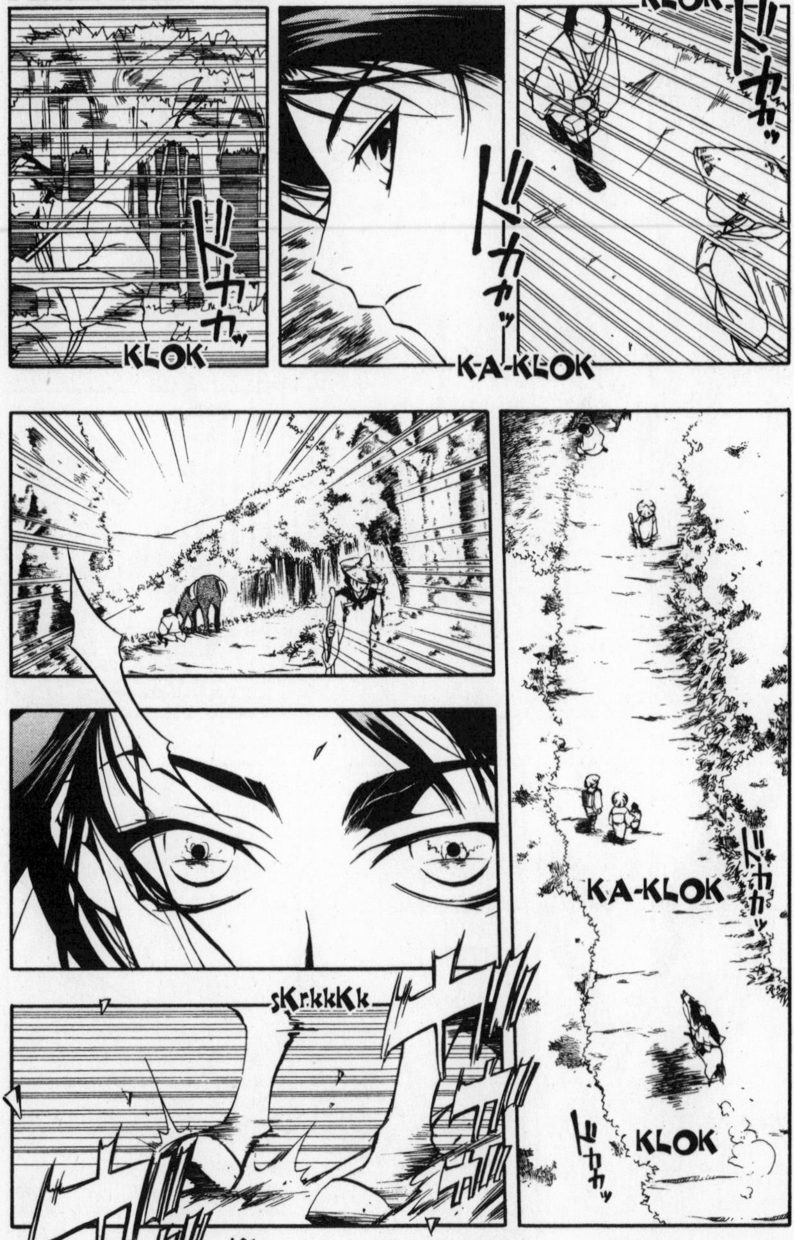
KLOK
K-A-KLOK
KLOK
KA-KLOK
KLOK
sKr.kkKk
sKk

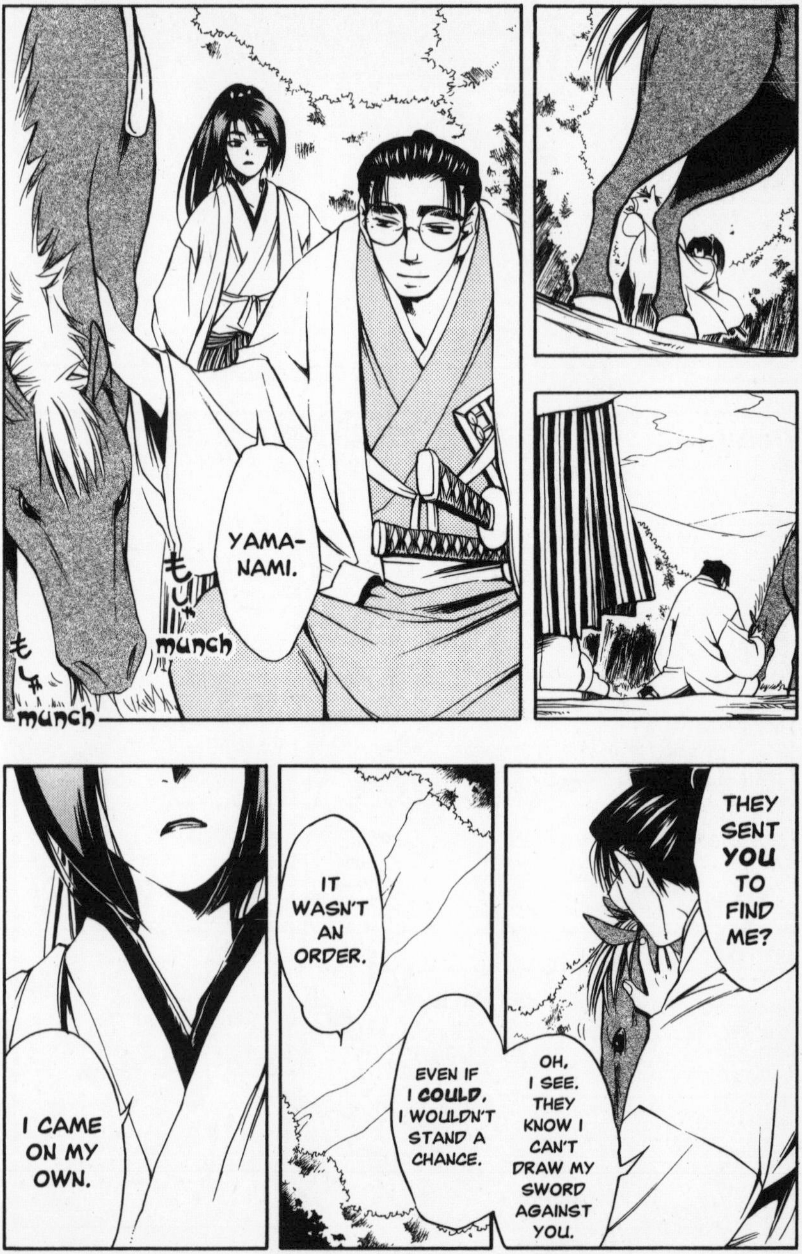

YAMA-NAMI.
もしゃ munch
もしゃ munch
THEY SENT YOU TO FIND ME?
OH, I SEE. THEY KNOW I CAN'T DRAW MY SWORD AGAINST YOU.
EVEN IF I COULD, I WOULDN'T STAND A CHANCE.
IT WASN'T AN ORDER.
I CAME ON MY OWN.

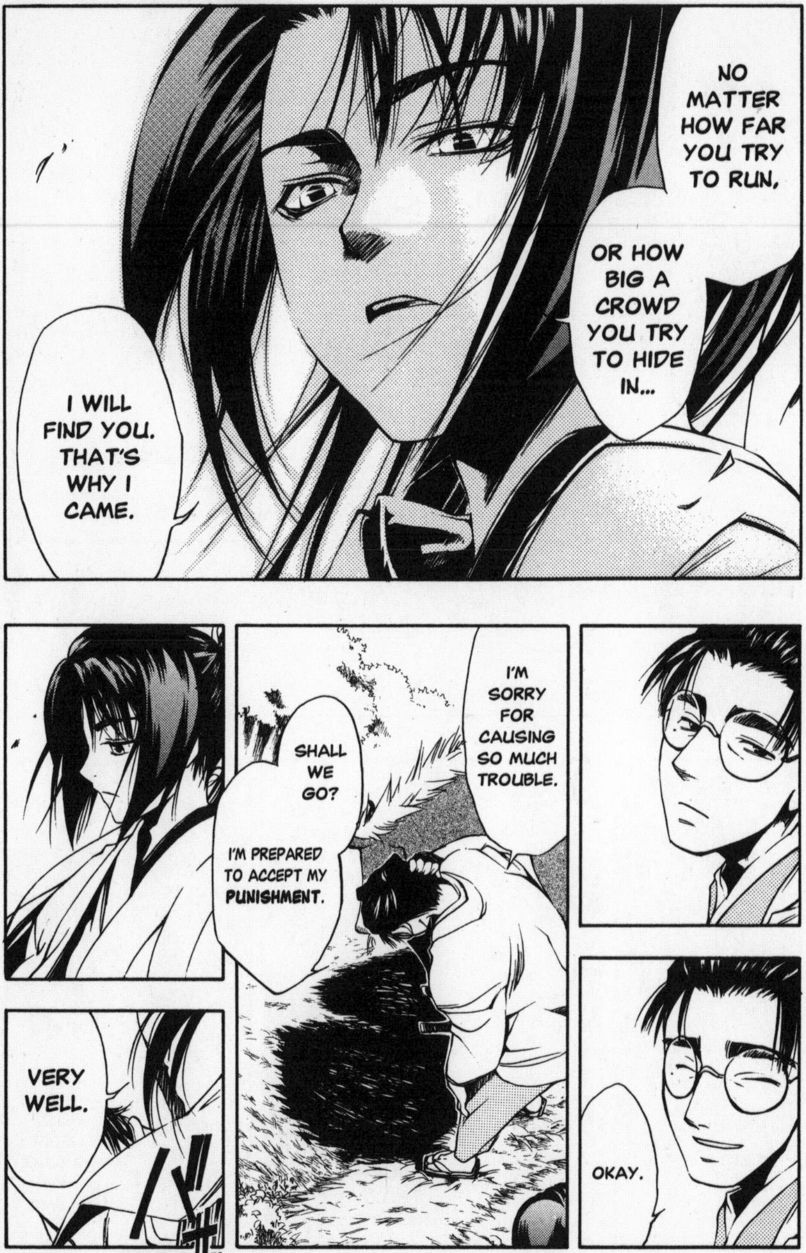
NO MATTER HOW FAR YOU TRY TO RUN,
OR HOW BIG A CROWD YOU TRY TO HIDE IN...
I WILL FIND YOU. THAT'S WHY I CAME.
I'M SORRY FOR CAUSING SO MUCH TROUBLE.
SHALL WE GO?
I'M PREPARED TO ACCEPT MY **PUNISHMENT**.
OKAY.
VERY WELL.
RUSTLE

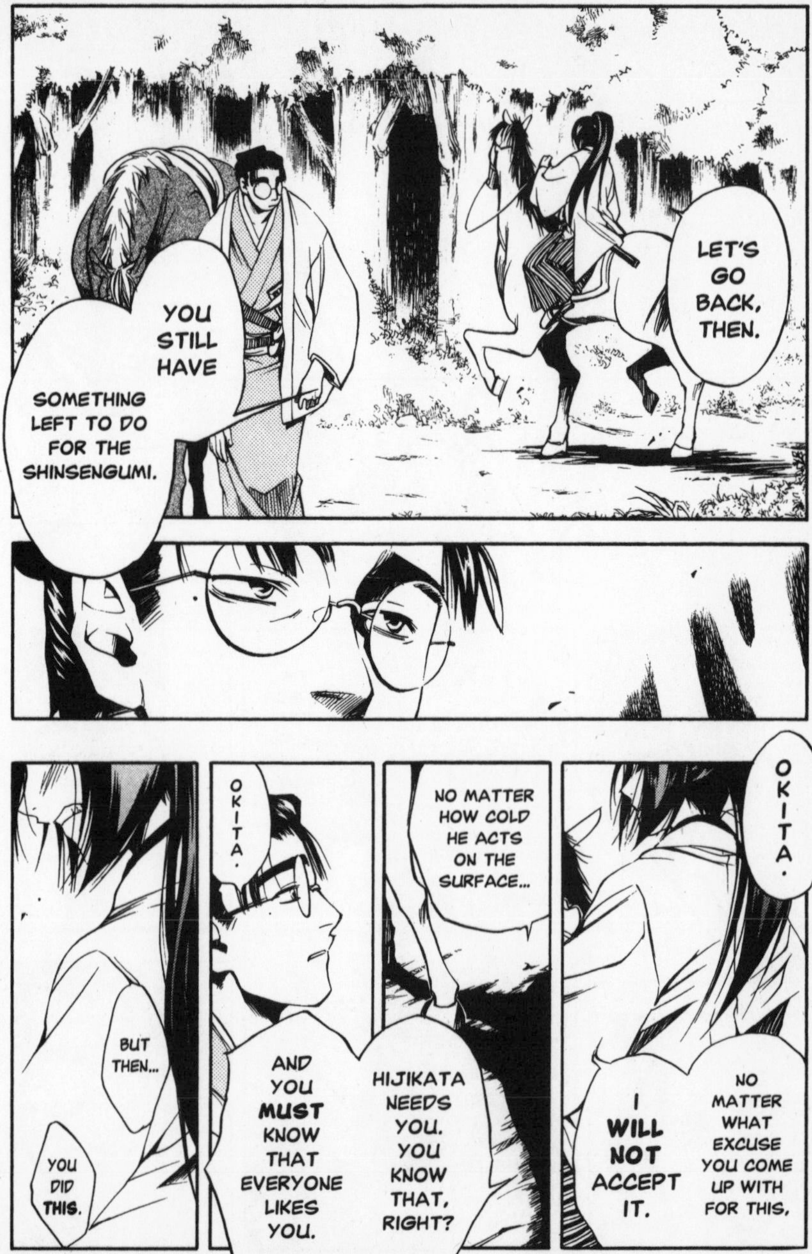
LET'S GO BACK, THEN.
YOU STILL HAVE SOMETHING LEFT TO DO FOR THE SHINSENGUMI.
OKITA.
NO MATTER WHAT EXCUSE YOU COME UP WITH FOR THIS,
I **WILL NOT** ACCEPT IT.
NO MATTER HOW COLD HE ACTS ON THE SURFACE...
HIJIKATA NEEDS YOU. YOU KNOW THAT, RIGHT?
OKITA.
AND YOU **MUST** KNOW THAT EVERYONE LIKES YOU.
BUT THEN...
YOU DID **THIS.**

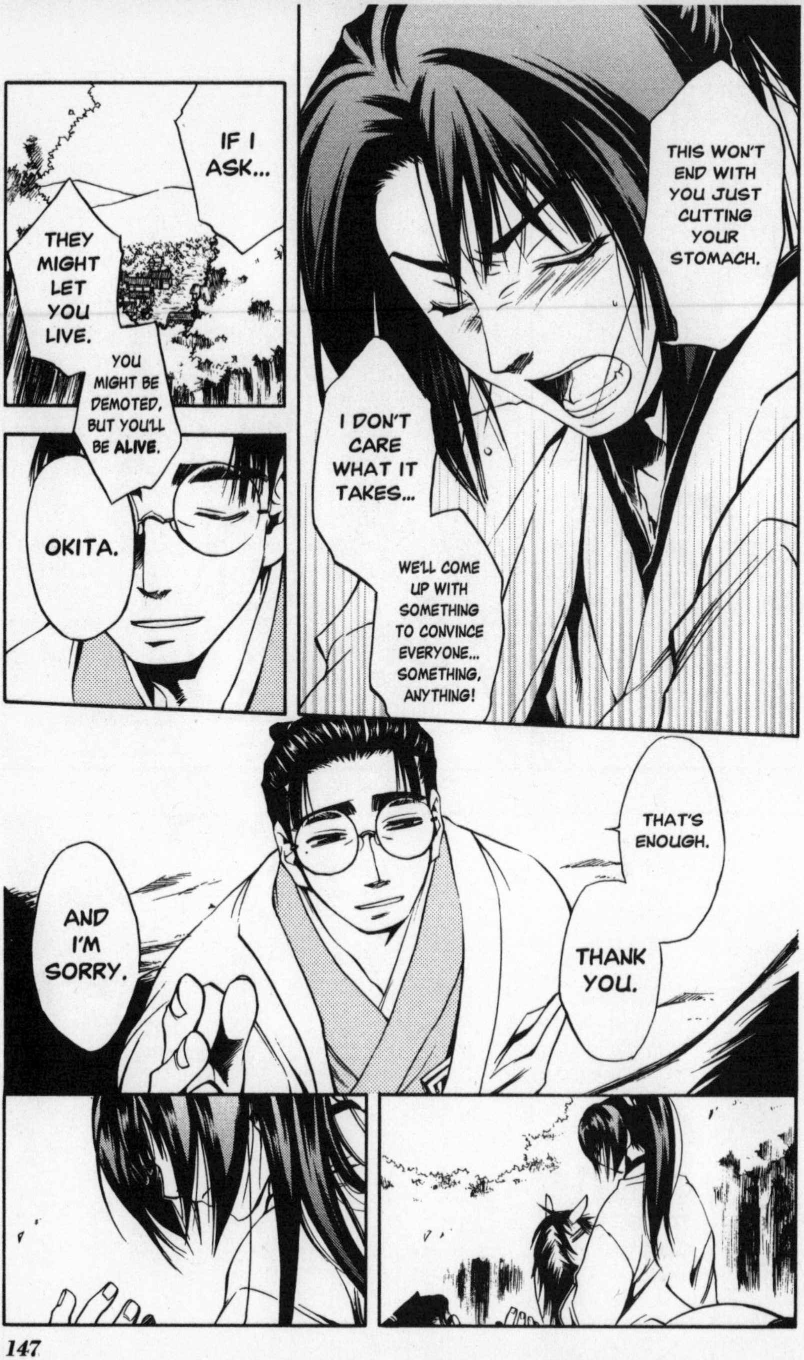
THIS WON'T END WITH YOU JUST CUTTING YOUR STOMACH.
I DON'T CARE WHAT IT TAKES...
WE'LL COME UP WITH SOMETHING TO CONVINCE EVERYONE... SOMETHING, ANYTHING!
IF I ASK...
THEY MIGHT LET YOU LIVE.
YOU MIGHT BE DEMOTED, BUT YOU'LL BE ALIVE.
OKITA.
THAT'S ENOUGH.
THANK YOU.
AND I'M SORRY.

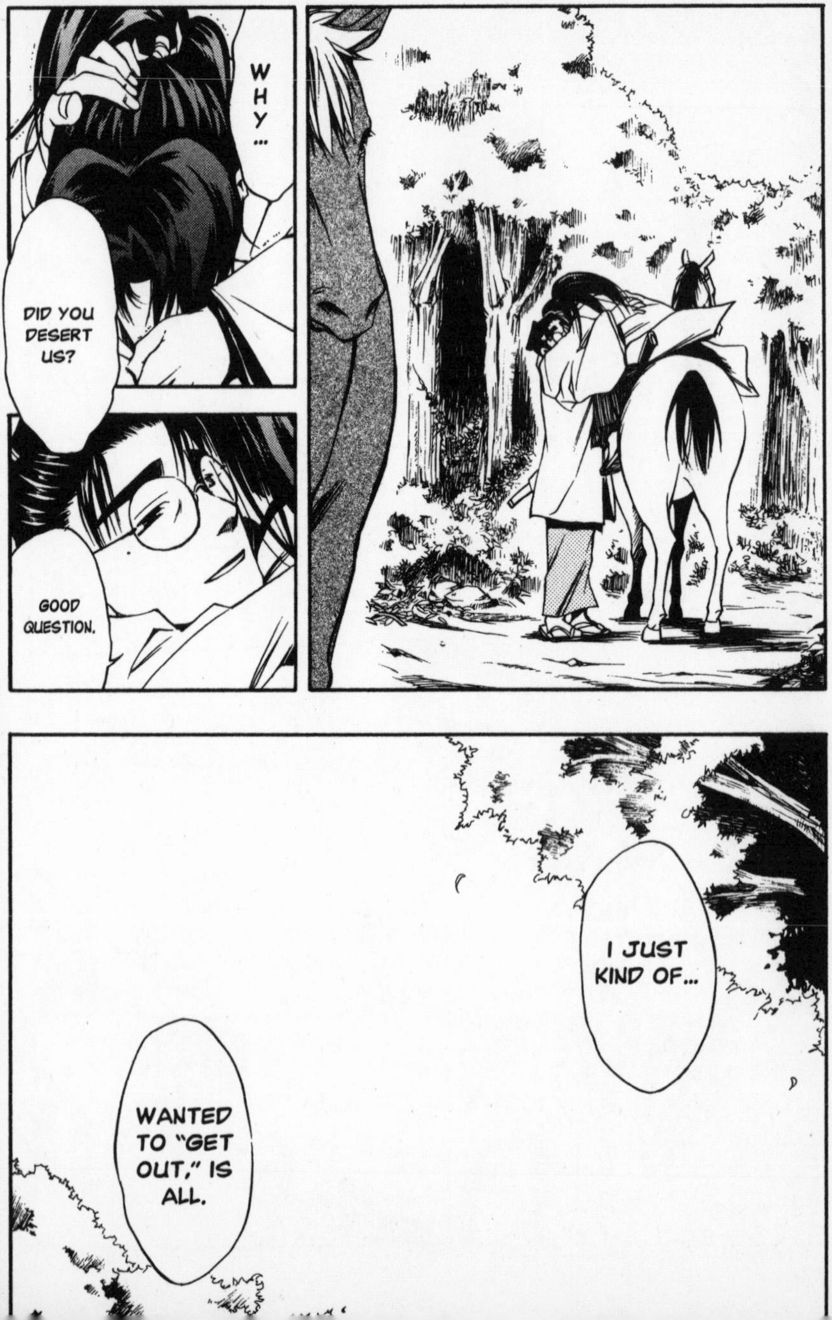
WHY...
DID YOU DESERT US?
GOOD QUESTION.
I JUST KIND OF...
WANTED TO "GET OUT," IS ALL.

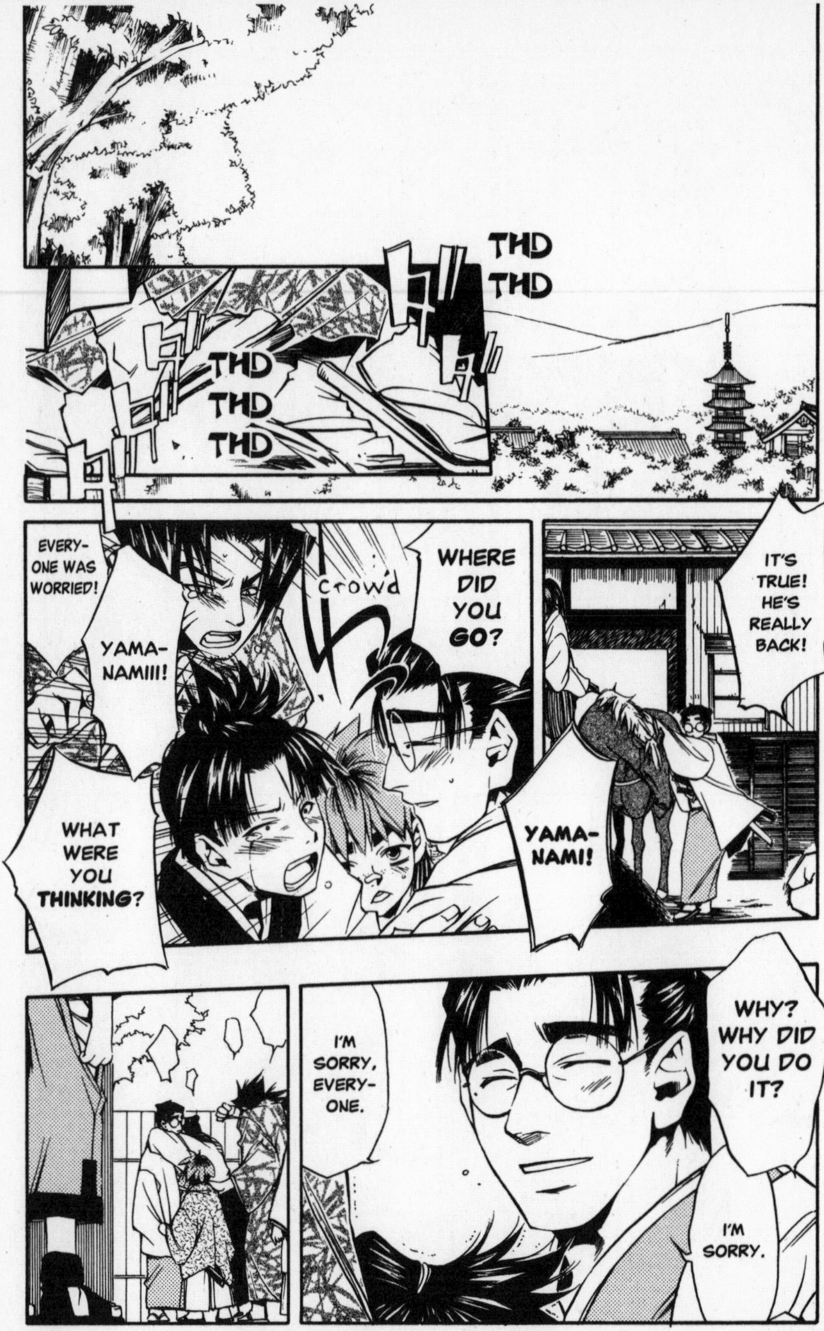
THD
THD
THD
THD
THD
IT'S TRUE! HE'S REALLY BACK!
YAMA-NAMI!
WHERE DID YOU GO?
crowd
EVERY-ONE WAS WORRIED!
YAMA-NAMIII!
WHAT WERE YOU THINKING?
WHY? WHY DID YOU DO IT?
I'M SORRY, EVERY-ONE.
I'M SORRY.

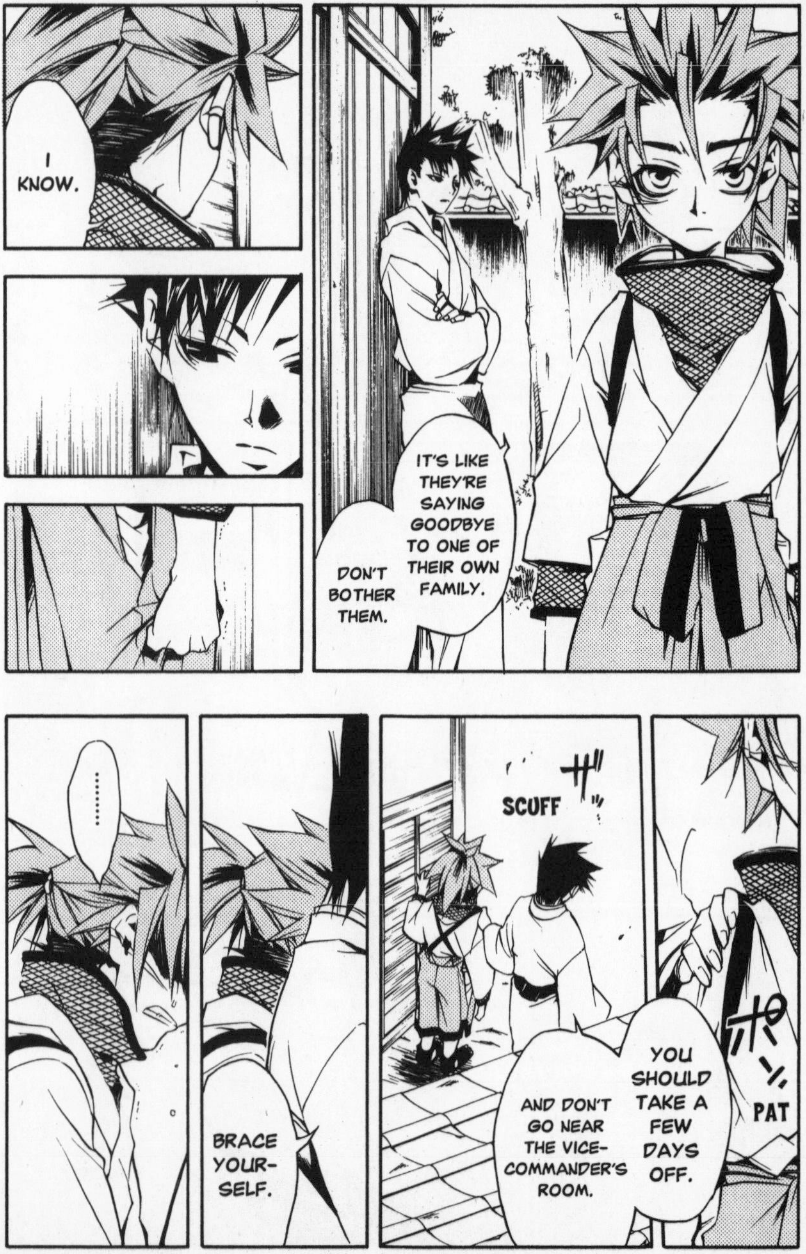
IT'S LIKE THEY'RE SAYING GOODBYE TO ONE OF THEIR OWN FAMILY.
DON'T BOTHER THEM.
I KNOW.
YOU SHOULD TAKE A FEW DAYS OFF.
PAT
AND DON'T GO NEAR THE VICE-COMMANDER'S ROOM.
SCUFF
BRACE YOUR-SELF.
......

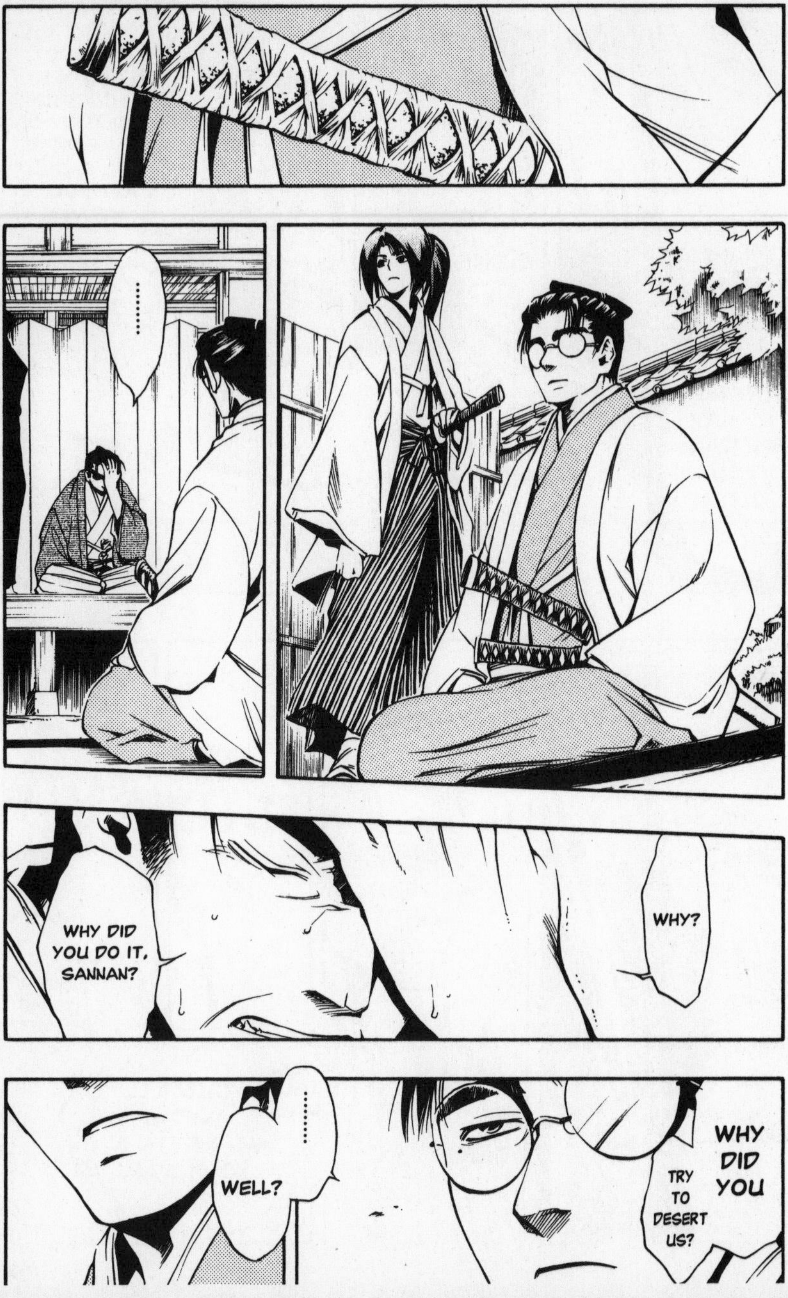
......
WHY?
WHY DID YOU DO IT, SANNAN?
WHY DID YOU TRY TO DESERT US?
......
WELL?

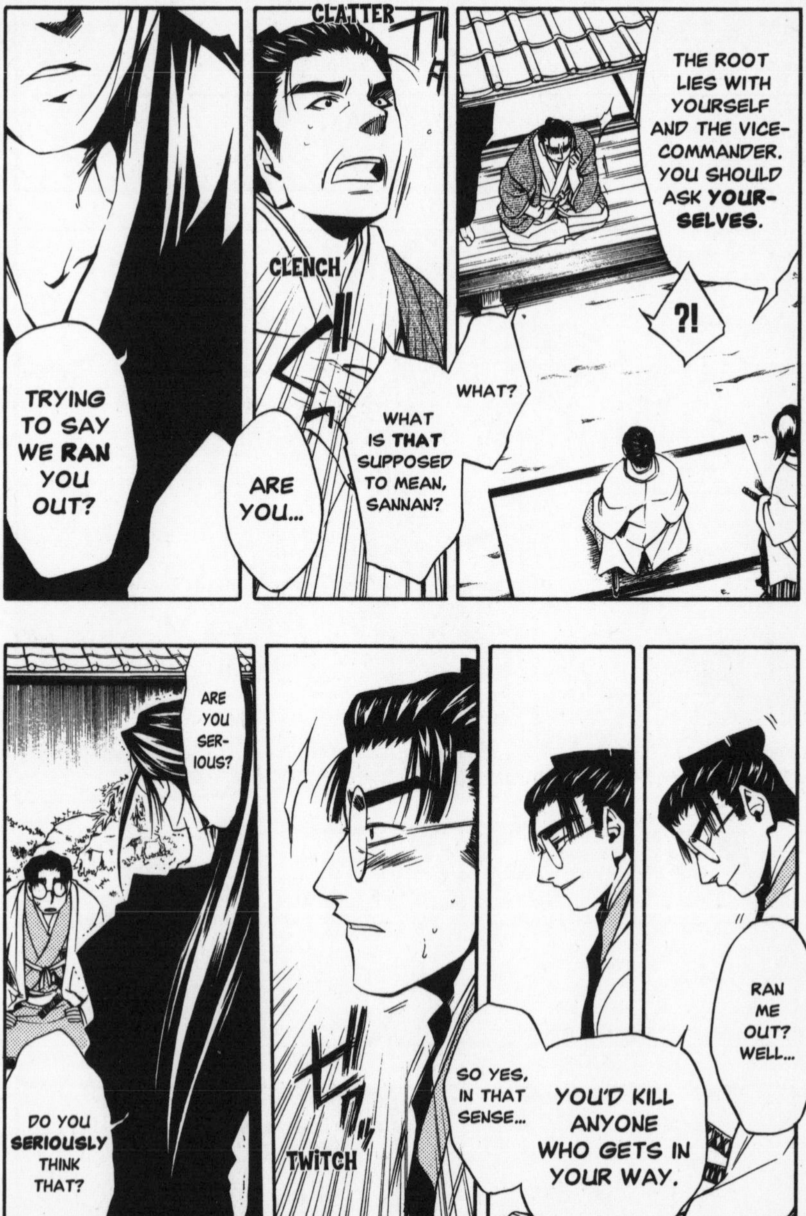
THE ROOT LIES WITH YOURSELF AND THE VICE-COMMANDER. YOU SHOULD ASK YOURSELVES.
?!
CLATTER
CLENCH
WHAT?
WHAT IS THAT SUPPOSED TO MEAN, SANNAN?
ARE YOU...
TRYING TO SAY WE RAN YOU OUT?
RAN ME OUT? WELL...
SO YES, IN THAT SENSE...
YOU'D KILL ANYONE WHO GETS IN YOUR WAY.
TWITCH
ARE YOU SERIOUS?
DO YOU SERIOUSLY THINK THAT?

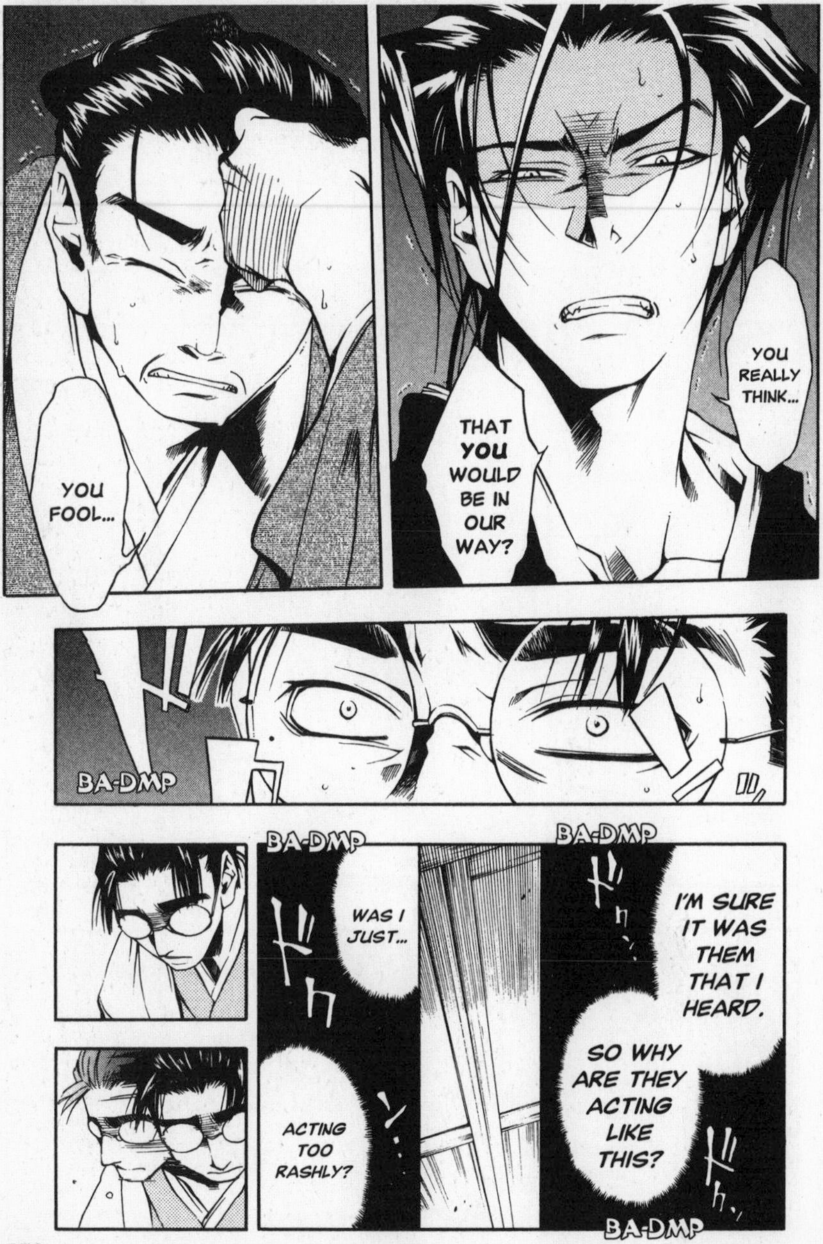
YOU REALLY THINK...
THAT YOU WOULD BE IN OUR WAY?
YOU FOOL...
BA-DMP
BA-DMP
I'M SURE IT WAS THEM THAT I HEARD.
SO WHY ARE THEY ACTING LIKE THIS?
BA-DMP
BA-DMP
WAS I JUST...
ACTING TOO RASHLY?

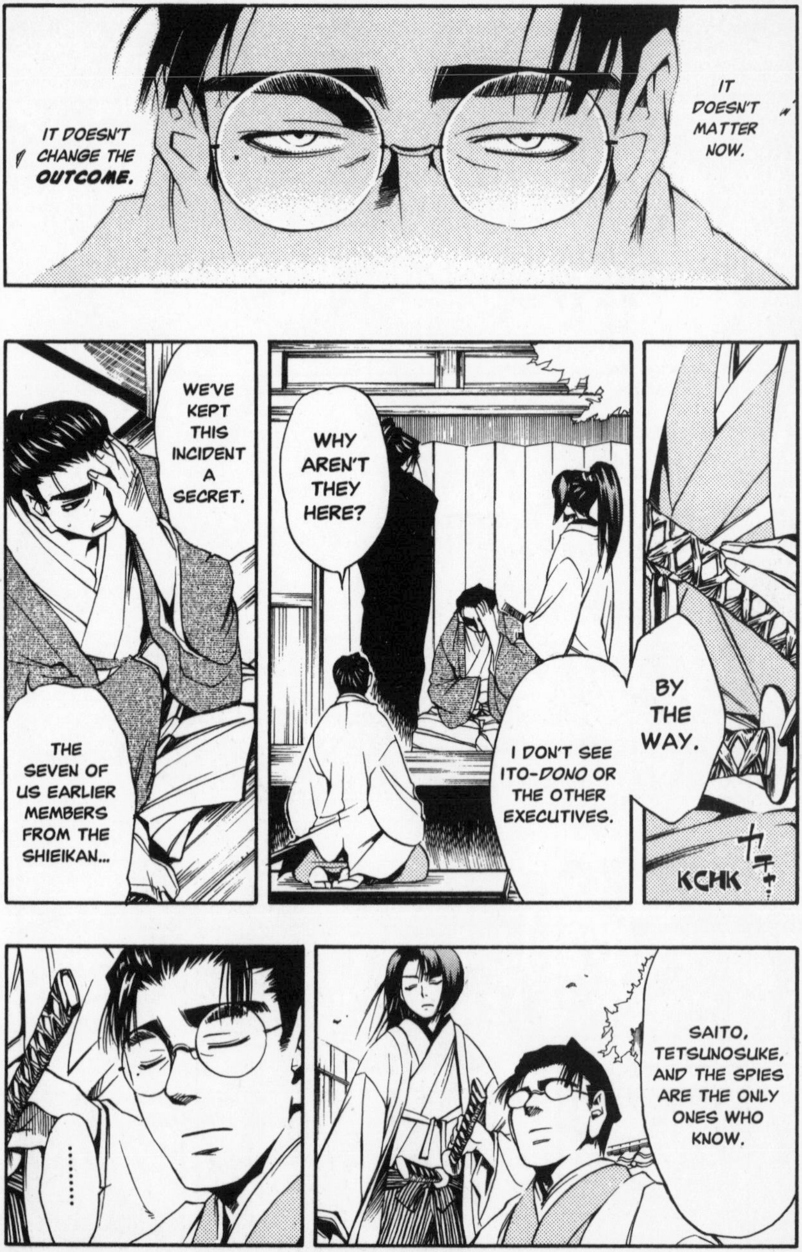
IT DOESN'T MATTER NOW.
IT DOESN'T CHANGE THE **OUTCOME.**
KCHK
カチャ
BY THE WAY.
I DON'T SEE ITO-*DONO* OR THE OTHER EXECUTIVES.
WHY AREN'T THEY HERE?
WE'VE KEPT THIS INCIDENT A SECRET.
THE SEVEN OF US EARLIER MEMBERS FROM THE SHIEIKAN...
SAITO, TETSUNOSUKE, AND THE SPIES ARE THE ONLY ONES WHO KNOW.
....

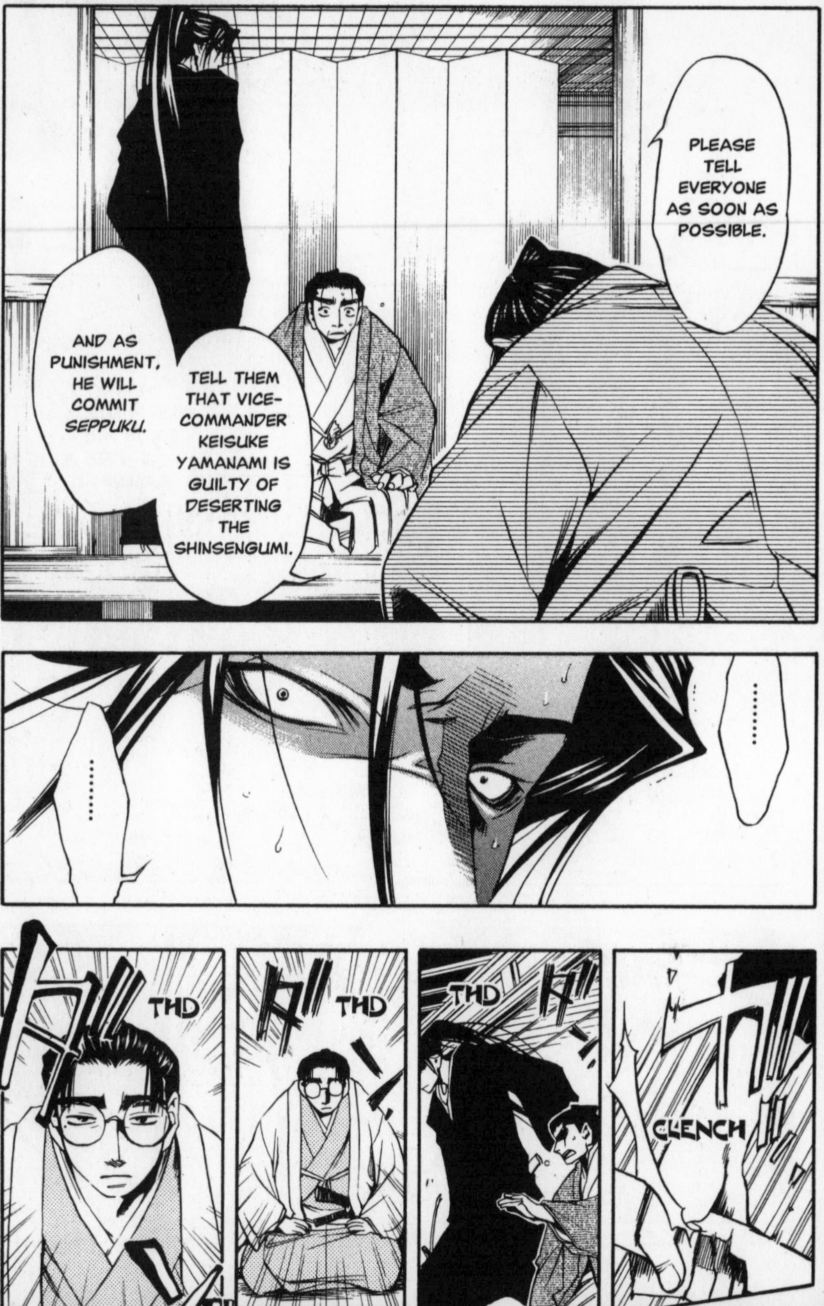
PLEASE TELL EVERYONE AS SOON AS POSSIBLE.
TELL THEM THAT VICE-COMMANDER KEISUKE YAMANAMI IS GUILTY OF DESERTING THE SHINSENGUMI.
AND AS PUNISHMENT, HE WILL COMMIT SEPPUKU.
......
......
CLENCH
THD
THD
THD

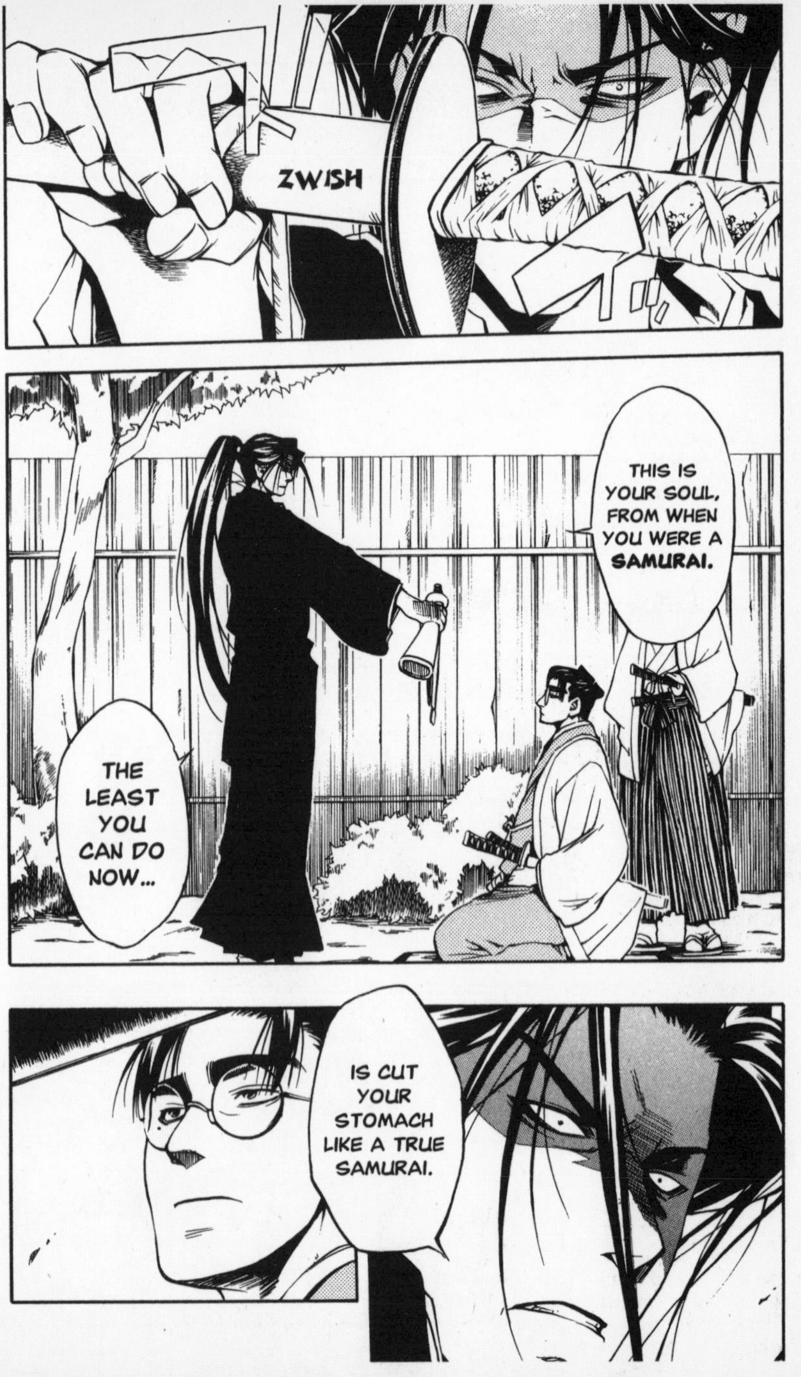
ZWISH
THIS IS YOUR SOUL, FROM WHEN YOU WERE A SAMURAI.
THE LEAST YOU CAN DO NOW...
IS CUT YOUR STOMACH LIKE A TRUE SAMURAI.

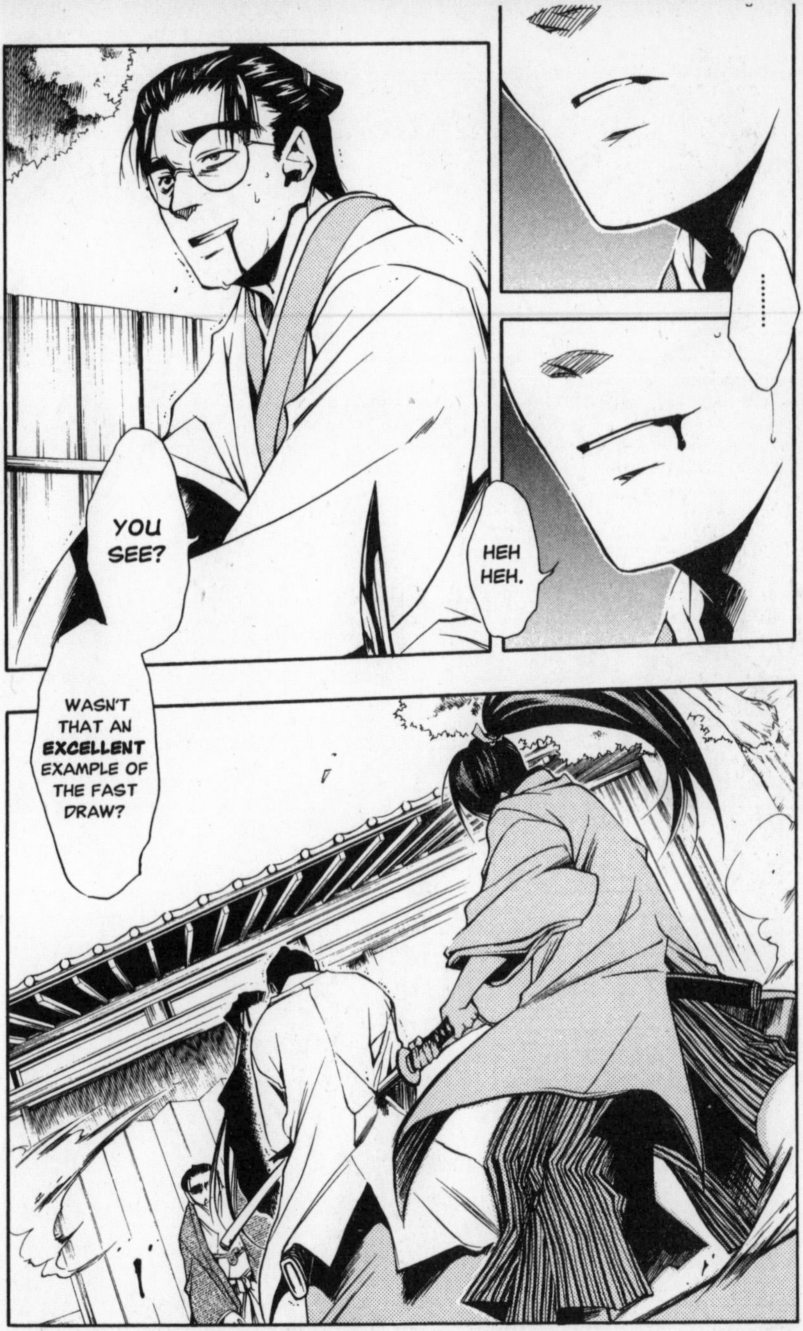
......
HEH HEH.
YOU SEE?
WASN'T THAT AN EXCELLENT EXAMPLE OF THE FAST DRAW?

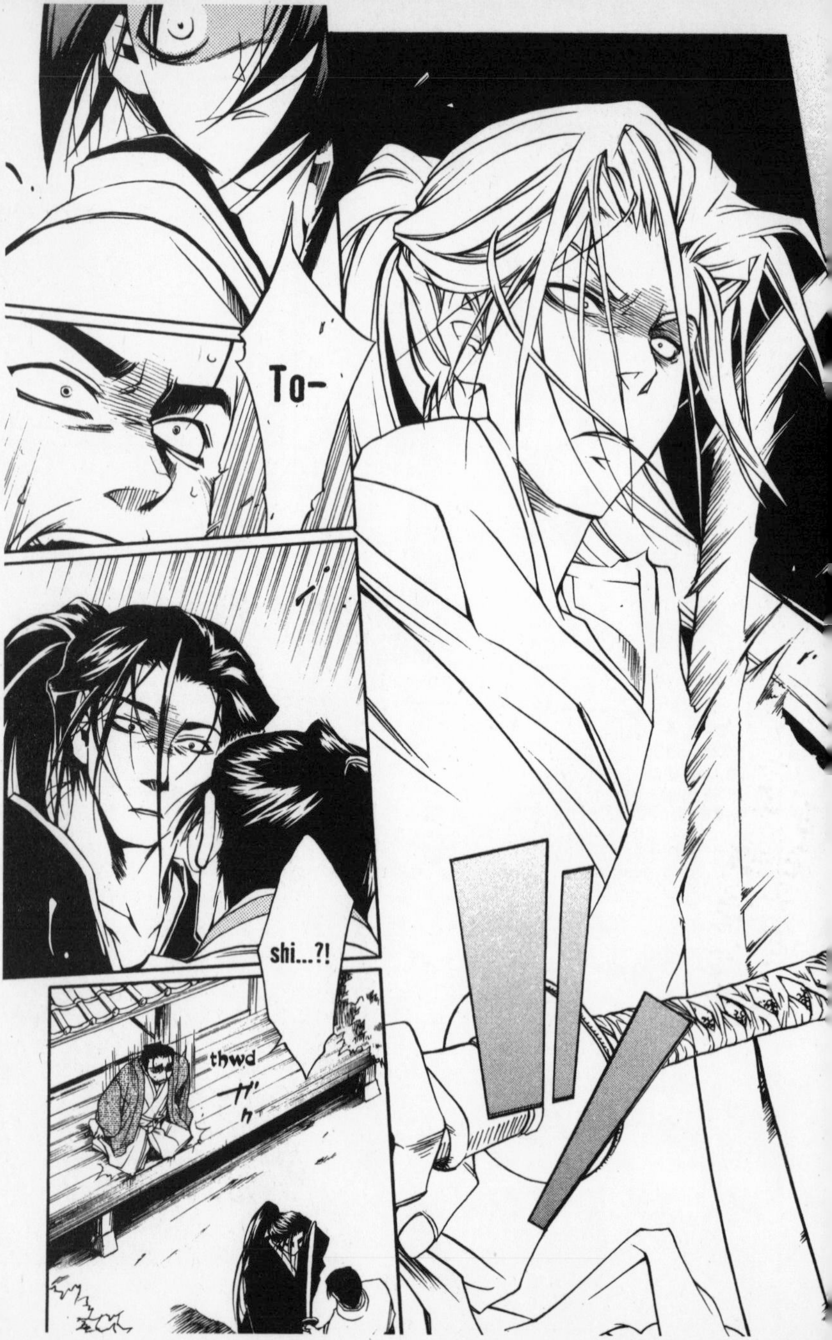
To-
shi...?!
thwd
ガッ

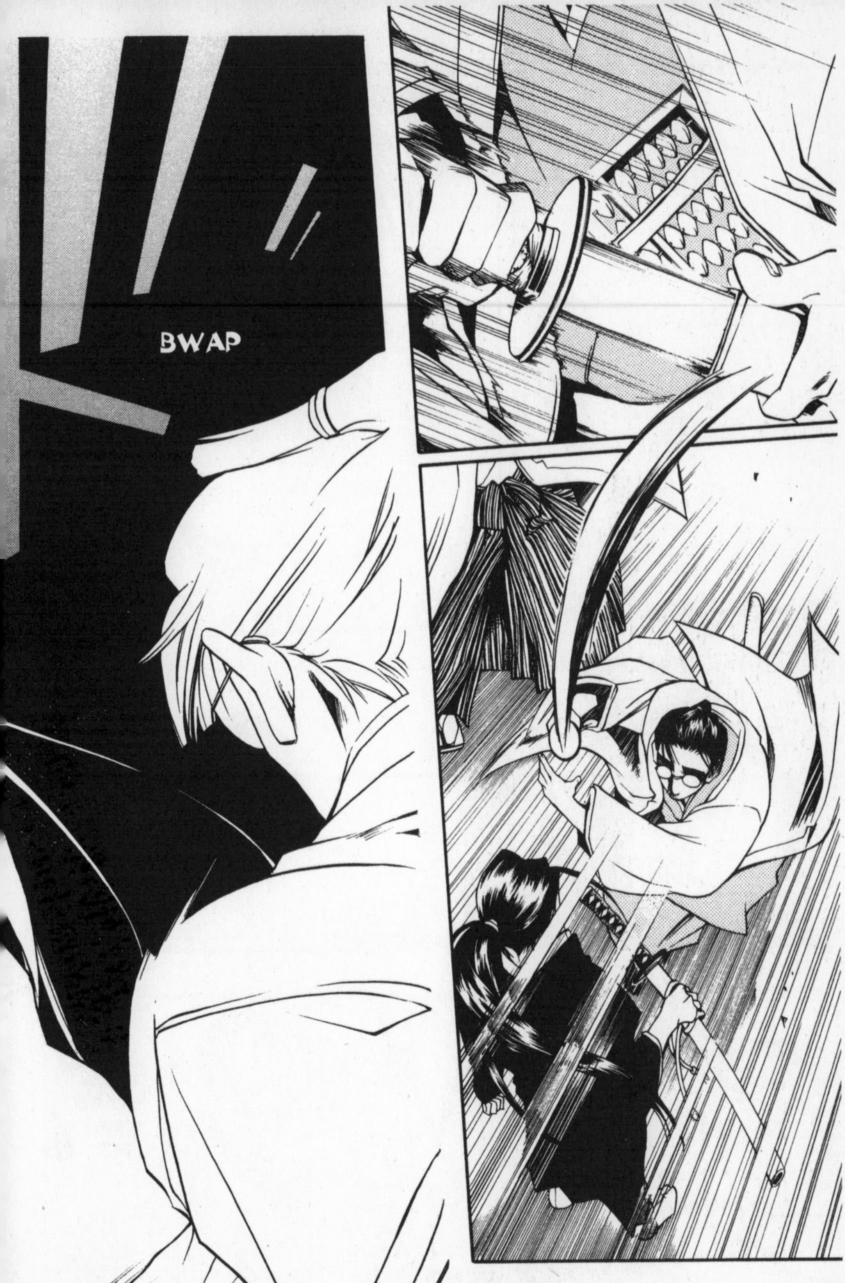
BWAP

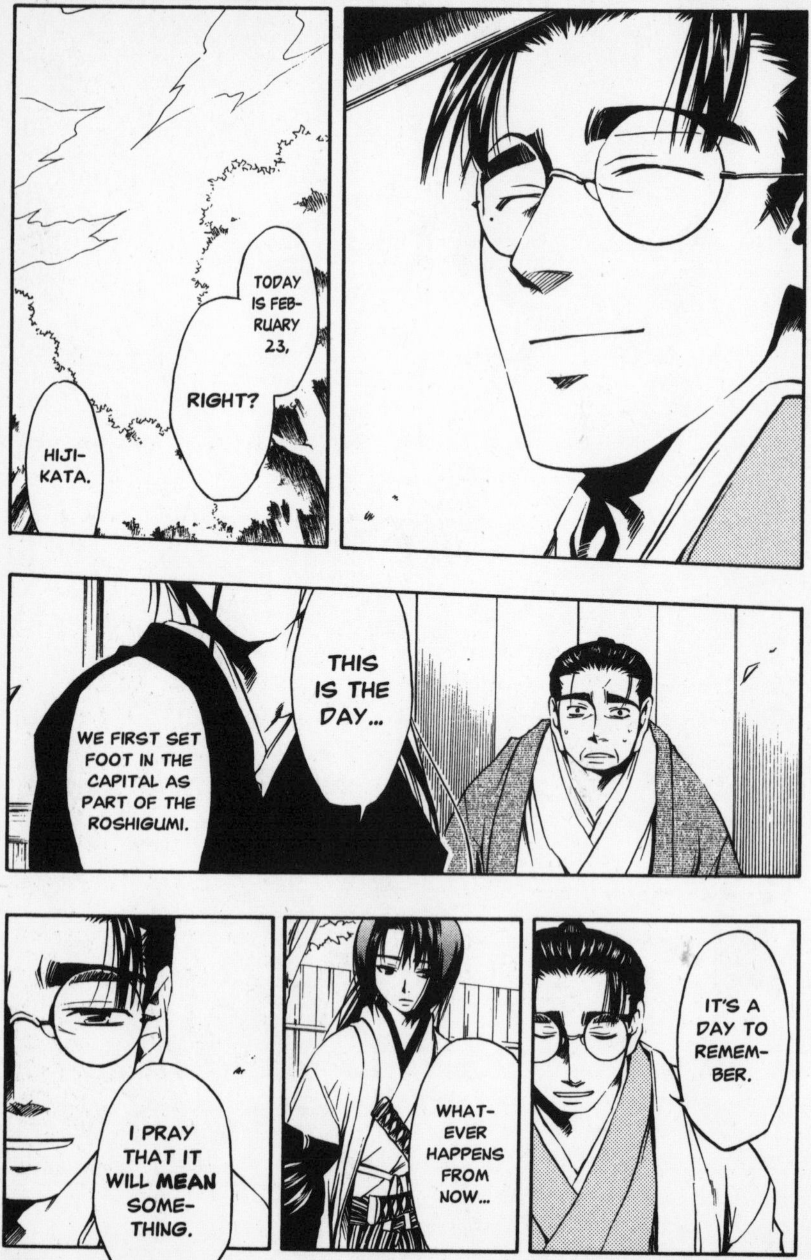
TODAY IS FEB-RUARY 23,
RIGHT?
HIJI-KATA.
THIS IS THE DAY...
WE FIRST SET FOOT IN THE CAPITAL AS PART OF THE ROSHIGUMI.
IT'S A DAY TO REMEM-BER.
WHAT-EVER HAPPENS FROM NOW...
I PRAY THAT IT WILL MEAN SOME-THING.

·········

ONCE YOU BARE YOUR FANGS...

HOFF

HOFF

DON'T HESITATE FOR A SECOND TO KILL...

COUGH

EVEN IF IT'S YOUR FRIEND.

KLAK

KLAK

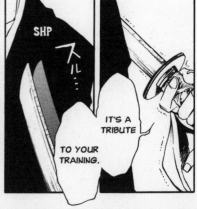

SHP

IT'S A TRIBUTE

TO YOUR TRAINING.

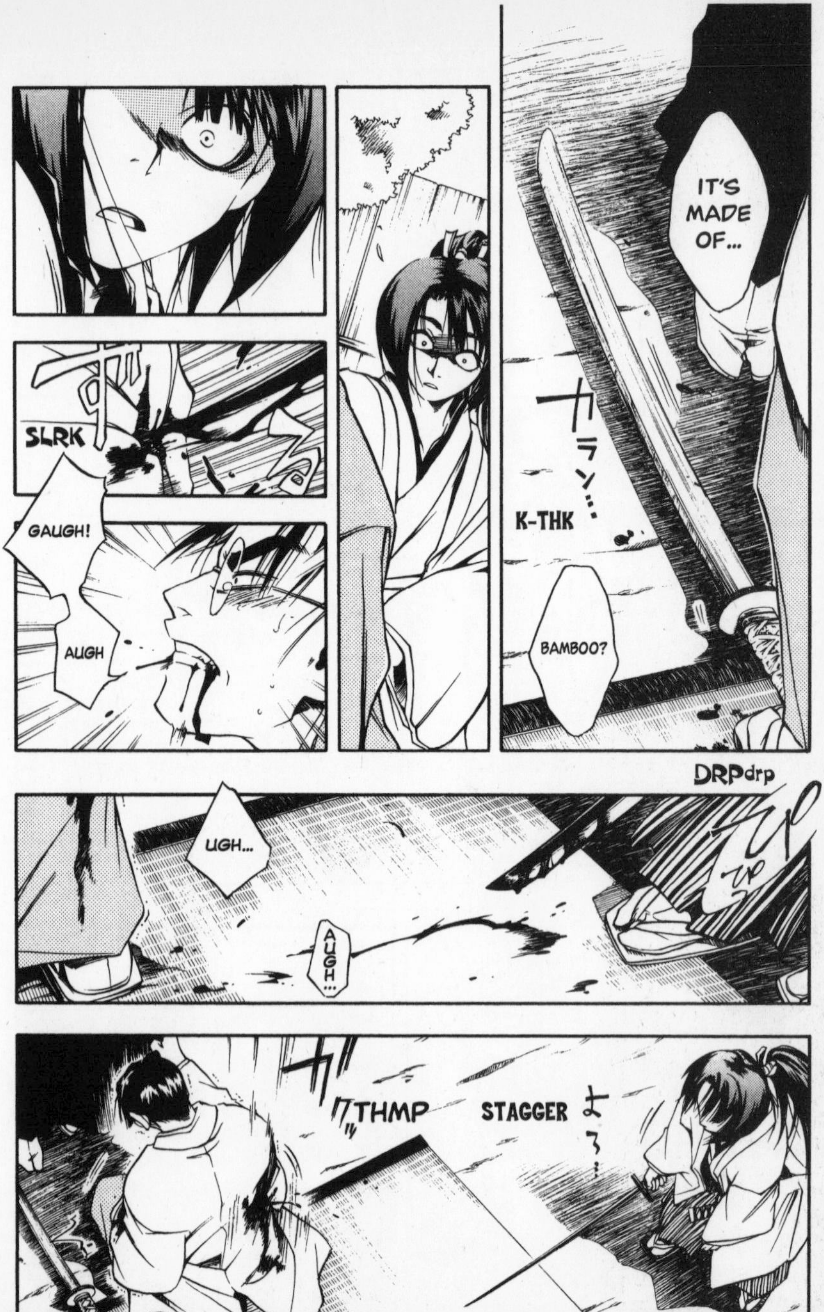
IT'S MADE OF...
K-THK
BAMBOO?
SLRK
GAUGH!
AUGH
DRPdrp
UGH...
AUGH...
STAGGER
THMP

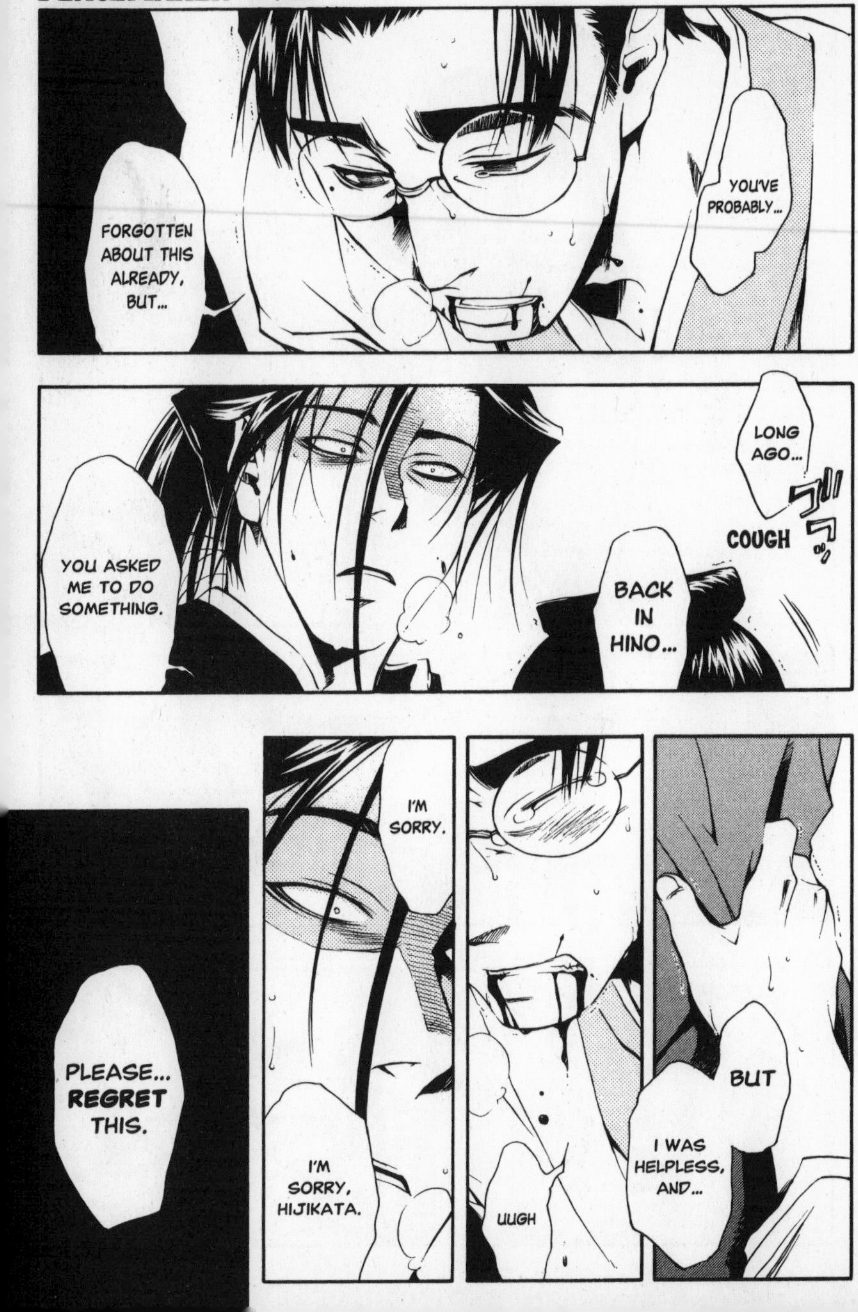
YOU'VE PROBABLY...
FORGOTTEN ABOUT THIS ALREADY, BUT...
LONG AGO...
COUGH
BACK IN HINO...
YOU ASKED ME TO DO SOMETHING.
BUT
I WAS HELPLESS, AND...
UUGH
I'M SORRY.
I'M SORRY, HIJIKATA.
PLEASE... REGRET THIS.

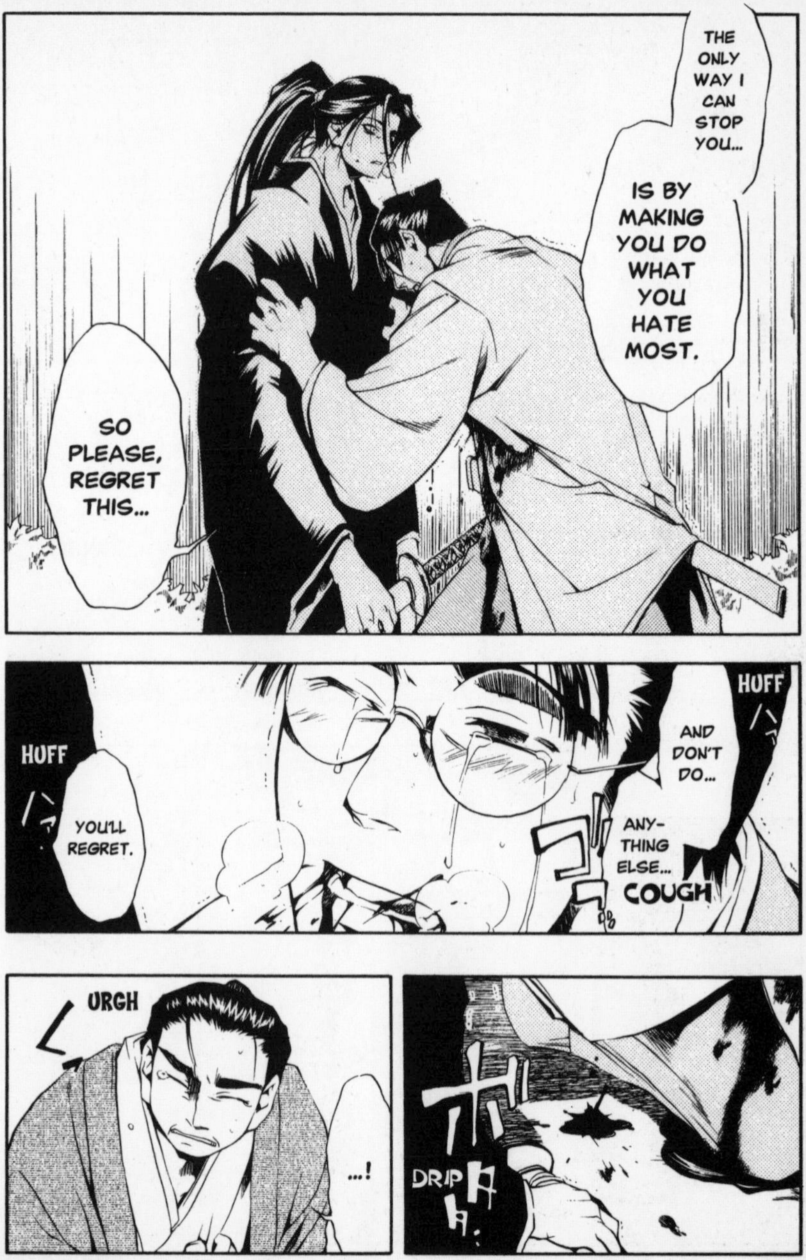
THE ONLY WAY I CAN STOP YOU...
IS BY MAKING YOU DO WHAT YOU HATE MOST.
SO PLEASE, REGRET THIS...
HUFF
AND DON'T DO...
ANY-THING ELSE... COUGH
HUFF
YOU'LL REGRET.
DRIP
...!
URGH

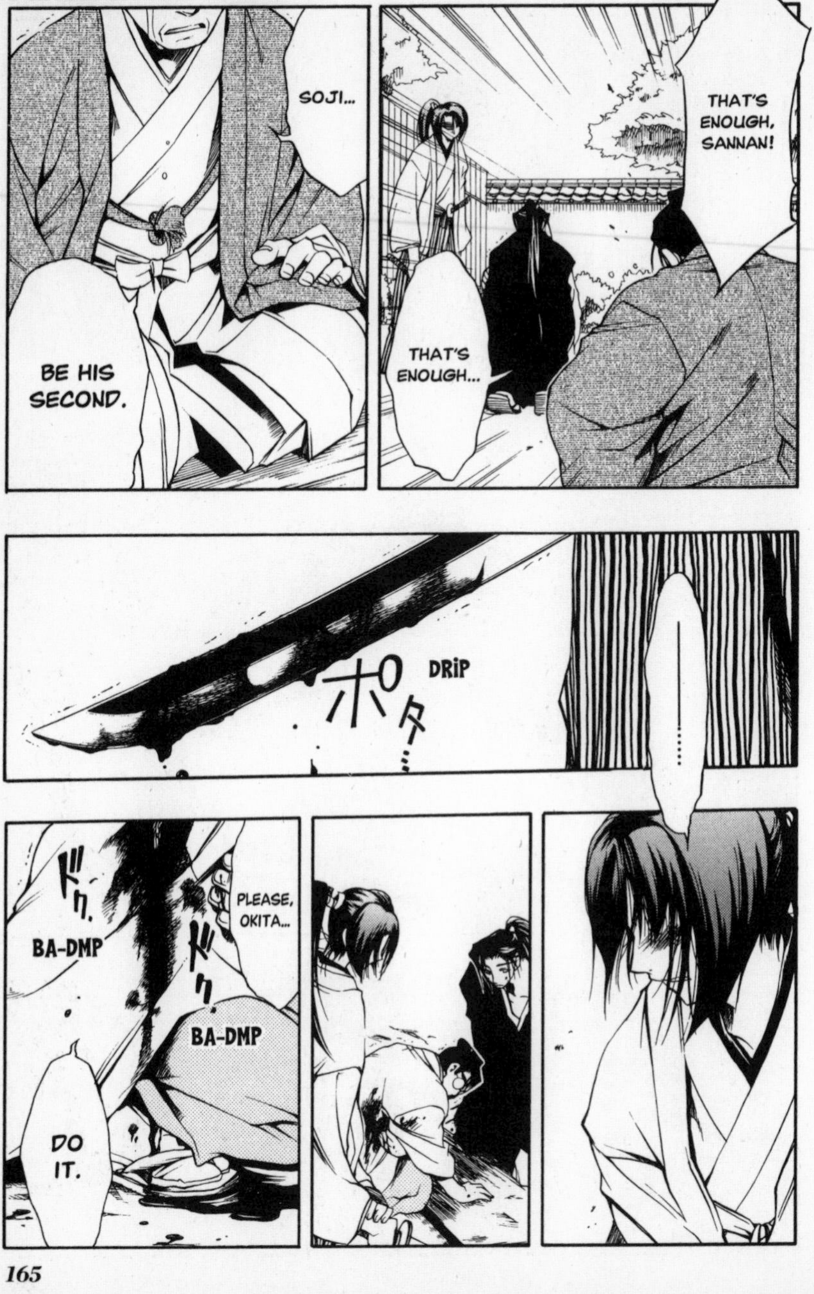
THAT'S ENOUGH, SANNAN!
THAT'S ENOUGH...
SOJI...
BE HIS SECOND.
......
ポタ…
DRIP
PLEASE, OKITA...
ドク
BA-DMP
ドク
BA-DMP
DO IT.

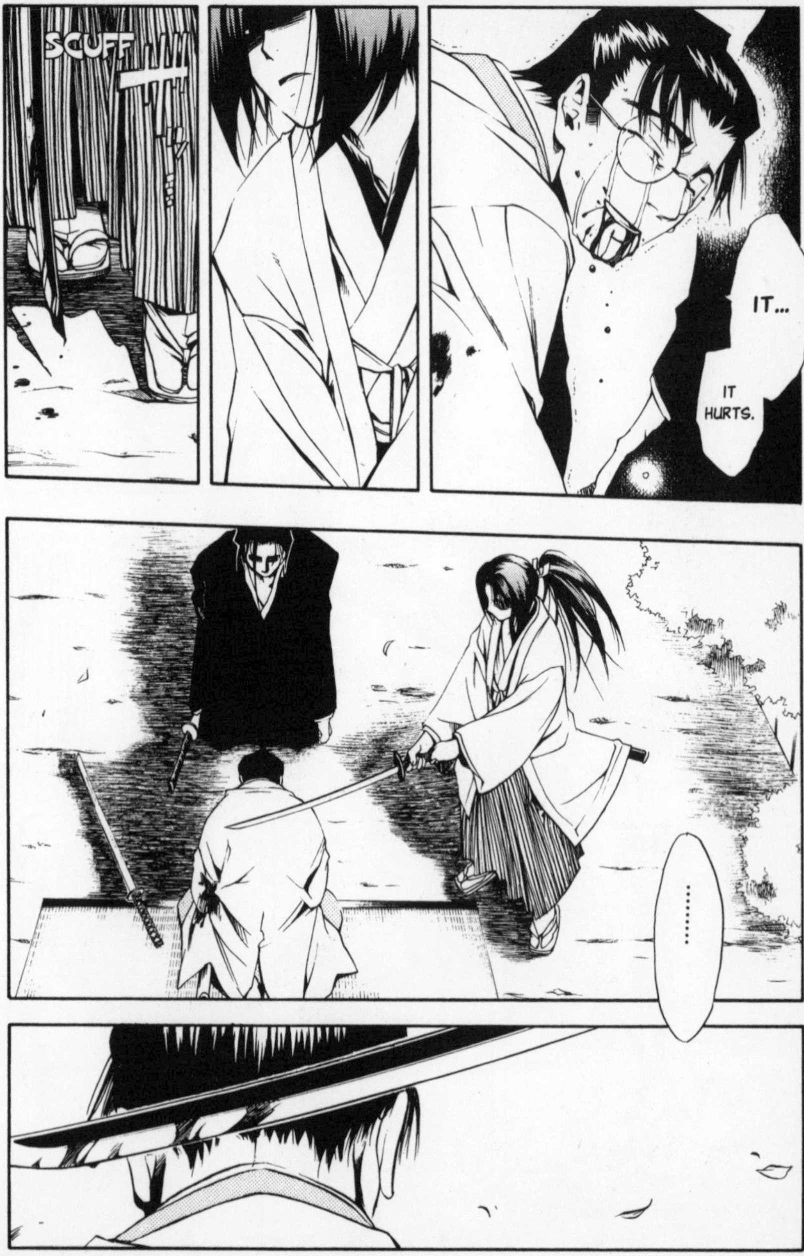
SCUFF
IT...
IT HURTS.
......

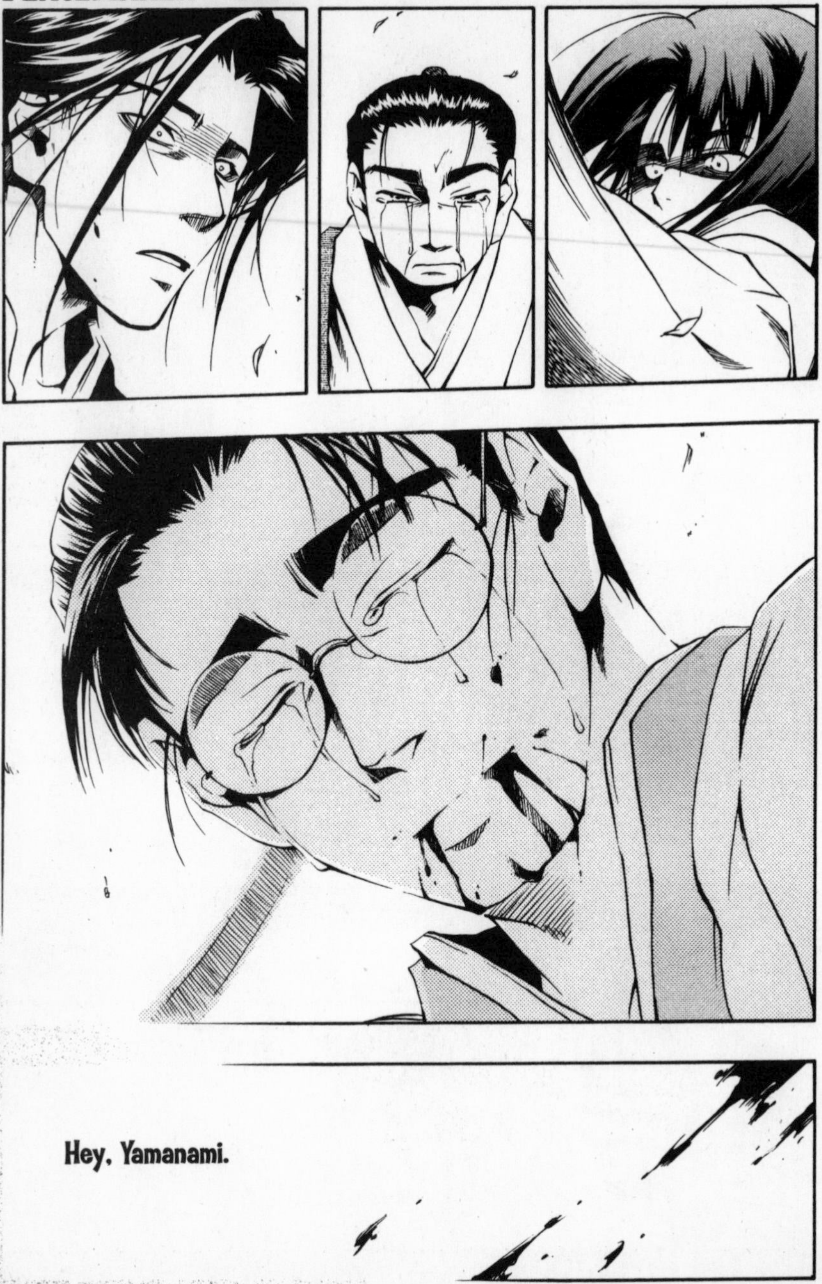
Hey, Yamanami.

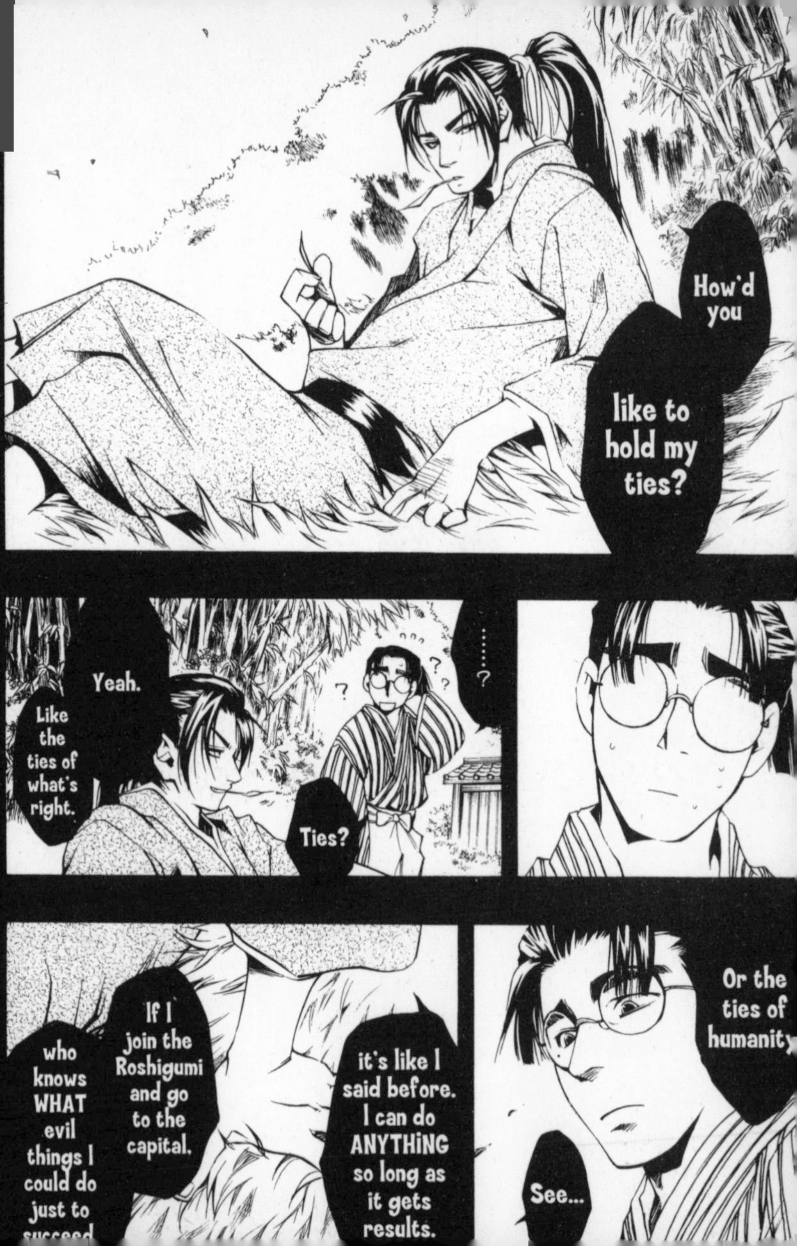

How'd you like to hold my ties?
......?
Ties?
Yeah.
Like the ties of what's right.
Or the ties of humanity
See...
it's like I said before. I can do ANYTHiNG so long as it gets results.
If I join the Roshigumi and go to the capital,
who knows WHAT evil things I could do just to

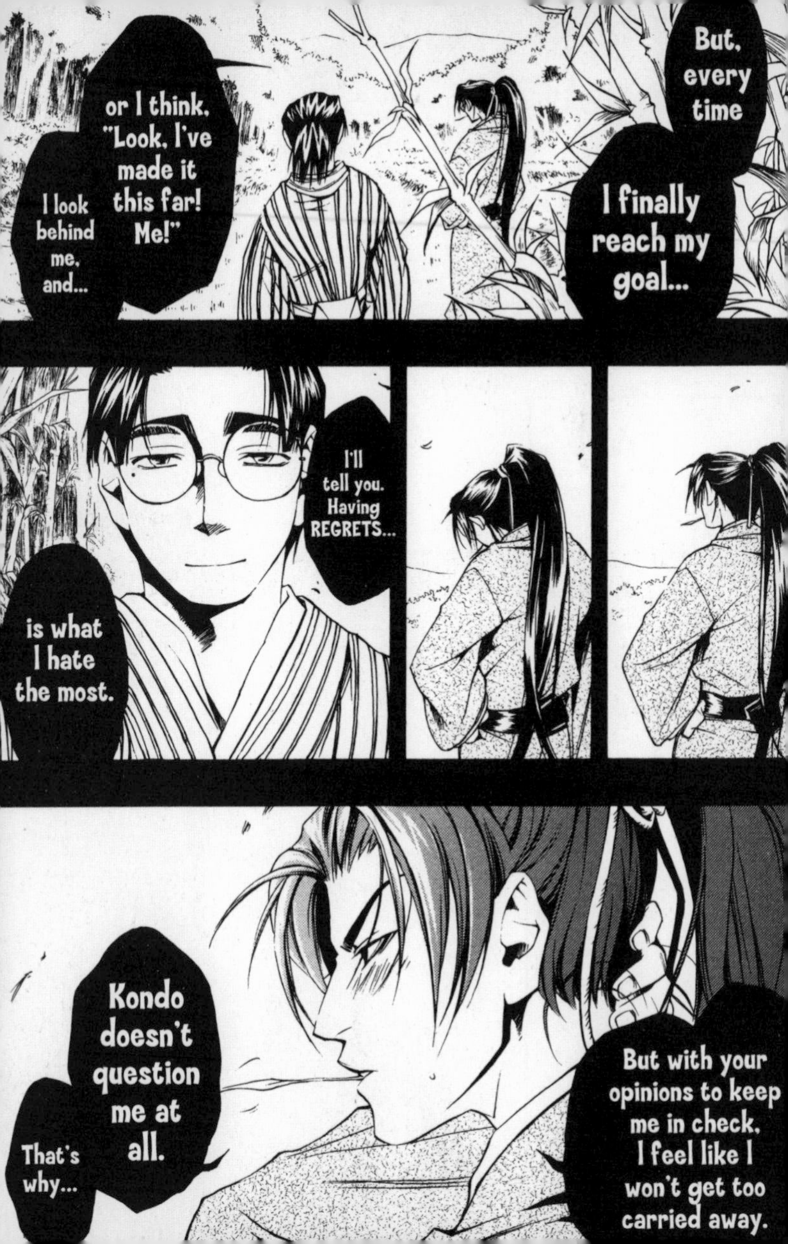
But, every time
I finally reach my goal...
I look behind me, and...
or I think, "Look, I've made it this far! Me!"
I'll tell you. Having REGRETS...
is what I hate the most.
But with your opinions to keep me in check, I feel like I won't get too carried away.
Kondo doesn't question me at all.
That's why...

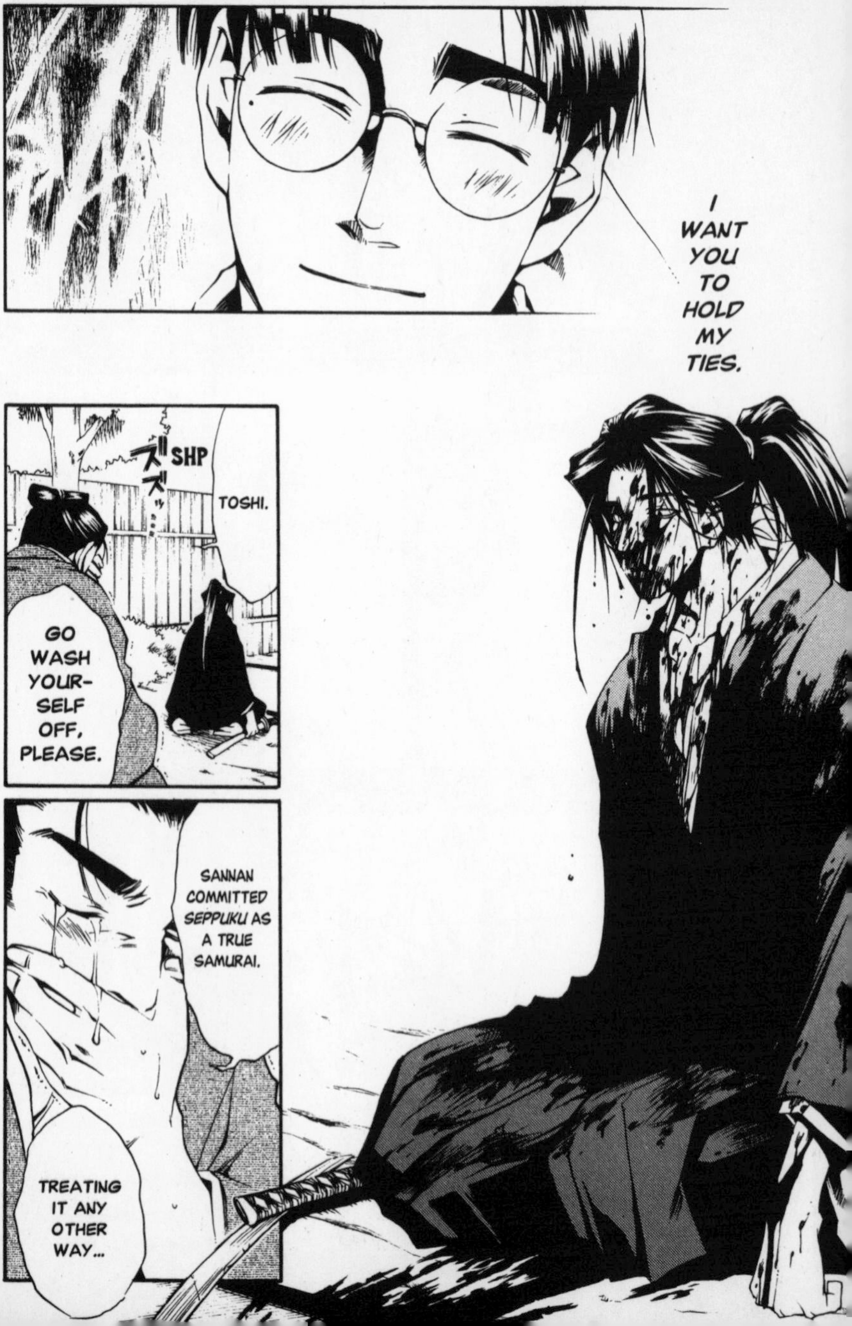
I WANT YOU TO HOLD MY TIES.
ズズッ…
SHP
TOSHI.
GO WASH YOURSELF OFF, PLEASE.
SANNAN COMMITTED SEPPUKU AS A TRUE SAMURAI.
TREATING IT ANY OTHER WAY...

WOULD BE...

FAR TOO CRUEL.

....

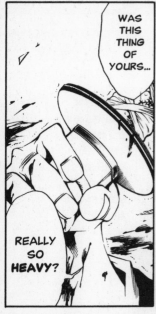

WAS THIS THING OF YOURS...

REALLY SO HEAVY?

WAS IT HEAVY?

KCHK

カチャ…

A BAMBOO SWORD.

I WON- DER...

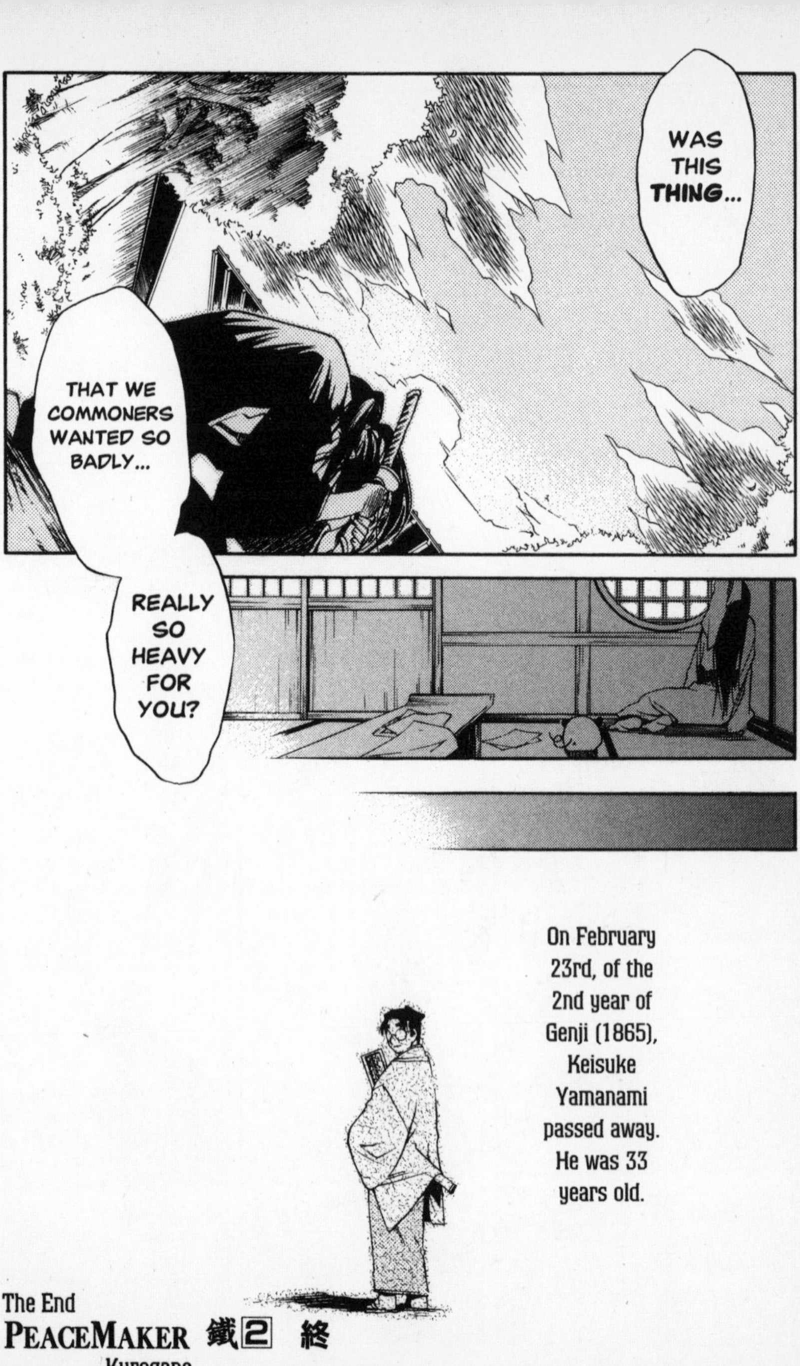
WAS THIS THING...
THAT WE COMMONERS WANTED SO BADLY...
REALLY SO HEAVY FOR YOU?
On February 23rd, of the 2nd year of Genji (1865), Keisuke Yamanami passed away. He was 33 years old.
The End
PEACEMAKER 鐵2 終
Kurogane

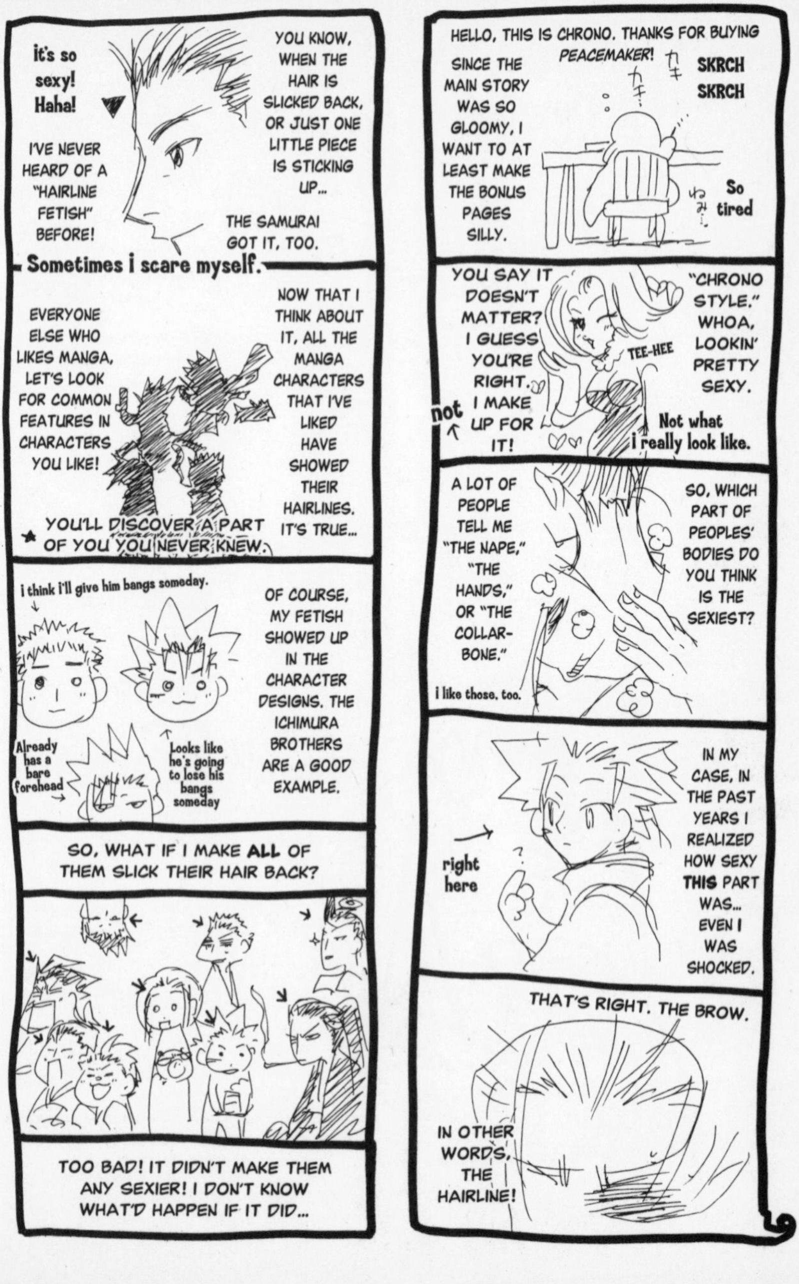

HELLO, THIS IS CHRONO. THANKS FOR BUYING PEACEMAKER!
SINCE THE MAIN STORY WAS SO GLOOMY, I WANT TO AT LEAST MAKE THE BONUS PAGES SILLY.
SKRCH SKRCH
So tired
"CHRONO STYLE." WHOA, LOOKIN' PRETTY SEXY.
YOU SAY IT DOESN'T MATTER? I GUESS YOU'RE RIGHT. I MAKE UP FOR IT!
TEE-HEE
not
Not what i really look like.
SO, WHICH PART OF PEOPLES' BODIES DO YOU THINK IS THE SEXIEST?
A LOT OF PEOPLE TELL ME "THE NAPE," "THE HANDS," OR "THE COLLAR-BONE."
i like those, too.
IN MY CASE, IN THE PAST YEARS I REALIZED HOW SEXY **THIS** PART WAS... EVEN I WAS SHOCKED.
right here
THAT'S RIGHT. THE BROW.
IN OTHER WORDS, THE HAIRLINE!
YOU KNOW, WHEN THE HAIR IS SLICKED BACK, OR JUST ONE LITTLE PIECE IS STICKING UP...
it's so sexy! Haha!
I'VE NEVER HEARD OF A "HAIRLINE FETISH" BEFORE!
THE SAMURAI GOT IT, TOO.
Sometimes i scare myself.
NOW THAT I THINK ABOUT IT, ALL THE MANGA CHARACTERS THAT I'VE LIKED HAVE SHOWED THEIR HAIRLINES. IT'S TRUE...
EVERYONE ELSE WHO LIKES MANGA, LET'S LOOK FOR COMMON FEATURES IN CHARACTERS YOU LIKE!
YOU'LL DISCOVER A PART OF YOU YOU NEVER KNEW.
OF COURSE, MY FETISH SHOWED UP IN THE CHARACTER DESIGNS. THE ICHIMURA BROTHERS ARE A GOOD EXAMPLE.
i think i'll give him bangs someday.
Already has a bare forehead
Looks like he's going to lose his bangs someday
SO, WHAT IF I MAKE **ALL** OF THEM SLICK THEIR HAIR BACK?
TOO BAD! IT DIDN'T MAKE THEM ANY SEXIER! I DON'T KNOW WHAT'D HAPPEN IF IT DID...

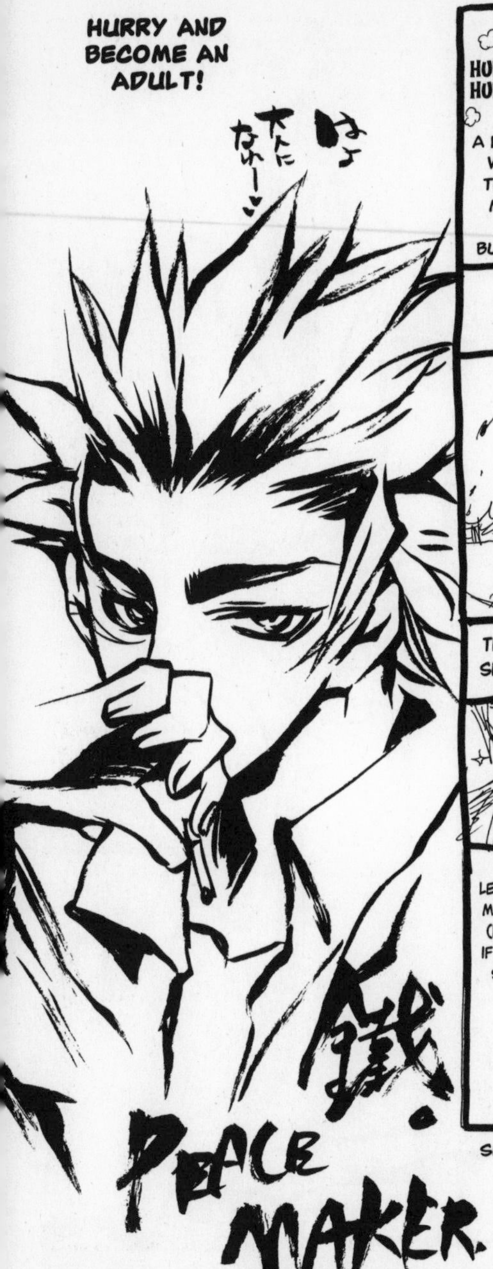
HURRY AND BECOME AN ADULT!
はよ大人になれーっ
鐵
PEACE MAKER.

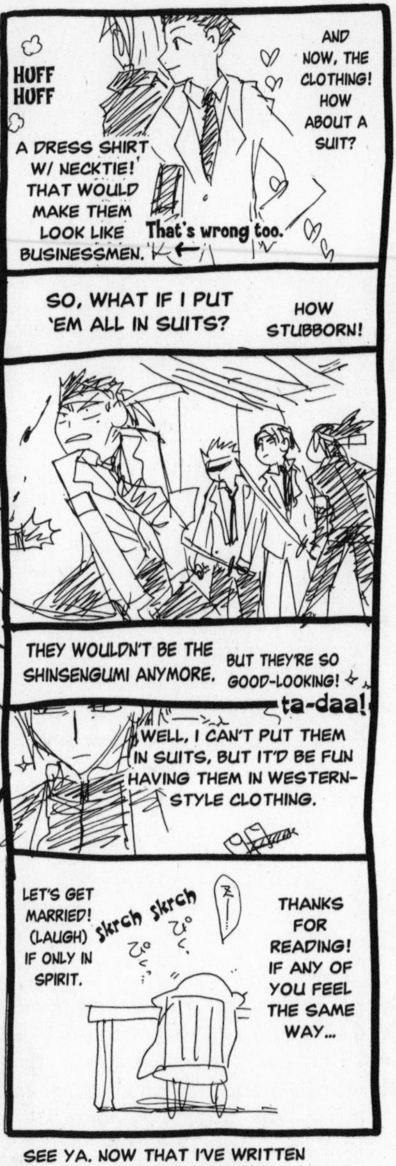
HUFF HUFF
A DRESS SHIRT W/ NECKTIE! THAT WOULD MAKE THEM LOOK LIKE BUSINESSMEN.
That's wrong too.
AND NOW, THE CLOTHING! HOW ABOUT A SUIT?
SO, WHAT IF I PUT 'EM ALL IN SUITS?
HOW STUBBORN!
THEY WOULDN'T BE THE SHINSENGUMI ANYMORE.
BUT THEY'RE SO GOOD-LOOKING!
ta-daa!
WELL, I CAN'T PUT THEM IN SUITS, BUT IT'D BE FUN HAVING THEM IN WESTERN-STYLE CLOTHING.
LET'S GET MARRIED! (LAUGH) IF ONLY IN SPIRIT.
Skrch Skrch
THANKS FOR READING! IF ANY OF YOU FEEL THE SAME WAY...

SEE YA. NOW THAT I'VE WRITTEN THAT, I'M OUTTA HERE!

I was going to talk a bit about the way Yamanami died, but it seemed like I was just making excuses, so I decided not to. But if I managed to surprise the readers who know how it actually happened, then I think it was a success.

Well then, I'm sorry for writing so hurriedly, but I have to go now! Starting with the next volume, some of the characters will start to make their move. I'm looking forward to it, too. I hope to see you again next time!

NANAE CHRONO.

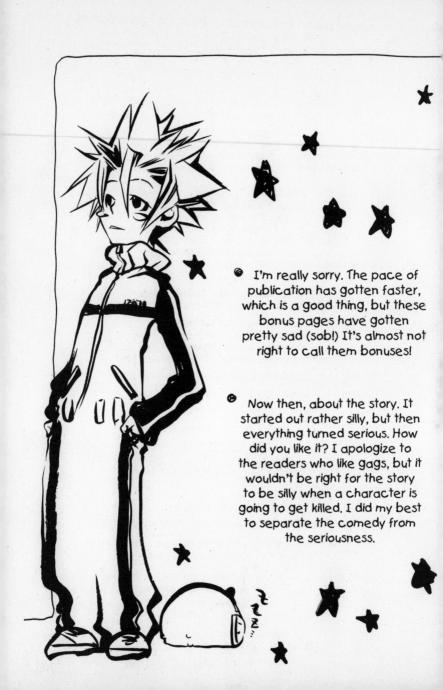

I'm really sorry. The pace of publication has gotten faster, which is a good thing, but these bonus pages have gotten pretty sad (sob!) It's almost not right to call them bonuses!

Now then, about the story. It started out rather silly, but then everything turned serious. How did you like it? I apologize to the readers who like gags, but it wouldn't be right for the story to be silly when a character is going to get killed. I did my best to separate the comedy from the seriousness.

PEACEMAKER KUROGANE
VOLUME 2

© Nanae Chrono 2002

All rights reserved.
First published in 2002 by MAG Garden Corporation.
English translation rights arranged with MAG Garden Corporation.

Translator **AMY FORSYTH**
Lead Translator/Translation Supervisor **JAVIER LOPEZ**
ADV Manga Translation Staff **KAY BERTRAND, JOSH COLE, BRENDAN FRAYNE,
HARUKA KANEKO-SMITH, EIKO McGREGOR AND MADOKA MOROE**

Print Production/Art Studio Manager **LISA PUCKETT**
Pre-press Manager **KLYS REEDYK**
Art Production Manager **RYAN MASON**
Senior Designer/Creative Manager **JORGE ALVARADO**
Graphic Designer/Group Leader **SHANNON RASBERRY**
Graphic Designer **GEORGE REYNOLDS**
Graphic Artists **HEATHER GARY, SHANNA JENSCHKE and KERRI KALINEC**
Graphic Intern **MARK MEZA**

International Coordinator **TORU IWAKAMI**
International Coordinator **ATSUSHI KANBAYASHI**

Publishing Editor **SUSAN ITIN**
Assistant Editor **MARGARET SCHAROLD**
Editorial Assistant **VARSHA BHUCHAR**
Proofreaders **SHERIDAN JACOBS AND STEVEN REED**

Research/Traffic Coordinator **MARSHA ARNOLD**

Executive VP, CFO, COO **KEVIN CORCORAN**

President, CEO & Publisher **JOHN LEDFORD**

Email: editor@adv-manga.com
www.adv-manga.com
www.advfilms.com

For sales and distribution inquiries please call 1.800.282.7202

ADV MANGA™ is a division of A.D. Vision, Inc.
10114 W. Sam Houston Parkway, Suite 200, Houston, Texas 77099

English text © 2004 published by A.D. Vision, Inc. under exclusive license.
ADV MANGA is a trademark of A.D. Vision, Inc.

ISBN: 1-4139-0192-1
First printing, December 2004
10 9 8 7 6 5 4 3 2 1
Printed in Canada

Peacemaker Kurogane Vol. 02

PG. 4 — **Edo** The old name for Tokyo, before it was the capital. At this point in time, Kyoto is the center of the nation's power.

PG. 5 — **Chinese calendar and symbology** According to the Chinese astrological calendar, 1864 was the first year of the 60-year cycle. It is written with the characters for "armor" and "child," and is pronounced *jia-zi* in Chinese (or *kinoene* in Japanese).

PG. 6 — **Kashitaro Ito** The name "Kashitaro" (or more specifically, the *kashi* part) is written with the same character for "armor" and "child" mentioned above.

PG. 24 — **Seppuku** Often translated as "ritual suicide," this is performed by cutting one's stomach with a small dagger. Another person (the "second") then beheads this person to keep them from suffering for too long. See the note for p. 165 for more.

PG. 40 — **Katamori Matsudaira** The last *daimyo* of the Aizu domain. He was the one who appointed the Shinsegumi defenders of Kyoto. He really did give the order to assassinate Kamo Serizawa, because he was arrogant, brash, and caused too much trouble.

PG. 109 — **Sano-stupid Hara-dork!** In the original Japanese, this was *Ahosuke Bakada*. This is a play on his name, Sanosuke Harada, and the words baka and aho, both of which mean "stupid," "dork," "moron," etc.

PG. 121 — **Kyoto accent** Just like English, Japanese has varying accents and dialects. Akesato has been speaking with an accent distinctive of people from Kyoto.

PG. 125 — **Around 4:00** The original Japanese said the "hour of the tiger." The Chinese zodiac system divides the day into 12 segments of 2 hours each. Each 2-hour interval is "ruled" by a certain animal. The interval ruled by the tiger is between 3:00 and 5:00 AM.

PG. 137 — **Roshigumi** The Roshigumi was a group of masterless samurai organized by the shogunate. It would eventually become the Shinsengumi.

PG. 154 — **Shieikan** The Shieikan was a *kenjutsu* dojo where the *Tennen Rishin* style of swordsmanship was taught. A few of the earliest members of the Shinsengumi, including Isami Kondo (who once owned and ran the dojo), Soji Okita, Toshizo Hijikata and Genzaburo Inoue practiced swordsmanship there. Other early Shinsengumi members also frequented this dojo, including Keisuke Yamanami, Sanosuke Harada, and Shinpachi Nagakura.

PG. 156 — **This is your soul…** The sword was said to be the soul of the samurai.

PG. 165 — **The second** When someone commits *seppuku* and cuts his stomach, the *Kaishaku* (or "second") is the one who puts this person out of his pain by beheading him.

Notes On Titles Used...

Dono A term of respect that can be used between people (mostly samurai) of same or similar ranks. It's not used as much today as it was during the time period of *Peacemaker Kurogane*. In modern days, actually *dono* is less formal than *sama* and mostly used in written forms, such as letters, public notice, etc.

Sama Another term of respect. This is still in common use in modern times, and is sometimes translated as "Master" or "Lady."

Sensei Teacher, instructor, or master. This is used for teachers in any field (not just the martial arts), as well as for doctors. It may also be used as a term of respect for someone who isn't necessarily a teacher, but who has gained some level of proficiency or notoriety.

NANAE CHRONO PRESENTS
PEACE MAKER
KUROGANE
3
ARTWORK SUBJECT TO CHANGE

© Nanae Chrono 2003

...WILL HIS DEATH HAVE BEEN IN VAIN?

While he died with honor, the death of beloved Keisuke Yamanami enshrouds the Shinsengumi in a veil of uncertainty. Will his death have been in vain? News surrounding his passing reaches some of the other members of the samurai squad, piquing Ito's curiosity. Later, a reunion of sorts brings Suzu Kitamura back into Tetsunosuke's life, but will the passage of time have strained their once friendly acquaintance? The saga of imperial Kyoto's samurai protectors resumes in the intriguing next edition of **Peacemaker Kurogane**, Volume 3!

PEACE MAKER 3
KUROGANE

ADV Manga™
www.adv-manga.com

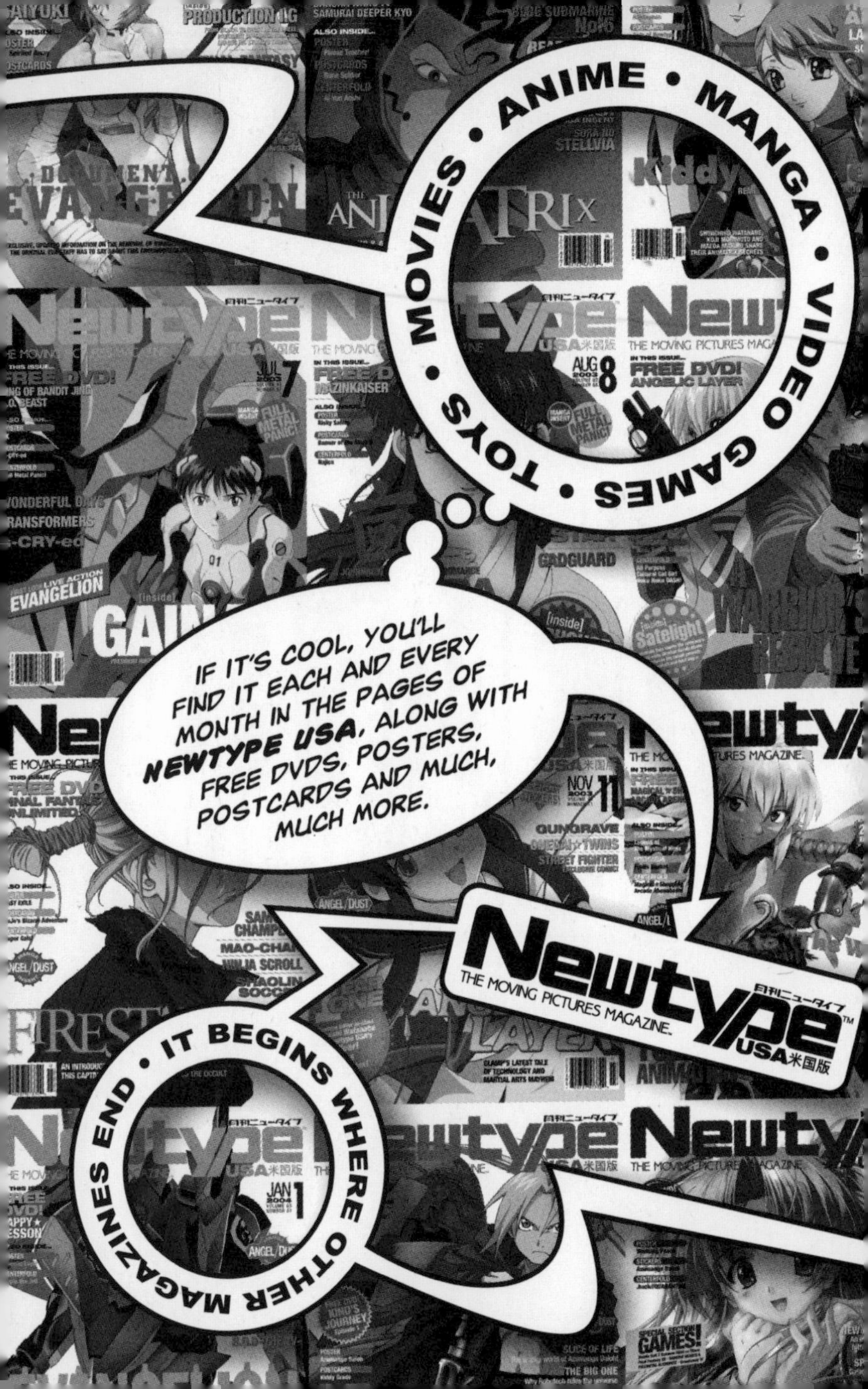
ANIME • MANGA • VIDEO GAMES • TOYS • MOVIES •
IF IT'S COOL, YOU'LL FIND IT EACH AND EVERY MONTH IN THE PAGES OF NEWTYPE USA, ALONG WITH FREE DVDS, POSTERS, POSTCARDS AND MUCH, MUCH MORE.
Newtype USA 米国版 THE MOVING PICTURES MAGAZINE. 月刊ニュータイプ ™
IT BEGINS WHERE OTHER MAGAZINES END •

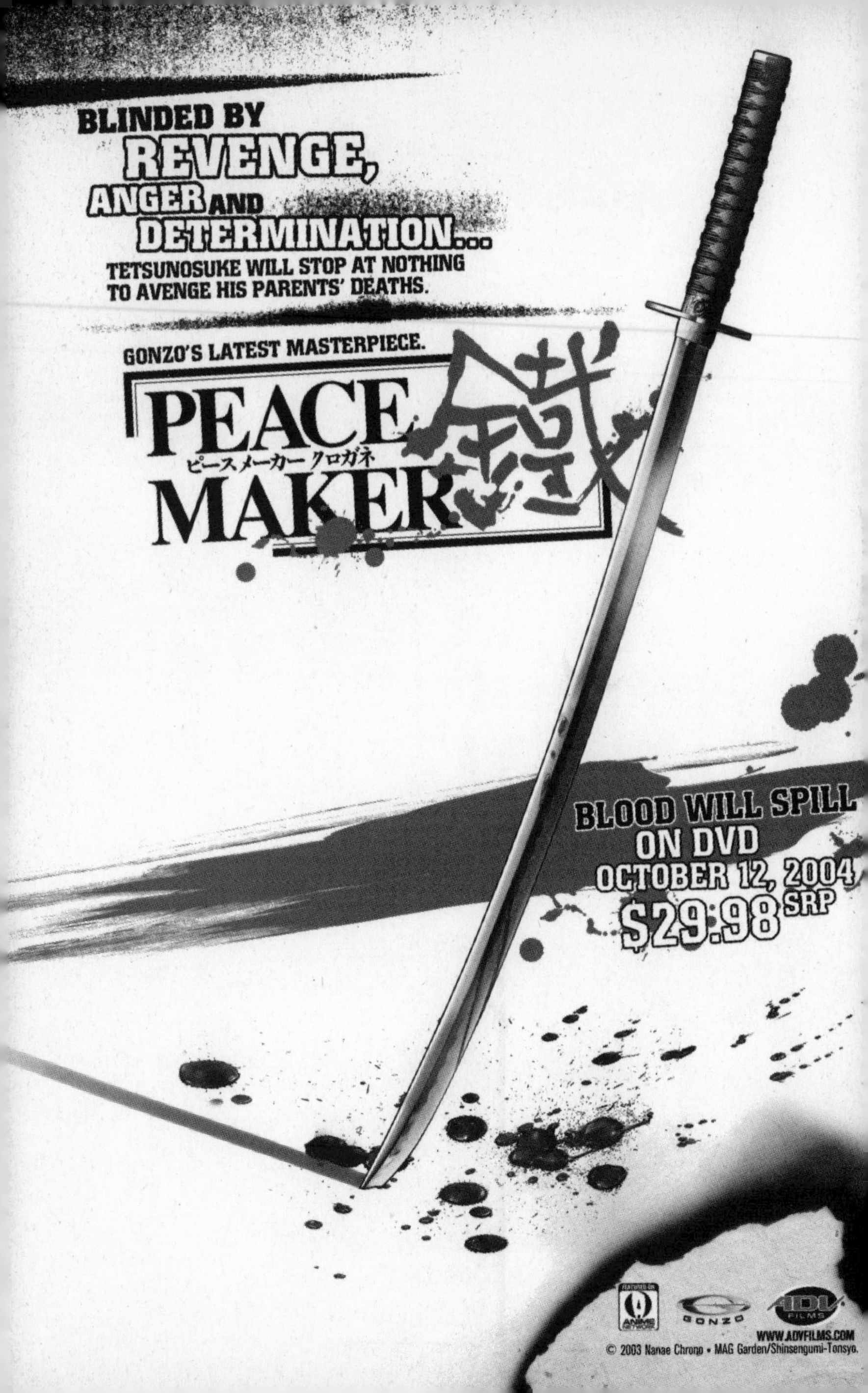
BLINDED BY REVENGE, ANGER AND DETERMINATION...
TETSUNOSUKE WILL STOP AT NOTHING TO AVENGE HIS PARENTS' DEATHS.
GONZO'S LATEST MASTERPIECE.
PEACE MAKER 鐵
ピースメーカー クロガネ
BLOOD WILL SPILL ON DVD
OCTOBER 12, 2004
$29.98 SRP
GONZO
ADV FILMS
WWW.ADVFILMS.COM
© 2003 Nanae Chrono • MAG Garden/Shinsengumi-Tonsyo.

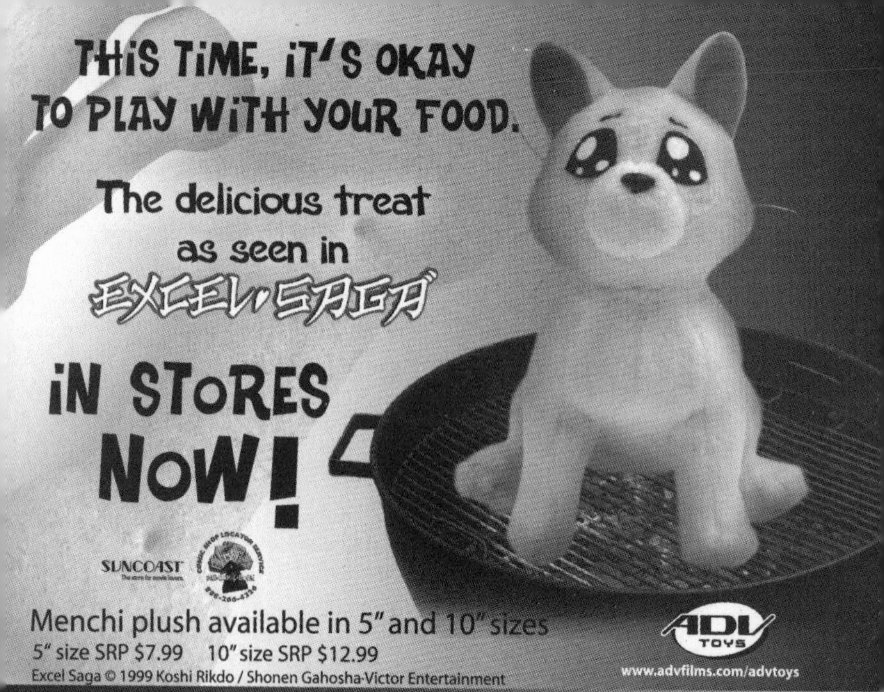
THIS TIME, IT'S OKAY
TO PLAY WITH YOUR FOOD.
The delicious treat
as seen in
EXCEL SAGA
IN STORES
NOW!
SUNCOAST
Menchi plush available in 5" and 10" sizes
5" size SRP $7.99 10" size SRP $12.99
Excel Saga © 1999 Koshi Rikdo / Shonen Gahosha-Victor Entertainment
ADV TOYS
www.advfilms.com/advtoys

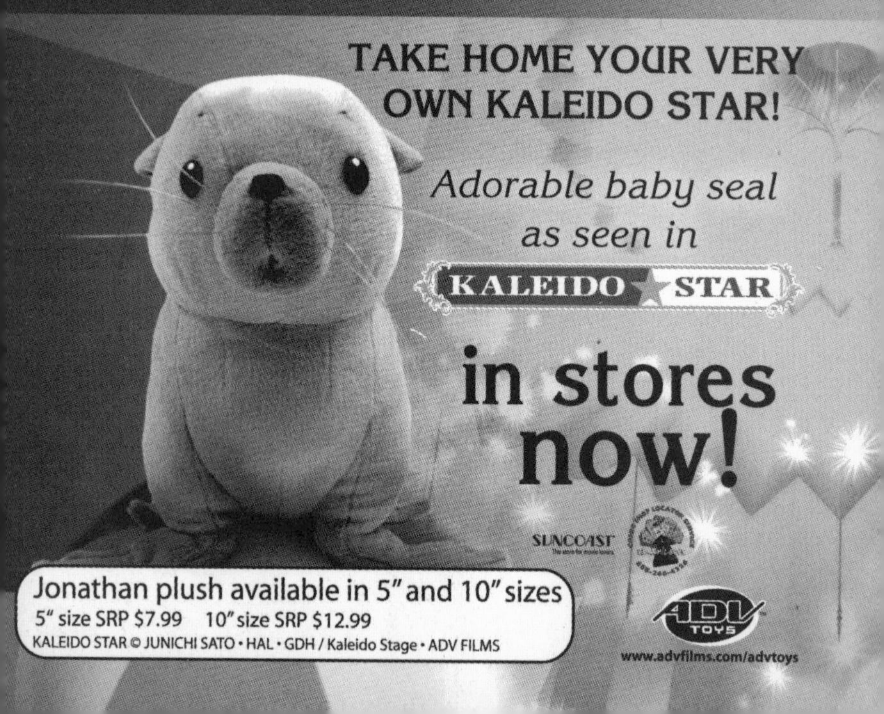
TAKE HOME YOUR VERY
OWN KALEIDO STAR!
Adorable baby seal
as seen in
KALEIDO STAR
in stores
now!
SUNCOAST
Jonathan plush available in 5" and 10" sizes
5" size SRP $7.99 10" size SRP $12.99
KALEIDO STAR © JUNICHI SATO • HAL • GDH / Kaleido Stage • ADV FILMS
ADV TOYS
www.advfilms.com/advtoys